AMERICAN ECCENTRICS

Carl Sifakis

Facts On File Publications
New York, New York ● Bicester, England

AMERICAN
ECCENTRICS

Library of Congress Cataloging in Publication Data

Sifakis, Carl.
  American eccentrics.

  Includes index.
  1. Eccentrics and eccentricities—United States—Biography.
I. Title.
CT9990.S53   1984   920'.073   [B]   82-15424
ISBN O-87196-788-X
ISBN 0-8160-1387-X (PB)

Printed in U.S.A.
10 9 8 7 6 5 4 3

Composition by Centennial Graphics
Printed by R.R. Donnelley and Sons, Co.

For my daughter Karen

ACKNOWLEDGMENTS

Special thanks must be given to Ed Knappman of Facts On File for his advice and guidance in the writing of this book. Additional important contributions were made by "Filers" Joseph Reilly, Kate Kelly, Eleanor Wedge, Robin Smith, Susan Brooker, and Debbie Glasserman, as well as designer Oksana Kushnir and copy editor Marcia Golub.

CONTENTS

INTRODUCTION

It is not easy to be an eccentric in America today. At first glance, it might not seem too difficult. All that appears necessary is a bit of engaging, or perhaps obnoxious, deviant behavior and you are an instant eccentric. However, we Americans no longer are the tolerant social beings we once were.

Today, more than ever in our history, we accept in only a few the sane whimsy or crazy sanity that marks a true eccentric. An ordinary person is no longer trusted with such traits. We generally apply a class test to judge behavior: If you are poor and act bizarrely, you're crazy and perhaps dangerous.

If few poor persons can make the grade, virtually no middle-class person would dare to try, preferring strict conformity over eccentric chic. Only the very rich can be humored in their eccentricity. This was not true in colonial days or in the first three or four generations of the new nation. Rich, poor, and in-between, early American eccentrics were, if not honored, regarded as a diverting and even beneficial ingredient in a new nation without completely fixed social hierarchy or identity.

As American society came of age, we somewhere along the line lost our appreciation for poor or middle-class eccentrics; only the super-rich now seem to be both amazing and unthreatening in their deviations from normal standards of behavior. Most important, they have the wherewithal to cater to their whims without becoming public charges. For example, there was Horseback Billings, the chairman of the board of Union Carbide, who threw the most grotesque dinner in American history. He had his guests, horse lovers all, eat in the ballroom of Louis Sherry's famous New York restaurant while mounted on their steeds, partaking of a $250-a-plate pheasant dinner from feed bags and guzzling champagne from large rubber casks. The cost of the feast came to $50,000, including the planting of sod on the ballroom floor and its later removal with a rather noticeable amount of manure, a fact of nature, the society writers sniffed, that diminished the elegance of the event. Still,

Billings' squandering ways brought him fame, just as the fabulously rich and miserly Hetty Green was celebrated for hardly ever parting with a dime. We still celebrate the recluse if he is a millionaire, a la the Collyer brothers, or, if only a poor man, one who turns out to be a secret miser like Stephen Senior who played the poor beggar, but used thousands of dollar bills to insulate the porous walls of his rude shack from the subzero blasts of wind.

Overall, we prefer the rich who flaunt it. Berry Wall could change his attire at Saratoga Springs forty times in a single day to win the nickname "King of the Dudes." Mrs. Jack Gardner, a mainstay of Boston society, could indulge herself by paying Paderewski $3,000 to conceal himself behind a screen and play at teatime for an elderly friend and herself.

This book is arranged in rough chronological order, and what becomes apparent as we read about 20th-century eccentrics is that most of them are rich. Those not blessed with wealth—such as compulsives Burro Schmidt, the human mole; Edward Leedskalnin, the builder of Florida's amazing coral castle; Shipwreck Kelly, the flagpole sitter; and One-Eyed Connelly, the great gatecrasher—were required to perform impressive deeds. Johnny Appleseed may be celebrated in story and verse today, but he and other strange itinerants such as Jules Bourlay, the Old Leather Man, would more likely be rousted as cranks or derelicts, striking chords of fear in the minds of modern Americans, rather than treated with the charity and respect earlier Americans gave them. Rather than being permitted to practice their acts of ethics or contrition, and even offered bed and board, they would be relegated to fringe society and regarded as outlaws. The 20th-century counterparts of Calamity Jane, as well as the grizzled loner prospectors who had no real interest in striking it rich, are to be found in every big city in America—as bag ladies and homeless men. We no longer honor such individuals with colorful nicknames. They are suffered in silence while our gaze is fixed elsewhere. A century or two ago the rules of social intercourse were broader, and eccentrics, rich or poor, were tolerated and excuses sought for their behavior.

Each society creates the ground rules for its own eccentrics, and the standards constantly change. Many well-known eccentrics of the 18th and 19th centuries find no place in this volume because they cannot meet present-day criteria. The Reverend George H. Munday is one. He was noted in Philadelphia in the first quarter of the last century for an idiosyncrasy that would not cause a ripple today. Yet, Philadelphians gathered by the hundreds to listen to the torrential sermons of the Reverend Mr. Munday whom they referred to as the "Hatless Preacher." For that was the sum total of his erratic behavior, that he was a man of the cloth who wore no hat in this capital of hat-wearing Quakers.

Of more lasting fame, although his deviations would be of minor mettle today, was Joseph Palmer who became one of the most hated eccentrics of the 1830s, subjected to what is now mind-boggling persecution. His offense: wearing a beard at a time when no Americans did so. For this he was sneered at, denounced as a "degenerate," stoned, and finally arrested. Ironically, within two decades beards became commonplace, and not long afterward Abraham Lincoln became the first of several U.S. presidents to sport whiskers.

As the fabric from which the eccentric is cut changes, some say eccentricity is vanishing from the American scene. They are unimpressed by the so-called nonconformists of the recent past—the longhairs, the acidheads, the bearded ones (again)—denying that these are true eccentrics. They are probably correct: These supposed aberrations are in fact the conformity of their own generation. As sociologist Werner Cahnman has stated: "Eccentricity frequently becomes only the transition between two conformities."

Not long ago *Time* magazine bewailed what it called "the sad state of eccentricity" in the United States. Where were those, it asked, with "the grand style and creative bursts . . . that marked the golden age of English eccentrics, among them one exotic aristocrat who habitually dined with dogs dressed as humans and another who spent his life trying to breed a symmetrically spotted mouse."

In what may have been almost an act of desperation, the publication tried to churn up interest in possible eccentrics among some of its own targets; it settled especially on atheist Madalyn Murray O'Hair, whom it saw as a person with "more religious fervor than anyone since Cotton Mather," and twitted for her announcement, "I'm no eccentric. I'm the leader of a valid movement." In any event *Time*'s effort to pin the label of eccentricity on O'Hair by citing such statements of hers as "I will separate church and state, by God!" falls a bit short of convincing.

Dismissing one's opponents as eccentrics has become the American way of battle. When Ralph Nader first set his aim on the least enviable accomplishments in matters of car safety, the officials of General Motors sought to tar him with the eccentric brush. What else could a male American be who didn't even own an automobile?

Who then is the real eccentric in modern America? Harvard

sociologist Peter McEwan described him as a person who is "extraordinarily secure. Other people are either wrong or going about life ineffectually. He thinks that he has the answer."

The U.S. Census, alas, does not classify and count eccentrics, but even the most casual research makes it readily apparent that an earlier America had many more, from the likes of Appleseed to Thoreau, marching to their own drummers.

Is the record different elsewhere? The British Isles have long been reputed to be the most fertile breeding ground for eccentricity, and it is said that the British embrace engaging practitioners of the odd and bizarre in a manner no other people has achieved. That may well be more myth than reality, especially in the present. Dame Edith Sitwell in her 1957 classic *English Eccentrics* finds no way to break the 20th-century barrier in quest of delightful deviates.

The study of eccentrics hardly achieves the level of a science, and most generalizations prove no more dependable than their subjects. Are there really more English eccentrics than Americans; if so, why? Do the English truly honor their eccentrics more, or is it simply a case that they produce more eccentric people? There are those observers who insist an island country that suffers over 200 days of rainfall a year has a running start toward unusual behavior. On the other hand, England's colonial cousins certainly have no trouble matching their overseas eccentric counterparts, quirk for quirk.

Major Peter Labellière, described by Sitwell as "a Christian patriot and Citizen of the World," was so disenchanted with the state of the planet that he declared in his will that "as the world was turned topsyturvy, it was fit that he should be so buried that he might be right at last." An American counterpart in odd burials could well be Texas-born millionairess Sandra Ilene West who had a love affair with automobiles; upon her death at the age of 37 she was buried, according to her instructions, "next to my husband . . . in my Ferrari, with the seat slanted comfortably." A shade more materialistic in outlook than the good major perhaps, but Labellière made his departure in 1800 and West in 1977; materialism by the later date had had its impact on the appreciation, and indeed the definition, of eccentricity.

Among odd members of the clergy Sitwell offers the Reverend Mr. Jones, curate of Blewberry in Berkshire, who wore the same hat and coat during the 43 years of his curacy. When, after some 35 years the brim of his hat had worn away, he stole the hat from a scarecrow and appropriated its brim; jet black and tar-twined, it fit rather jarringly to his own brown crown. Then too there was the Reverend Mr. Trueman who stole turnips in the field as he trekked on his works of righteousness among the farms of Daventry. Cajoling invitations to spend the night, the Reverend Mr. Trueman would pinch "the red or white worsted out of the corners of the blankets, and with these variegated pickings he mended his clothes and his stockings."

These gentlemen suffered from the sin of parsimony, but their behavior passes as trivial oddity compared to Handkerchief Moody, a pastor in York, Maine, who for the final two decades of his pastorage wore a fold of crepe knotted above the forehead, covering all his facial features. In church he preached with his back to the congregation, his masked appearance adding unneeded elements of dreariness to both weddings and funerals. Of course, the Reverend Mr. Moody had a heavier cross to bear—complicated motivation best left to his entry—than either Reverend Messrs. Jones or Trueman.

The writing of any book requires the author to start with preconceived notions, but even the most logical-sounding theories on eccentrics teeter. It certainly seems logical, and rather profound, to declare we can measure a society by the way it treats its eccentrics. Sadly, the facts soon intervene. As surprising as it seems, the true eccentric probably thrived as much in Nazi Germany as in democratic England, despite the latter's concept of personal liberty for the individual.

Nazi Germany may have been barbarous to its mental defectives, yet, even under the stress of war, the Nazis could not escape what may be called the Captain of Kopenick Syndrome, named after Wilhelm Voight's character who won the hearts of the German people by his eccentric belittling of the German army.

Thus, even though during World War II the rooting out of "defeatists" became a Hitlerite obsession, scores of offenders picked up by security forces for declaring the war was lost suffered no worse fate than a lecture by the Gestapo. Then they were released (after a check on possible Jewish ancestry, of course). Belittling of Nazi demigods was far more rife than Germany's opponents could have guessed. All of Munich could laugh about the fish peddlar who was snatched up for hawking his wares: "*Hering, Hering, so fett wie Göring.*" ("Herring, herring, as fat as Göring.") Arrested and interrogated by the Gestapo, the man was back peddling his wares after a mere three weeks imprisonment, announcing: "*Hering, Hering, so fett wie vor drei Wochen.*" ("Herring, herring, as fat as three weeks ago.")

Naturally, the fact that Himmler's S.S. and Göring's Luftwaffe were jealous rivals helped the heroic peddlar. But even the Gestapo itself could be hoaxed, as was Luftwaffe intelligence, by a young Austrian private named Elfried Schmidt, celebrated by author Joseph Wechsberg as *The Man Who Fooled Hitler*.

Before he was even 20, Schmidt far outdid Voight's Captain from Kopenick of 30-odd years earlier. Schmidt masqueraded as *Ingenieur Honoris Causa*, claiming to have been personally so dubbed by the Führer himself in the Reich Chancellery in Berlin. He got this "award" for having provided the Third Reich with the designs of an electric diesel rail car. Hitler had been supposedly so impressed by Herr Engineer Schmidt's invention that he had even slipped him his secret telephone number in case he ever had any problems.

Of course, none of this ever happened, but Schmidt parlayed his daring tale into an honored position of fame in his home village outside Vienna. He strutted through town wearing a special silver *fourragère* or cord on his left side—also an alleged special dispensation from Hitler.

Later Schmidt was drafted into the Luftwaffe and served as a common private until his superiors were made aware—circuitously by Schmidt—of his special standing. Why had he not informed them, flustered officers asked. He said he simply wanted "to do my duty like any other soldier."

Kanonier Schmidt was immediately relieved of all military duties and provided with private quarters where he could perform his special work. He didn't stay in barracks but slept in Vienna, reporting to the base at 8 A.M. When he entered, the sentry called out the guard of honor, which was done only for the garrison commander and general officers.

Later Schmidt was transferred to Luftgaukommando XVII and assigned to Secret Projects, studying drawings of foreign aircraft engines that had been obtained by the German Secret Service. Schmidt's downfall came when Colonel-General Eduard von Löhr decided that, despite the Führer's fascination with a brilliant private, the young Austrian deserved officer rank. He forwarded his recommendation to the Air Ministry and in due course Schmidt was exposed.

Brought before a Luftwaffe court, Schmidt was charged with being a foreign spy, a far more rational view than the one Schmidt was to advance. Happily for Schmidt he wrote a letter to a girl friend in his home village, bewailing his fate and that he was charged with spying when actually he had taken up the impersonation simply to impress her. The letter was seized when he tried to have it smuggled out of his cell.

By the time the trial started, the military was convinced that Schmidt was not a foreign agent, but rather merely *"verrückt,"* or eccentric. The judges frequently tittered during the trial and even the chief prosecutor had trouble keeping a straight face. The presiding judge burst into laughter as testimony revealed Schmidt's frustrated love life.

The espionage charge against him was dropped; Schmidt was convicted of "forging an official diploma," of "unjustified use of an academic title," and of "insolently exploiting the name of the Führer and Reichskanzler." It was clear the order had come down from high—one can only speculate how high—to end the matter expeditiously.

Schmidt was sentenced to six months imprisonment, did only three, and served out the war as an ordinary soldier. When Schmidt married in 1940 the army forced him to wear his old uniform with the silver *fourragère* so that his home villagers would not be suspicious. At the time the Nazis did not want the truth out.

The eccentric label is often applied loosely and too frequently. It is easy now to view with amusement the babblings of erratic pseudoscientists and flat-earthers, as well as those we have dubbed UFO-nuts, but that was the same fate suffered in their respective days by both Galileo and Freud. It would be easy to classify the Wright brothers, Thomas Edison, and Henry Ford as eccentric because they all held to some wild-eyed theories or suffered from bizarre conduct or belief, but their serious accomplishments far outweigh their peccadilloes. In fact, their touches of madness may have sparked their genius. Nonetheless, they fail to qualify as fulltime, card-carrying eccentrics. Nor will Douglas "Wrong Way" Corrigan qualify as one, even though he achieved fame in July 1938 for taking off from New York for Los Angeles, flying instead through fog to Dublin, Ireland, allegedly by mistake. He captured the imagination of the country and was dubbed by journalists as an eccentric of the clouds but, alas, he did nothing for an encore and his feat remains, the suspicion never downed, more commercial than erratic.

The true eccentric follows his own rules of behavior 24 hours a day—because he knows his code is the right one and everyone else is wrong; because he does not want to compete by conventional standards; or because eccentricity seems the only way to gain recognition as an individual. Even among the super-rich, there are those who turn to the outrageous in their desire not to be considered just another millionaire.

Even Howard Hughes, the so-called billionaire recluse dubbed by *Fortune* "the Spook of American capitalism," is given more credit for bizarre behavior than he is entitled to. If Hughes was a true eccentric, he was only one in his final years, when age tipped the scale. His earlier loner behavior was more often a convenient and calculated method of avoiding subpoenas that would have hauled him before various judicial and legislative bodies. Hughes' behavior during his moviemaking days reflected little more than that of a big-shot Hollywood lecher. And certainly Hughes did not buy up so much of Las Vegas' real estate because, as the lurid press hyped the facts, he wanted a city in which to be alone. Rather it represented a vital multimillion-dollar dodge to avoid the undistributed profits tax. It was a matter of either spending the money or giving it to the government. Howard Hughes was simply too cunning to be dismissed as a compleat eccentric.

When we shut ourselves off from authentically unconventional people, we lose an important way to put conventional wisdom to the test. When we fail to nurture eccentrics, we run the risk of turning conventionality into the greatest eccentricity of all. We rob ourselves of joy. The "town character" is becoming less of a fixture. Widespread conformity is allowing fewer and fewer exceptions.

New York's Mohawk Valley is renowned for its historical legends, but it is just as rich in its heritage of "characters." Fort Plain may be regarded as a sleepy sort of community, but it has its own legends, one of which concerns an unlikely 19th-century pair, Wells Grant and Winnie (no one alive and no written records provide us with the latter's last name), who became the talk of the village because of their physical statures. Wells was all of two feet four inches tall, and he never saw a big woman without falling in love. By contrast Winnie towered seven feet six inches, and he loved most of all his dogs and of course Wells. The pair was inseparable. Shy with women, Winnie took delight in the town's first fire company and was deeply touched when it was named the Winnie Hose Company. Winnie and Wells were the grand masters of all parades in the town as long as they lived, and when they died, Fort Plain buried them next to each other.

Another charmer of Fort Plain was John Baxter whose greatest thrill was watching boats on the canal. Young John one day decided he was going to build his own boat with which to navigate the canal, and he spent an entire winter constructing a stream runabout in his cellar. Only when he was finished did John realize his craft was too big to get out of the cellar.

Undaunted, John ripped a gaping hole in the cellar wall and got his beloved creation to the water. The whole town turned out the day John was ready to launch. John polished his equipment, tooted his whistle, and shouted to his beaming mother on the canal bank, "Here I go, Ma!"

John certainly did go—straight to the bottom of the canal.

John Baxter had his fill of boat-building, and he never made another one, but for decades thereafter he never forgot his first one. The children would follow him, shouting, "Toot, toot, here I go, Ma," and old John would chase them with his cane.

Wells, Winnie, and John are still remembered fondly in Fort Plain, their eccentricities still worth a chuckle.

In Queens, New York City, today there is an elderly man who shops at a Queens Boulevard supermarket. After he pays, his custom is to leave a tip of $2 and some silver for the cashier. As he leaves, the cashier, pocketing the money, will shake his or her head and, twirling a finger at the temple in a familiar motion, explain to other customers, "The nut does that with all the cashiers."

Queens is today's reality. We will not see Fort Plain and its eccentrics again.

Bachiler, Stephen (1561–1662)

THE AMOROUS PARSON

Playing the game of ascribing "firsts" is a pastime filled with pitfalls, but there seems to be good reason, chronologically speaking, to believe the Reverend Stephen Bachiler was the first man of the cloth in America to fall victim to the adoring women of his parish (or vice versa). Mr. Bachiler arrived in New Boston aboard the *William & Francis* on June 5, 1632, after a voyage of 88 days.

During that long voyage, a chronicler noted, he "found it necessary to have 'spiritual understanding' with almost every woman on board." What made Mr. Bachiler all the more noteworthy was his age—71. Mr. Bachiler over the next 30 years—apparently something in his doings agreed with him—was the epitome of the naughty parson.

Some observers, including Governor Winthrop, record his doings with considerable distaste. Wrote Winthrop:

> Mr. Bachiler, the pastor of the church at Hampton, who had suffered much at the hands of the bishops in England, being about eighty years of age and having a lusty, comely woman to his wife, did sollicit the chastity of his neighbour's wife, who acquainted her husband therewith; Whereupon he was dealt with, but denied it, as he had told the woman he would do, and complained to the magistrate against the woman and her husband for slandering him.

The record is unclear, but there were some—"mostly daughters and sons-in-law"—who contended that until that invigorating ocean voyage Mr. Bachiler was devoid of lecherous conduct. If that were so, perhaps it was his very age and appearance—tall, with white hair that created the impression of a halo—that caused the feminine heart to thrill at being in the presence of a "saint." Whatever it was, Mr. Bachiler had his way with the women aboard the

William & Francis, and through his veins surged the sensations of a youth.

Over the next 19 years of his busy life, Mr. Bachiler was a demon for his church. Well ahead of his time, he argued for a "Holy House without ceremonies," a church totally free of the influence and control of the state. This was a century and a half before the Founding Fathers were to write the Constitution, which incorporates that separation. But in the Massachusetts Bay Colony of Mr. Bachiler's time, church and state were inseparable.

Mr. Bachiler first set up his Holy House in Saugus, which was later to become Lynn. Among his flock were six of his relatives and a few friends, especially some of the women with whom he had dallied aboard ship. Some were single or widowed, others married; these wives apparently pressured their husbands to follow the good reverend.

The "strange power" Mr. Bachiler had, which, he was to aver, perplexed him considerably, enabled him "to convey the word of God lucidly to goodwives and turgidly to men." Trouble started within a matter of months, and it was seized on quickly by Winthrop and the civil authorities in Boston, who resented such talk about a church separable from the state. It was exactly for such talk and other "churchly grounds" that he had been condemned by the English bishops. In the New World, he was again condemned, this time for his "moral frailty" and his magnetic power over the weaker sex.

Thus, in October 1632, the reverend was arraigned in court in Boston. The verdict brought in that "Mr. Bachiler is required to forebeare exercising his gifts as a pastor . . . until some *scandles* be removed."

Mr. Bachiler returned to Saugus with a heavy heart over the charge of "scandles." He asked permission to leave the place, but several women came to him, begging him to offer a prayer meeting. This led to new troubles and Stephen Bachiler's rearrest. Finally, in February 1636, Mr. Bachiler removed to Ipswich with his family and a few friends.

Matters proved no different there. All the women of the parish left the church their husbands had formed to take up worship under Mr. Bachiler. In exasperation a few husbands joined the new church, but most remained hostile. It was only a matter of time, Mr. Bachiler knew, until they would take their complaints to the magistrates, and he would again be refused permission to preach.

Mr. Bachiler decided to leave before he was overwhelmed by new "scandles," and so he led his flock to land granted on the peninsula of Cape Cod. Between the community of Sandwich and one down the Cape at Eastham, they established a new home at Hampton.

Mr. Bachiler was happy. He preached, laughed a good deal, and drank too much wine; and when his wife Helena was not looking, he chucked the "maides of Hampton" under their pretty chins. Hampton attracted new residents and Mr. Bachiler's success as a leader of a new community attracted offers from other towns. Newbury promised much land if he would move there. Ipswich wanted him back and dangled a large grant for a stay of three years.

Mr. Bachiler preferred to remain in Hampton, where his holdings grew to 300 acres. He was comfortable with his flock, especially the women. Unfortunately, he could not restrain his amatory behavior. Husbands seethed and finally brought in a rival parson to establish another parish. Arguments arose in most Hampton homes as to which church to attend. Finally, in 1641, charges of unchastity were brought against him. Mr. Bachiler replied by calling the charges slanders, and his contention, much to the dismay of Governor Winthrop, was accepted.

Having been cleared, Mr. Bachiler, it might be thought, would have rejoiced. But the parson was overwhelmed by a sense of remorse. He stood before his congregation to fully admit his transgressions. He walked from his church back to his home, awaiting the call of the deacons to dispossess him. When they came, these men, many of whom had been constantly suspicious of their religious mentor, proved rather charitable, allowing him to keep his land.

Mr. Bachiler's conversion to righteousness had a stirring effect upon his parishioners. By late in the year they petitioned for his full restoration to the church. In an age of stern punishment, Mr. Bachiler's treatment was unusual, to say the least. It cannot be said to have been very salutary. He went on chucking pretty girls under the chin and calling on the housewives of Hampton. When he confessed, Stephen Bachiler showed perhaps that he had in him the stuff that made martyrs. But he was pardoned his sins, and he went on to demonstrate that he was incapable of being a saint—certainly not day after day.

The "troubles" ensued again. All through these tribulations his wife, Helena—his second wife, the first having died years earlier in England—tolerated him, fed him, and kept his house. Then one day it burned to the ground. An accident? The vengeful act of some cuckolded husbands? No one knew for sure. Mr. Bachiler was offered a post in Exeter, but the colonial court refused permission because of his "evil reputation." So Mr. Bachiler wandered north, trying a dozen different churches. Always there were the troubles.

When he was 89 his wife died. His daughter offered him a home in retirement in Sandwich. Mr. Bachiler refused. He could not take such inactivity, not with the heart of an 18-year-old.

When he was 90, Mr. Bachiler took a third wife, Mary. "Beautiful as dawn" she was, and the parson was happy, if only for a matter of a few months. Then he discovered she was an adulteress. He was crushed and asked for an immediate divorce. Mary was not averse. She denounced her husband as a hypocrite, one guilty of all the same sins she had committed.

If Mr. Bachiler was stung by the scandal of it all, his chagrin was to grow unbounded when the court refused his plea for divorce, stating:

> It is ordered by this Court that Mr. Bachiler and his wife shall lyve together as man and wife as in this Court they have publicly professed to doe; and if either desert one another then hereby the court doth order that the marshal shall apprehend both the said Mr. B. and Mary, his wife, and bring them forthwith to Boston.

The old parson was sickened at the thought of being forced to share his roof with a confessed adulteress. He would be a laughing stock. Cuckolded husbands would laugh at his plight, and Mary would do worse.

Secretly, alone and on foot, he set out for Boston, seeking passage on a ship bound for England, where he could be free of the disgrace. Mr. Bachiler was on board when he learned that Mary had been convicted of new offenses and had been sentenced to "receive forty stripes save one, at the first town meeting held at Kittery six weeks after her delivery, and be branded with the letter A (for adultery)."

It was a cruel punishment, and Mr. Bachiler debated returning to his errant wife and her bastard-to-be. He was torn over what to do. Then he met a young woman, barely more than a child, aboard ship. She was teary eyed, heartsick at going all the way to England, terrified of the travails.

Mr. Bachiler asked what he could do to comfort her; the words issued with the feel of a caress. "Wilt thou stay near me on the voyage?" she asked.

And so Mr. Bachiler returned to England. It would be fitting and proper to report that Mr. Bachiler mended his ways in his old age. Alas, it cannot be so. Although he had never been granted a divorce from the naughty Mary, he married again, to another young woman; and he lived on happily, an actively social being, until he died at the age of 101.

Anonymous (1589?—early 19th century)

THE OLDEST AMERICAN

We know not why or when the Old Hermit of Western Virginia went to his cave, but a broadside around 1817 tells his tale. In June 1816, John Fielding and Captain James Buckland went west from their Virginia homes to explore the wilderness. Their mapmaking was not as hardy and disciplined as their chronicling, and we do not know where precisely they were after 73 days of forded rivers and streams, scaled peaks, crossed flatlands, and battles with and evasions of wild beasts. But on an unnamed mountain they happened upon a cave and were startled indeed when, in answer to their shouts—a precaution in case of animals dwelling within—a hermit stepped out to greet them.

He was ragged and bearded, but extremely talkative. He was only too happy to tell them who he was, save for his name. He said he was born in London in 1589. His visitors were a bit puzzled. Did he not know that it was now 1816? The hermit nodded in agreement, noting that that was about the date he thought it to be. Then he went on. His father was an ordinary laborer, but he was fortunate enough to be placed with a landed gentlemen who saw to it that he received an education.

The boy thrived in his wholesome surroundings and, as was probably inevitable, he fell in love with his master's daughter. The noble's charity soon turned to boiling anger, in response to this. He forced them apart, a fate that proved too stern for the daughter, who died of grief. The boy too was sorrow-struck, and he ran away, shaking the dust of the English countryside from his boots. He made his way to the Continent, living by his wits until he reached Italy, where he shipped out as a sailor.

He was aboard a vessel that foundered off the American coast, and the youth, separated from the rest of the survivors, if indeed there were any, began a long vagrancy that pulled him further and further west. He evaded Indians, and when at last he came upon the cave that was to be his home, he decided to remain there; it seemed to be a safe refuge from the savages. The more the men questioned the hermit, the more he convinced them that his knowledge of the outside world ended in the early 1600s. He knew of Good Queen Bess and allegedly of little thereafter.

Some observers have speculated that Messrs. Buckland and Fielding might have fabricated their tale, but they seemed to be of "sound reputation." It could be that the hermit had heard of England's magnificent old man, Thomas Parr, who lived to be 152 years old and died in 1635, after having been presented at court, and who was honored by being buried at Westminster Abbey. Perhaps the hermit of the cave thought to outdo Old Parr, moving back his birth year in order to do so. But a man seldom achieves fame by hiding from the world. The blandishments of his visitors were not enough to lure the hermit—the oldest American?—from his wilderness home for the trivial comforts of civilization. As he pointed out, the animals were most gracious to him. Nightly they emerged from the forests and danced before his cave. Our anonymous hermit, whoever he was, evidently knew his Orpheus as well.

Hyde, Sam (1626–1732)

THE CRAZY INDIAN

Even today, although it is a custom changing with a changing society, the term "To lie like Sam Hyde" is a New England saying. Sam Hyde (or Hide) was an Indian in early colonial America, and he became the model for all the "crazy" Indians who inhabit the white man's lore.

Clearly Sam did try to fool the white man, being mendacious to the extreme as well as crazy enough to even try. Many of the tales concerning his attempts to fool whites merely serve to bolster the white man's ego; but others demonstrate Hyde's cunning as well as indicate, at least by the whites' standards, exercises in eccentricity in and of itself.

Sam could become lost trying to fathom the white man's logic, and delighted whites told many tales about him, some perhaps exaggerations. One story often attributed to Sam concerns his being hired to guide two travelers through the forests. At a certain point, the white pair separated in order to study different areas of the woods. The one Sam remained with found some unusual berries, and he sent Sam, with a note specifying their number, to his companion. When Sam arrived with the berries, the fruit were far less in number than the note indicated. The second traveler accused Sam of eating the berries, and he sent him back for more. When Sam returned the second time, again the berries were short in number. Accused again, the puzzled Indian fell to his knees and kissed the note, indicating that he thought it had witch-doctor powers. He confessed he had eaten the berries, but the second time he had tried to make allowances for the paper's magic. He had carefully put it under a rock so it could not *see* him eating the berries.

In 1841 Samuel Drake wrote his famed *The Book of the Indians*, and because Sam Hyde was still noted as a crazy and lying Indian, for a time Drake hesitated to include him—for fear "we might not be thought *serious* in the rest of our work." Still, Sam was too engaging to be omitted, and Drake could not resist the following anecdote:

"*Sam Hide* was a notorious cider-drinker as well as liar, and used to travel the country to and fro begging it from door to door. At one time he happened in a region of country where cider was very hard to be procured, either from its scarcity, or from Sam's frequent visits. However, cider he was determined to have, if lying, in any shape or color, would gain it. Being not far from the house of an acquaintance, who he knew had cider, but he knew, or was well satisfied, that, in the ordinary way of begging, he could not get it, he set his wits at work to lay a plan to insure it. This did not occupy him long. On arriving at the house of the gentleman, instead of asking for cider, he inquired for the man of the house, whom, on appearing, *Sam* requested to go aside with him, as he had something of importance to communicate to him. When they were by themselves, *Sam* told him he had that morning shot a fine deer, and that, if he would give him a crown, he would tell him where it was. The gentleman did not incline to do this, but offered half a crown. Finally, *Sam* said, as he had walked a great distance that morning, and was very dry, for a half crown and a mug of cider he would tell him. This was agreed upon, and the price paid. Now *Sam* was required to point out the spot where the deer was to be found, which he did in this manner. He said to his friend, *You know of such a meadow,* describing it—Yes—*You know a big ash tree, with a big top by the little brook*—Yes—*Well, under that tree lies the deer.* This was satisfactory, and Sam departed. It is unnecessary to mention that the meadow was found, and the tree by the brook, but no deer. The duped man could hardly contain himself on considering what he had been doing. To look after *Sam* for satisfaction would be worse than looking for the deer, so the farmer concluded to go home contented. Some years after, he happened to fall in with the Indian; and he immediately began to rally him for deceiving him so; and demanded back his money and pay for his cider and trouble. *Why,* said *Sam, would you find fault if Indian told truth half the time?*—No— *Well,* says *Sam, you find him meadow?*—Yes—*You find him tree?*—Yes— *What for then you find fault* Sam Hide, *when he told you two truth to one lie?* The affair ended here. *Sam* heard no more from the farmer."

Clearly there can be a dispute on whether Sam Hyde was more crazy or cunning, but he imparted his characteristics, whatever they were, to many of his race as seen through white man's eyes.

Drake adds: "He died in Dedham, 5 January, 1732, at the great age of 105 years. He was a great jester, and passed for an uncommon wit. In all the wars against the Indians during his lifetime, he served the English faithfully, and had the name of a brave soldier. He had himself killed 19 of the enemy, and tried hard to make up the 20th but was unable."

If Sam Hyde made that claim about his killings, he was lying once more. The account, as it turns out, can be traced to earlier accounts; clearly the hero involved was not him. He was simply lying like Sam Hyde.

Rogers, John (?–1721)

TUMULTUOUS JOHN

No man can be said to have more riled up religious Connecticut in the late 1600s than John Rogers. He led his disciples, called Rogerenes, in noisy, often violent confrontations with the more established churches.

To quote Benjamin Trumbull's long-yellowed *Complete History of Connecticut*:

> The Rogerenes were a sort of Quaker, who had their origin and name from one John Rogers of New London. He was a man of unbounded ambition and wished to be something more than common man. . . . To gratify his pride, and that he might appear as the head of a peculiar sect, he differed in several points from the Quakers. . . .
>
> The madness, immodesty and tumultuous conduct of Rogers and those who followed him, at this day, is hardly conceivable. It seemed to be their study and delight to violate the Sabbath, insult magistrates and ministers and to trample on all law and authority, human and divine. They would come on the Lord's Day into the most public assemblies, nearly or quite naked, and, in the time of public worship, behave in a wild and tumultuous manner, crying out and charging the most venerable ministers with lies and false doctrines. They would labor upon the Lord's Day, drive carts by places of public worship and from town to town, apparently on purpose to disturb Christians and Christian assemblies. They seem to take pains to violate the law in the presence of officers that they might be complained of, and have an opportunity to insult the laws, the courts and all civil authority.

There may be some exaggeration in Dr. Trumbull's account, but John Rogers was truly a "shaker," and he stands out because he so rattled the unity of worship in his native New London. The Rogerses were an old family in the town and well-respected; it came as a thunderbolt in the 1670s when John Rogers joined the Seventh Day Baptists, later joining the Quakers, and finally starting his own sect.

John Rogers preached in the streets and certainly sought to

disturb public worship with which he disagreed. From 1676 on, Rogers was arraigned at every session of the local court. He was fined and imprisoned, usually for blasphemy, but once he was implicated in the burning of the New London meeting house. To the good Congregationalist minds of New London, his most irritating offense involved his sitting on the town gallows beneath a halter, for which he was jailed for blasphemy. Rogers spent roughly one-third of his life, after he converted, in jail for the practice of his faith.

None of these punishments and fines, not the stocks, not tar and feathers, not even jail terms would stop Rogers and the Rogerenes who, over the years, grew in numbers, clearly in reaction to the closed New England mind. Whenever Rogers was hauled into court, he insulted officials; and his followers, as one historian put it, "tuned their pipes and screamed, roared, shouted and stamped."

His wife finally had enough of Rogers' constant assault on the establishment. She was granted a divorce and custody of their two children. She later remarried and the children promptly deserted her, returning to Rogers and becoming two of his most devoted followers. Rogers for his part recognized neither the courts nor the marriage laws. He insisted he was still married to his ex-wife, and once even tried to kidnap her from the bed of her most respectable second husband.

Yet later he himself decided to take a new wife and did so without constraint, since it was Rogerene doctrine that spouses could be acquired and discarded without benefit of court or clergy. His new wife was Mary Ransford, a young indentured servant and one of his stoutest followers, capable of as bizarre actions as Rogers. She once poured scalding water from a second-floor window onto a constable seeking to collect certain fees.

The couple's marital life proved very Rogerenian, marked by violent spats that required legal interference. Eventually the courts ruled that the couple had not been legally married and, under threat of forty stripes, Mary agreed to a separation, eventually marrying someone else respectably.

Rogers cared little. He had many jousts to partake and continued the violent practice of his religion. Almost as strong as his antipathy toward Congregationalists was Rogers' distrust of medicines, which he taught his flock to forego. Rogers regarded himself to be immune to all diseases and frequently exposed himself to sick persons to prove his point. In 1721 he insisted on going to Boston while the city was in the midst of a smallpox epidemic. He sat beside the afflicted and announced he was safe from the disease. He went home and a few days later died of smallpox. Within a few days his daughter-in-law and grandson met the same fate, having been exposed to Rogers.

As late as the 1830s the Rogerenes were still a hefty force in New London, Groton, and the vicinity, and they still bore an antipathy to all other denominations. When a new church was being built in New London, the Rogerenes allowed none of their number to work on the construction.

Cornbury, Edward Hyde (1661–1723)

THE PECULIAR GOVERNOR

In 1702 Queen Anne of England faced a serious problem concerning what to do with a wastrel spendthrift cousin, Edward Hyde Cornbury, the grandson of the famed first earl of Clarendon, who was the so-called Greatest of the Royalists. Unlike his ancestor, Lord Cornbury was a monumental eccentric who compounded his difficulties by running up huge debts he could not pay. Queen Anne nonetheless had a fond feeling for her cousin and, to save him from debtors' prison, she offered him the post of royal governor of the colonies of New York and New Jersey. It was a form of "transportation" that disgusted American colonists even more than the much condemned practice of shipping English criminals across the ocean.

The leading Tory historian William Smith was later to concede, "We never had a governor so universally detested."

Cornbury offended colonial sensibilities upon his arrival by announcing that he literally wanted to represent the queen; thereupon, he went about town wearing the most elegant dresses, some the gifts of Her Majesty (but whether for Lord or Lady Cornbury was a matter of some speculation).

Cornbury, in addition to flaunting his feminine finery in public, had the annoying habit of sneaking up on unsuspecting gentlemen and pulling their ears. Once, when scheduled to make a political address, he proceeded to irritate the assembly by delivering

Dressing in women's clothing was but one of the eccentricities New York colonists found galling in their Royal Governor, Edward Hyde Cornbury.

an ode dedicated to his wife's ears. He then invited the gentlemen present to feel the delightful contours of his wife's ears.

Besides his taste for female dress, Cornbury developed other unpopular habits. He was soon known to the colonists as, among the more genteel terms, a spendthrift, grafter, bigot, and drunken, vain fool. He appears never to have turned down any bribe offered, especially from the aristocratic faction in New York, and when he obtained a grant for raising armed units, he promptly embezzled a huge portion of the funds for his personal use. He wined and dined in luxurious style at home, and the bills for his foods, drink, and finery were staggering. Despite all the dipping into the public till, Cornbury's debts mounted, but he remained legally untouchable because of his official position.

Finally, after being deluged by colonial petitions against this "peculiar, detestable maggot," Queen Anne was forced to recall him. However, as soon as the official decree reached New York, in effect stripping him of his immunity, irate creditors had him flung into prison. He might well have rotted there but for the fact that his father had died, making him the third earl of Clarendon, thus once more immune from prosecution. Leaving his creditors powerless to act, he blithely returned to England, where the queen saw to it that he was able to continue a political career under her aegis, despite all the obvious peculiarities of his character.

Bowers, Bathsheba (1671–1718)

LOVE'S SOLITAIRE

One observer of odd personalities, Richardson Wright, noted many years ago that the difference between the male and female of the species is rather pronounced when they are tainted by a sad affair of the heart. Women, he observed, tended to "grow tight-lipped and acidulous." Men, he added, "become unconscionable rakes or dour penny-pinching grouches." Quite a few female crossed lovers, it seems, do turn recluse or take to religion for consolation. Bathsheba Bowers did both.

Bathsheba's grandmother was the niece of Henry Dunster, the first president of Harvard. Bathsheba's father was a Quaker, a fact that caused his eviction from England. Settling in New England, he often ran afoul of the Puritan code. Still, he was a plucky sort and, despite intolerance, managed to maintain a farm of 20 acres near Boston, raising 12 children in reasonable comfort.

At that time, the late 1600s, Philadelphia was much more a haven for the Friends, so Father Bowers shipped off four of his daughters, including Bathsheba, to live there. By the age of 18

Bathsheba had obtained numerous admirers and, common to the affairs of maidenhood, also suffered the sadness of an undependable lover. Thus she had a broken heart to nurse.

Living on her own, Bathsheba maintained a beautiful home and garden in what is now South Second Street, but she also built a small cottage out a bit further, under Society Hill. She began to spend more and more time in the simple cottage, furnished with books, a table, a hard bed, and a cup. The place became known as Bathsheba's Bower and, as a descendant's account reads, "she retired herself as free from Society as if she had lived in a cave underground, or on the top of a high mountain."

Bathsheba read her Bible, and contemplated and wrote of religious matters. She lived an ascetic life, eating neither meat nor fish. In 1709 she wrote a pamphlet about her own religious experiences, entitled "An Alarm Sounded to prepare the Inhabitants of the World to meet the Lord in the way of His Judgement." This brought her considerable fame. From the balcony of her bower George Whitefield, the noted revivalist, once preached to a large crowd.

But Bathsheba generally preferred being very much alone. She wrote a history of her life—her advice to young girls who suffered defeat in love was for them to develop green thumbs and garden their troubles away—which she distributed without charge. She also kept a remarkable diary and several manuscript books filled with visions and dreams, "and a thousand romantic notions of her seeing various beasts and bulls in the heavens."

Bathsheba, one would have thought, had found solace and bliss in her retirement, yet after two decades she suddenly left her bower. She moved out further in the country, to be more alone, and then she up and left Pennsylvania entirely for a backwoods settlement in South Carolina.

It was an area beset with problems: wild animals, ravaging diseases, attacking Indians. However Bathsheba was happy and very involved in the affairs of the colony. Then a harsh plague hit and, while Bathsheba was abed with fever, the Indians attacked. In a cottage next to hers several persons were killed before the Indians were driven off for a short time.

Bathsheba, despite the pleas of friends, refused to rise from her bed, insisting Providence would protect her. Thus the woman who had for so long deserted her fellows now refused to give up her place with a community of humans. Finally, two men, ignoring her protests, lifted her, bed and all, and carried her away to a boat for safety, all amid a hail of Indian bullets and arrows. It was a dramatic scene long celebrated in American literature. More than two centuries later it was vividly portrayed in more than one Hollywood film, including *Drums Along the Mohawk*.

Shortly after the excitement of Bathsheba's grand escape, she died—in 1718.

Lay, Benjamin (c. 1681–1759)

THE REBELLIOUS GNOME

Men go underground for many reasons—fear, penitence, disgust with humanity. But Benjamin Lay was a troglodyte cut from different cloth. He went to his cave as a protest, but he was of too fiery a temperament to bury himself there; instead he would charge forth constantly on various crusades. He was a little man, barely four feet six inches, and capable of acting in the most eccentric manner, without grace and obstinately. There are many Quaker families today who own heirloom portraits of Lay; for fifty years after his death few Quaker households were not so graced.

Lay was, in the words of John Greenleaf Whittier, "the irrepressible prophet who troubled the Israel of slave-holding Quakerism, clinging like a rough chestnut-burr to the skirts of its respectability and settling like a pertinacious gad-fly on the sore places of its conscience."

Born in Colchester, England, to Quaker parents about 1681, Lay went to sea in his early twenties. After seven years, he quit the sailor's life, after being shamed by the behavior he witnessed. Settling in London, he took a wife, Sarah, a quiet woman who must have found her 25 years with him a tribulation. But she followed him loyally, starting when he decided to leave London—twice he had been expelled from Friends' Meetings for his fiery temperament, and twice he ventured to the courts of both George I and George II to tell them the errors of their ways.

The Lays emigrated to Barbados, where Lay became a merchant. However, he was depressed by the overwhelming presence of slavery, and on the Sabbath hundreds of slaves gathered before

Benjamin Lay, the fiery crusader, lived in a cave home outside Philadelphia. He settled here with his wife to live as a gnome, secluded from the evils of slavery and barbarianism.

the Lay cottage to hear this flamboyant little man denounce the system that exploited them. Not surprisingly, the planters did not think highly of Lay and so, within a year, they went on to Philadelphia.

But Benjamin Lay was shocked to find slavery rampant there as well, and in disgust he moved to the countryside, where he would be less offended by mankind's wickedness. He had become a vegetarian in Barbados, after witnessing the slaughter of so many animals, and vowed for the rest of his life to eat no food and wear no article of apparel that involved the killing of any animal. Since he resolved never to utilize the work of slave labor, he wore only clothes that he made himself.

His vegetarianism struck meat-eating Philadelphians as odd, while his constant antislavery preachments led to embarrassment for those who tried to befriend him. While it was true that the Germantown Mennonite Friends had written against slavery since 1688, Lay became the first active public declaimer against slaveholding. As a protest, he moved himself and his wife into a country cave which, although still furnished like a house within, left him buried away from the sins of humanity.

This, however, did not mean that Lay could not issue forth to joust with evil. He harangued the Friends at their meetings, and when he could not get universal condemnation of slavery, he took more direct action. Once he stood in deep snow outside the Abington Meeting with his right leg bare. When others remonstrated with him, he said, "You pretend compassion for me, but you do not feel for the poor slaves in your fields who go all winter half clad."

On another occasion, at the Friends' Meeting in Burlington, New York, Lay showed up with a bladder filled with red berry juice concealed under his greatcoat. Midway through the meeting, Lay arose, railing against slavery and stabbing the bladder open, sprayed many of the congregation with symbolic blood.

It became common practice for Friends to eject Lay from meetings. Once he was forced out of the Market Street Meeting, and he immediately let himself fall in the gutter, remaining there until the meeting ended. Several Friends asked if he needed help, but he replied with indifference, "Let those who cast me here raise me up. It is their business, not mine."

He once fasted for 21 days, slightly more than half the time he had planned, but he had weakened so much that he finally bowed to the pleas of his wife and friends, and took nourishment. Lay, despite his eccentricities, had many friends, among them Benjamin Franklin, who published tracts Lay wrote, although not without much tribulation and editorial conflicts.

In 1741 Lay's own aching body and the sickly condition of his wife forced him to leave his cave, and the couple took up residency with friends in Abington. Sarah died the following year. The solitary life did not still Lay's temperament. He continued to rail against slavery and tea drinking—a practice almost as vile, he said. He spent his free time spinning, and he also made beehives, launching a detailed study of the social existence of those insects.

He was in his late seventies when he slowed to near inactivity. He lay near death on February 3, 1759, when acquaintances brought him word that the Society of Friends had voted to put out of their meetings any who did not free their slaves. Lay sat up, shouted a hallelujah, and cried, "I can now die in peace." He did.

In death, the little man of the erratic ways became endeared to the Friends. The most popular portrait of him that became a common possession in Quaker households shows him with his untrimmed beard and white scraggly hair, standing before his cave, his finger upraised in protest. The caption of the portrait reads: "Benjamin Lay, Lived to the Age of 80, in the Latter Part of Which he Observed extreme Temperance in his Eating and Drinking, his Fondness for the Particularity in Dress and Customs at times Subjected him to the Ridicule of the Ignorant, but his Friends who were Intimate with him Thought him an Honest Religious man."

Richardson, John (c.1690–1738)

THE GREAT SEDUCER

It could be said that John Richardson earned the title of the Most Wanted Lover in Colonial America. Certainly many broadsides told of his depredations, warning females of all ages to beware of his roguish charms. Whether such warnings were wise is a matter of dispute. In any event John Richardson seldom had trouble with the ladies wherever he stayed.

It is for the sexology texts to measure Richardson's romantic compulsions, ascribing to them possibly neurotic bases; but there can be no doubt that Richardson suffered from an incurable compulsion, one that he vowed on numerous occasions to curb, a promise lost in the crackle of a skirt.

Richardson's early forays are not recorded by his profilers, hence not much detail is known. We know he was born in New York and therein broke several maidens' hearts. He was what was known as a "Maiden Lane Rogue." Maiden Lane was a small New York street just beyond Wall Street that earned its name because so many maidens lost their maidenheads there. Some of Richardson's more enthusiastic profilers of the 20th-century male-magazine stripe have attributed the naming of the street to his efforts, but historical accuracy requires it be noted that Maiden Lane was so called when Richardson was still in swaddling clothes. Still, the fact remains that Richardson was so practiced he could find his way along the lane in the pitch of night.

The first offense specifically attributed to the great seducer concerned the daughter of a carpenter with whom Richardson found work. John had to flee the city. The carpenter stalked the streets after him, hammer in hand, looking for the young despoiler.

In due course we discover Richardson at sea. As a sailor he landed in Amsterdam. There he found a Dutch seaman's wife whose husband was on an extended cruise. Richardson settled in until news arrived of the husband's imminent return, whereupon the American decamped with a considerable amount of the Dutch couple's savings.

Richardson sailed to Boston where, with his substantial money hoard, he could retire to a county hamlet, living in the home of a farmer as a well-paying guest. From an Indian maid he acquired a large number of Indian handkerchiefs, for a payment that was not in the coin of the realm. And thereafter several farm girls were sporting Indian handkerchief mementos from Richardson. Richardson engaged in affairs with no more discretion than a cock-of-the-walk; soon he had managed to get a good half-dozen girls pregnant, including his landlord's daughter.

Richardson decided to do the right thing and marry one of his lovers; it was, he felt, the least he could do. Not surprisingly, he chose as his intended the landlord's daughter since her dowry would be the most bountiful. However this decision did not sit well with his other ladies. They promptly had him arrested, agreeing to his release only upon his giving surety for the maintenance of his future brood.

Richardson's marriage went forward upon his receipt of £300 dowry from his bride's anxious father; in a short time John announced he had better go to New York to find work to meet all his outstanding obligations. Amazingly, his wife and father-in-law allowed him to go, apparently believing his assurances that he was a moral man reborn who would make amends for all his sins.

Richardson was of course aware that his amorous activities were getting him into constant trouble. He made a public avowal to the courts that he would change. In New York the incorrigible Richardson secured work and lodging with a Quaker shipbuilder, and the Quaker's wife gained a bed partner. Caught flagrante delicto, Richardson decamped for Philadelphia. He knew now he could never go back to Boston.

In Philadelphia Richardson found lodgings with a handsome widow who had two teenage daughters. Soon all three were pregnant. Again limited to how much he could do right, lusty John offered to marry one of the daughters, and the widow apparently was so happy with at least a partial solution to the family dilemma that she agreed to a dowry of £100 and half her plate.

Did Richardson see himself supporting three newborn babes? The more he thought about it, the more he thought not. He sold the plate and moved south.

Wherever he went, the tribulations of young maidens and old

maids increased. Tales of John Richardson grew, and he was continually on the move. We have testimony of the drinking companions of this rogue in South Carolina that his problem was that he simply did not know how to resist the amorous advances of women.

He secured a berth as navigator on a vessel going from Carolina to Jamaica. When it returned Richardson was ensconced where else but in the shipowner's home. There was the inevitable daughter and the inevitable lunar developments. Being his usual good-natured self, John proposed marriage and the relieved father not only settled a dowry on him but provided his new son-in-law with a vessel.

Richardson put to sea just in time to elude a warrant from up north. He was identified as *the* John Richardson. Here nature lent a hand, and in a storm Richardson lost his vessel. He was barely rescued and taken ashore in Barbados. Soon he was living well, informing the Barbadians that he was the son of a prominent man and would reward them for the kindnesses they showed him. It turned out that the women were even more kind than the men. But by now he was somewhere in his late forties, and the ravages of a long love life were taking their toll. Some women actually *could* resist his charms.

Barbados was not so far removed from the American shore that Richardson would not eventually be identified, so he signed on to a British vessel as a common seaman. The ship was bound for Turkey and also on board was another adventurer named Richard Coyle. The men talked of gaining money, an enterprise that interested Richardson as much as his failing libido worried him.

So it was that the Great Seducer passed on to a new activity, that of murder. He and Coyle conspired to kill the captain and dispose of the cargo. The deed was done but the plot was unsuccessful, both men being apprehended. On January 25, 1738, Richardson and his accomplice were hanged on Execution Dock, London.

When news of John Richardson's tragic end spread throughout the colonies, there were numerous cries of satisfaction but also, we are told, many wails of anguish. As one of Richardson's profilers of past years put it: "To this day, Richardson is also a fairly common family name up and down the Atlantic seacoast."

Moody, Joseph (1700–1753)

HANDKERCHIEF MOODY

It was said that when the yound Reverend Joseph Moody succeeded his father as pastor of the Second Church in York, Maine, in 1732, the congregation was not a bit above quietly rejoicing. Reverend Samuel had been noted as one of the greatest "exhorters" in all New England and, after half a century of his damnation sermons, the parishioners were ready for almost anything else. Anything, it was to turn out, save Joseph Moody.

After but two years in his pastorate, Reverend Joseph fell into a deep melancholy. No one could understand it, and in time he was to become more a burden to his flock than his father had ever been. The young pastor developed such a pronounced phobia that he suddenly desired that no one see his face, a most disconcerting quirk indeed for a man of the cloth. Moody took to walking through York with a fold of crepe knotted above the forehead, hanging down and covering all his facial features. He was quite a sight to see in church, preaching with his back to the congregation, turning only to give the benediction, and then of course he was covered with the crepe or a silk handkerchief.

Not surprisingly, Moody's bizarre behavior, a permanent life-style for his last two decades, did not induce an added measure of joy at weddings, christenings and other celebrations. It got so that his flock avoided him on the road. To escape such slights he usually ventured abroad only at night and restricted much of his nocturnal prowlings to the area of the local graveyard, a beat that assured him an added degree of solitude.

Eventually "Handkerchief Moody," as he became widely called, resigned his post, never offering an explanation for his odd behavior; that secret was to be kept until his death. As he lay on his deathbed, a fellow minister afforded him spiritual comfort, and he relieved his soul to him. It developed that Moody had inadvertently shot a friend. The townspeople had laid the killing on a marauding Indian, never suspecting their minister. The torment of the shame he felt, and the fear of facing the scorn of his friend's family, forced silence on him. However, his feeling of guilt became so obsessive he finally vowed never to allow his face to be subjected to the open view of humanity.

Just before Handkerchief Moody's body was committed to the

ground, the clergyman lifted the cloth that covered his face, now forever safe from human censure. We are assured by one old account that it was "serene and majestic."

Peters, Samuel Andrew (1735–1826)

"THE LYING EPISCOPALIAN PARSON"

It has been suggested that the Reverend Sam Peters, rector of Hebron, Connecticut, took an awful vengeance on the new nation of the United States of America for the fact that he was mistreated, even tarred and feathered, for his Tory sympathies during the Revolution. He fled back to England and there went to work on his *General History of Connecticut.* The state is often said not to have lived down yet what the parson wrote. However, that theory of the origin of Reverend Peters' wrath grants him more justification than he deserves. It would have been difficult in 18th-century America to find a more compulsive liar or teller of tall tales—certainly one who was wearing the cloth—than Peters. He told fantastic lies in several other books and had a reputation for extracting powerful if nonsensical meaning from biblical events for use in his sermons.

Yet there is no doubt that his Connecticut "history" topped all his other efforts. To this day preposterous laws supposedly passed by Puritan lawmakers still are written of in popular histories as true; many such "laws" were in fact fabrications by Peters. Historians have found no traces of these ridiculous laws in records of that time; serious scholars now say there were no blue laws enjoining parents from kissing their children on the Sabbath, or restricting people from making mince pies or playing any musical instrument except the drum, trumpet, or Jew's harp.

Nor did such an earthshaking event as a caterpillar invasion along the Connecticut River ever occur. With an unquivering quill, Peters reported that the thorny little insects were so numerous that they marched in a phalanx three miles wide and two miles long, and ate every bit of green for 100 miles. Peters described these prickly little monsters as being two inches long with red throats.

Even more fearsome were the giant bullfrogs who marched through Windham in 1758 and virtually laid waste to the town with a ferocity unmatched even by raiding Indians.

Peters had a knack for mixing real events with improbable fantasies so that the former legitimized the latter, making the hodgepodge believable. His "histories" became bestsellers; he returned to America in 1805 to enjoy for the remaining two decades of his life a comfortable existence on the royalties his hoaxes earned him. It was only after his death that scrupulous historians studied his works in detail. Then he was given the sobriquet in learned circles of the "lying Episcopalian parson."

Lee, Mother Ann (1736–1784)

ANN THE WORD

The illiterate daughter of a Manchester, England, blacksmith, Ann Lee was to become a religious leader in America, dedicated to the proposition that she was the second (this time female) incarnation of Christ.

At the age of 22 Ann joined a small pentecostal group known as Shaking Quakers or Shakers, a name deriving from their highly active or agitated physical method of public worship. In 1762 she married a Manchester blacksmith named Abraham Standerin and had four children, all of whom died in infancy. These sad events had a profound psychological effect on her, and when she was imprisoned in 1770 for "profanation of the sabbath," she started experiencing revelations and visions that were to lead to her being accepted by many Shakers as the prophetess of the group. Mother Ann or Ann the Word, as she was called, had a lot of words to say about many matters. On the subject of coitus she was rather opinionated, describing it as "filthy gratification . . . a covenant with death and an agreement with hell . . . the root of all depravity." She promised those who copulated severe treatment in the Afterlife, including being bound up and tortured genitally. It may be noted that by this time her husband had left her for another woman.

Released from prison in 1772, she had a number of revelations that profoundly impressed her followers. In 1774, a vision instructed her to take her followers to America. Mother Ann and some of her disciples worked at washing and ironing in New York City, then purchased some property in what would later become Watervliet, near Albany, New York. The established rules called for communal ownership of property and the rigid practice of celibacy, which in due course could have had a profound influence on the growth of the community. Ann Lee passed the word that it was permissible to adopt orphans, thus solving the problem.

In the meantime Mother Ann, who had become known as a faith healer, ventured into Massachusetts and Connecticut, recruiting more followers. The movement continued to grow during the Revolutionary War, although Mother Ann spoke out against the conflict and ordered the Shakers neither to take oaths nor bear arms. For this, she and a number of her disciples were accused of treason and jailed in Albany for several months, without benefit of trial. Released in December 1780, Mother Ann went on with her work, including at times allegedly raising the dead back to life. Some of her disciples seemed to have a remarkable faculty for dying and, with the proper exhortations from Mother Ann at public gatherings, of miraculously reviving.

Not surprisingly Mother Ann gained the reputation, among the faithful, of being immortal. It must have come as quite a shock to them when she suddenly died on September 8, 1784. Had she lived a fuller life, the American Shaker movement undoubtedly would have achieved greater acceptance. As it was, the Shakers continued as a thriving, if small, sect, having established 11 communities in New York and New England by the 1790s. In the 19th century the Shakers spread into Ohio, Kentucky, and Indiana, and the movement reached its zenith in midcentury when there were some 6,000 adherents.

But by the middle of the 20th century, Shakerism was nearing extinction; its adherents to the end held to the worship of a Father-Mother God, with Mother Ann as the female principle of Christ. If the female founder of American Shakerism was bizarre in some of her beliefs, the fact remains that she inspired what were by far the most successful, longest-lasting communal societies to appear in this country. The Shakers also developed handicrafting and furniture making that were famed for their quality and design.

Perkins, Elisha (1740–1799)

THE FIRST AMERICAN QUACK

The first medical quack in American history—or at least the first to achieve a considerable following—was Dr. Elisha Perkins, who became obsessed with the idea that human ailments could be yanked literally from the body by the correct combination of metals acting in magnetic concert. He patented a device consisting of two three-inch-long rods. One rod was composed of an alloy of copper, zinc, and gold, and the other of silver, platinum, and iron. Exceedingly simple to use, the "Perkins' Patented Metallic Tractor" simply had to be pulled downward over the sickly portion of the body, and the disease, presto, was pulled free.

Virtually all experts on the subject agree that Elisha was a firm believer in his Tractor; he saw confirmation of its value in the many cases in which it seemed to help patients through what we now know was obviously the power of suggestion in psychosomatic ailments. Among his more notable customers were George Washington, who had his entire family use it, and Chief Justice Oliver Ellsworth.

Elisha's son, Benjamin (Yale, class of 1794), made a huge amount of money selling the Tractors in England. In Copenhagen, 12 medical men published a learned volume in defense of "Perkinism." Experts, including Oliver Wendell Holmes, said that Benjamin was no fool, that he knew his father's obsession was medical humbuggery, but he nevertheless cashed in on the device. In 1796 he published a book offering hundreds of enthusiastic testimonials from intelligent people, among them doctors, scholars, ministers, and members of Congress.

How could such stirring tributes be countered by a mere medical man who did some tests with phony tractors resembling the genuine item but actually nonmetallic in content? His results, of course, were equally "excellent." Holmes, first dean of the Harvard Medical School, could not help being somewhat amused by Perkinism, often relating the tale of a woman who immediately lost the pains in her shoulder and arm when a fake tractor of wood was applied. "Bless me!" she exclaimed. "Why, who could have thought it, that them little things could pull the pain from one!"

The younger Perkins lived to retire a very rich man in New York City, and Elisha Perkins went to his grave fully deluded that his Tractor was a boon to mankind. In 1799 Elisha took his Tractor to New York City, which was then being ravaged by a yellow fever epidemic. He would, he said, put things right. Within four weeks, Elisha himself was dead of yellow fever. He was 59 years old.

Burton, Mary (c.1741)

THE GREAT INFORMER

Mary Burton was an insignificant prostitute and thief well known for her lack of brainpower. However, she stands as an example of how an eccentric may be embraced by society when he or she appeals to its basic needs. In 1741 fear swept the colony of New York that its blacks, both slave and free, planned to revolt and murder the whites in their beds. At the time Mary Burton (sometimes known as Margaret Kelly) was in jail; authorities began making inquiries about the supposed black plot.

Eager to please her jailers, Burton quickly acknowledged that she had been in the company of several blacks while such discussions were held. Although she was noted as "weak-brained," her testimony was eagerly seized on and, as she happily produced further revelations, persecution of blacks ensued. In all, 71 blacks were transported out of the colony, 20 were hanged, and 14 were burned at the stake, a toll much greater in fact than had been taken during the Salem witchcraft hysteria.

Mary Burton now walked the streets of New York as a heroine of great prestige, gaining in stature with each conviction. Soon Burton came to regard herself as a real lady with few equals, and she started making shocking accusations linking a number of the colony's leading citizens with the black conspiracy. While the testimony of a white eccentric might be more than sufficient to doom any black, it was another matter when concerning prestigious whites. Furthermore, the great dignity exhibited by many doomed blacks at their executions (much like that of the Salem victims) sparked additional doubts regarding Burton's babblings. She was cast out of decent society once again to finish her years with her imaginings not paid any attention.

Cook, Tom (1741–?)

THE LEVELLER

It may be safely said that New England was this country's most fertile and tolerant ground for eccentrics. While the Puritan tradition was harsh in its treatment of malefactors, real or imagined, there can be little dispute that New England, much as its namesake across the ocean, suffered its fools with notable restraint.

Usually.

But what if the oddball suffered from the villainy of near wholesomeness? What if he had the ethics of a real-life Robin Hood? Here was behavior to grate the Yankee conscience indeed, mischief carried beyond all acceptable bounds, evil deeds in compact with the devil.

Tom Cook, born in 1741 to a blacksmith family in Westborough, Massachusetts, became known far and wide as a most incredible thief. Scores of New England towns reported his transgressions, and since most records were kept by men of property, his virtues, carried out with a compulsive nosethumbing of authority, were not noted in favorable terms.

Tom called himself "the leveller." It is a matter of fact that he stole from the rich and well-to-do with flair and cunning, bestowing much of what he took on the poor and needy. Such traits are fine for a Robin Hood when it serves the political purpose of battling tyranny but, as a redistribution of wealth for mere altruistic purposes, the behavior seems tinged with the most vicious rascality—at least to the rich.

That Tom so often absconded with a shank of meat from a wealthy farmer's kitchen and deposited it on the spit in a poor man's house made him a hero to one man but, just as equally, a rogue to the other. Also true was the fact that there was no universal approval of the leveller when a poor woman lay ill in bed, and Tom decided to find her the best feather comforter available. He sneaked into a wealthy farmer's house, tied one in a sheet, and then went downstairs and around to the front door. He asked the mistress of the house if he could store the bundle with her for a few days, but the woman recognized him as the scourge of the area and slammed the door in his face. So Tom walked off with his prize with a clear conscience.

Tom appropriated goods and grain and meal from carters'

wagons and dispensed them to the needy, often before the drivers' eyes. And he was always cheered by village children, for they knew he always had pockets stuffed with toys—all stolen of course—for them. The children's elders did not share the high regard for Tom's actions, fearing his example would send their offspring on the same evil road he traveled.

Many wealthy farmers and businessmen found it better to pay him tribute, to guarantee exemption from his depredations; but vengeance finally came their way when he was caught roasting himself a stolen goose in an abandoned schoolhouse in Brookline. Conviction could have confined him to jail for some time; but his many victims, who flocked to his trial, wanted more immediate and direct punishment. Tom was offered the option of jail or to run through a gauntlet of teamster whips, a punishment that often resulted in maiming or death.

Tom chose the gauntlet, and he was savagely lashed by men angered by a score of years of his misdeeds. Tom survived, but the record is not readily available to indicate if he ever strayed into the eccentric life of a Robin Hood again. On that day no doubt his victims felt that virtue, honesty, and, above all, sanity stood affirmed.

Dexter, Timothy (1747–1806)

THE LUCKIEST SPECULATOR

A fool and his gold, we have long believed, are soon parted. In the case of Timothy Dexter, a Yankee trader of considerable renown, that sentiment was pure balderdash. He blundered his way into an ever-increasing fortune, much to the chagrin of his many detractors. And Dexter was no run-of-the-mill fool but rather the complete idiot—authoring one of the stupidest books ever written to prove the point. Semiliterate at best, he nevertheless dubbed himself "First in the East, First in the West and Greatest Philosopher of all the Known World." He unilaterally proclaimed himself to be a lord, even offering the young American nation the opportunity to crown him king.

Born in Malden, Massachusetts, January 22, 1747, he had meager schooling. At the age of nine he was placed on a farm. At 16 he became an apprentice to a leather dresser, and in 1769 he set himself up in business in Newburyport, starting out with a capital in British coin worth about $8.20. The following year he made one of his shrewdest deals, marrying a well-to-do widow named Elizabeth Frothingham. Elizabeth in later years regretted her marriage, being appalled by her husband's many eccentricities, but Dexter did not. He used his wife's fortune well, although it hardly seemed so to her at the time.

During and after the American Revolution, the Continental currency fell in value until it was considered practically worthless. The only money instruments considered more worthless were the various state bonds which, the general consensus was, would probably never be redeemed. As a result, they sold at a fraction of their face value. Dexter proceeded to buy up as many of these bonds as he could, and he became pretty much of a laughingstock. In 1791, however, Alexander Hamilton won his point that the debt of the United States, and those of the individual states comprising it, was "the price of liberty," and the bondholders were paid off in full. Timothy Dexter, much to the chagrin of his Massachusetts compa-

LORD TIMOTHY DEXTER

Lord Timothy Dexter, who blundered from one fortune to another, was bufuddled when the newly freed colonies passed up his offer to become the new nation's king.

triots and, quite possibly, to his own surprise, overnight became a very rich man.

It was perhaps a form of resentment that caused so many businessmen thereafter to seek to hoax him and hurt him financially. Thus, when he once asked some merchants what he should do with a few hundred loose dollars, they maliciously advised him to buy a cargo of warming pans and send them to the West Indies. Dexter took the advice. Truly it may be said that Providence sometimes shows its contempt of wealth, by giving it to fools; for Dexter found a ready market for the warming pans. The tops were used by the West Indies inhabitants for strainers, and the lower parts became dippers in the production of molasses.

Later, other hoaxers suggested Dexter send Bibles and mittens to the same warm, "heathenish" climes. Both items arrived at the most opportune times, that of a burst of Christian interest and during the visit of ships bound for the Baltic Sea. Dexter sold his Bibles at more than double his costs, and an eager sea captain bought up the mittens for resale in frigid eastern Europe.

With the proceeds of his West Indies trade, Dexter built a fine vessel. Informed by the carpenter that "wales," were needed, he asked a businessman what the carpenter had meant. "Why, whalebones, to be sure," came the reply from someone eager to impose on Dexter's stupidity. Dexter set about buying whalebones with a vengeance, and when Boston could not supply him with enough, he emptied the stores of Philadelphia and New York as well. The story became a standing joke among the ship-carpenters, until the good fortune that always seemed to smile on Dexter struck again. New fashions dictated that ladies wear stays lined with whalebone, and it turned out Dexter had a lock on the market. He once more raked in a fortune.

Even when he violated the old adage warning against transporting coals to Newcastle in England, Dexter triumphed financially. His shipment arrived in the midst of labor troubles that had closed the mines there. Desperate buyers paid premium prices for Dexter's coal.

Was it any wonder then that Dexter thought it only reasonable that he make himself a lord and, indeed, seek the royal crown in America? Dexter affected regal pomp in his appearance and behavior, and once he even staged a mock burial for himself on a kingly scale. There were honorary pallbearers, a minister to pronounce a fitting eulogy, and enough funeral meats and drinks to sate some 3,000 guests to the rites. When Dexter noticed his wife was not into the spirit of the event and was shedding no tears, he proceeded to beat her in the presence of the mourners until she cried properly.

About this time Dexter also decided to make his mark in the literary world and published his autobiography entitled *A Pickle for the Knowing Ones, or Plain Truths in a Homespun Dress*. Written with utter disregard for punctuation and with capital letters hurled about willy-nilly, the book expounded Dexter's philosophy of life. "I wants to make my Enemys grin in time Like a Cat over A hot pudding and goe away and hang there heads Down Like a Dogg bin After sleep" As to his financial well-being, he explained with colorful modesty; "I was very luckkey in spekkelation"

Dexter expounded his theories on the nature of man, religion, and original sin, world politics, peace movements, college learning, and why he was so successful with the maidens. Almost anything that passed through his muddled mind went into his masterwork. *Pickle* went through four printings, not surprising since Dexter proudly gave copies away, and it had become a sort of word game to figure out what he had written.

Dexter answered complaints about his lack of punctuation by appending to the second edition a full page of commas, periods, question marks, and exclamation points for his critics so "thay may peper and solt it as they plese." One of Dexter's 20th century profilers, J. P. Marquand, has written, "Whether intentional or not, the 'Pickle' is like Dexter's life, a huge and ill-formed jest."

It may be difficult to fathom how it was noticed, but Dexter lapsed into senility in the last few years of his life, a condition aided along by his stupendous absorption of rum. Meanwhile, his writing, often using word combinations that no one understood, commented on such major topics as politics, the cost of funerals, and whether angels were truly adorned with wings.

It was almost a relief to all, friends and "Enemys" alike, when he passed from the living in his sixtieth year, in 1806. A long obituary in the local paper called him "perhaps one of the most eccentric men of his time. . . . His singularities and peculiar notions were universally proverbial."

In his will, he left his hometown of Malden three hundred dollars to buy a bell for the meeting house, plus another $2,000, the interest on which was to accumulate for 100 years and thereafter be used "for the support of the gospel." Dexter may have been as mad as a hatter, but he retained to the very end his knack for accumulating wealth.

Anonymous (early 18th century)

THE NAKED BEACHCOMBER

Nudism did not shock colonial America—as long as it was practiced by the Indians, who were of course "heathens." However, when the first white men publicly stripped down, the effect on the colonists' conscience was one of bitter rage, and it often resulted in violence for such blasphemy. However, that does not appear to have been the case in what may have been the first instance of nudism on these shores.

From whence or when the so-called hermit of the "dividing line" between Virginia and North Carolina came, we know not, only that he was there early in the 18th century—a fearsome-looking, long-bearded beachcomber from whom all kept their distance. Most likely he was a marooned seaman who, having made it somehow to this lonely coast, decided to go no further. By this time Defoe's *Robinson Crusoe* had gained wide circulation, and some of the inhabitants of the area tried to give their hermit a few of those romantic qualities. That was difficult to do; he appeared hostile, keeping intruders away not only by menacingly preparing to hurl rocks but by his lack of raiment. He generally went totally bare, protected in time only by a long beard.

This behavior was enough to keep the natives at a distance, and we can only imagine the shock they sustained when this naked beachcomber somewhere, somehow found himself a mate, a woman who dressed as immodestly as himself.

Our description of the pair comes from William Byrd, a New England surveyor who, in 1728, was engaged to mark the borders of the two colonies. Byrd may have been, if not our first gossip columnist, one of the merriest. He seems to have rejoiced telling of "A Marooner that modestly calls Himself a Hermit, tho he be forfeited that Name by Suffering a wanton Female to cohabit with Him."

What shocked, or at least impressed, Byrd was that this strange maroon seemed not to be afflicted with either ambition or conscience, and he let a woman wait on him. "His Habitation was a Bower, cover'd with Bark after the Indian Fashion which in this mild Situation protected him pretty well from the Weather. Like the Ravens, he neither plow'd nor sow'd, but Subsisted chiefly upon Oysters which his Handmaid made a Shift to gather from the adjacent Rocks. Sometimes, too, for a change of diet, he sent her to drive up the Neighbor's cows, to moisten their mouths with a little Milk."

No one dare protest such an expropriation. Even the most property-conscious farmer seemed to have considered it wise to ignore the situation. Byrd seems to have been the most conscientious observer of the pair, recording that this female at least had the decency to use the length of her hair as an apron "and the rest dangled behind quite down to her rump, like one of Herodotus' East Indian Pygmies. Thus did these wretches live in a dirty State of Nature and were Adamites, innocence only excepted."

Alas, we have no reliable record of what became of the naked hermit and his spouse, once observer Byrd departed the scene. Could they perhaps have one day entered clothed society? If so, they must have trekked far from the dividing line, to someplace where they would not have been recognized. Unfortunately solitaries and recluses have never felt obliged to fill in the blanks in their record. Our wonderment seems to be no concern of theirs.

McQuain, John (fl. late 18th century)

THE MAN WHO HATED WOMANKIND

The word "mankind" is no favorite with present-day feminists, but in the 1770s, in the neighborhood of Waterford, Massachusetts, there thrived a hermit farmer who can only be described as a dedicated hater of womankind. John McQuain left Bolton and showed up in Waterford as a young man in his twenties. He clearly demonstrated a dislike for women, shuffling away with downcast eyes when one approached him. What caused this strange but consistent reaction, which clearly went beyond shyness—an uncaring mother, an object of his affection who did not return his love? No one knew, but it soon became apparent to McQuain that he could not hope to avoid females in Waterford or anywhere else in civilization. And so he moved deeper into the forest, building a hut on a distant plot of land for $40. He owned no household furnishings other than a pail, a dish, and a spoon; all else he apparently held to be too feminine. His only companion was a dog—male.

For a number of years McQuain worked his land alone, clearing away trees and sowing crops. As he prospered, he kept extending his holdings, until he had 800 acres and 40 head of cattle. As his work load increased, he brought in day laborers, men only. However, none of the workers would take care of the cows, since they considered that to be a dairymaid chore. But McQuain would have no maiden, spouse, spinster, or widow on his land, and was content simply to dump the milk as feed for his hogs. The hogs waxed enormously on this rich diet and fetched huge prices.

Not once is it recorded that McQuain ever left his tract, although he proved to be a generous host whenever male passersby visited him. Food and liquor issued forth in generous volumes, but whenever McQuain was invited to return the visit or come to town, he demurred, explaining the farm required his constant presence.

If McQuain lost popularity with the women of Waterford, the townsmen and certain of the town fathers thought highly of him. His farm was so prosperous that he paid double the tax for any other landholding of like size. On several occasions, married men tried to imitate McQuain's success in deep-forest farming, taking their wives along. But all failed miserably. On the McQuain farm, cider and liquor flowed freely when McQuain learned of each failure, but he was never recorded as saying what he thought accounted for the misadventures of the married men.

With the passing years McQuain's history becomes lost, perhaps because he became a pariah to some. He made his own way, with a lonely sort of dignity, but his was clearly not the way for all mankind.

Phyle, Francis Adam Joseph (?–1778)

THE HERMIT OF MOUNT HOLLY

For almost 25 years in the 18th century, Mount Holly, New Jersey, hosted a penitential cave dweller about whom little was known. The local citizenry knew not his name, and he, speaking no more than a few words of English, provided them with none. Yet from the 1750s—perhaps 1755, but no one was sure when the hermit took up residence—he was treated with general kindness and charity.

In 1758, 21-year-old Hannah Callender of Philadelphia recorded in her diary a trip through New Jersey, during which she "Went to see the Hermit in a wood this side of Mount Holly. He is a person thought to travel along from Canada or the Mississippi about ten years ago, living in the woods ever since, partly on the charity of the neighborhood, partly on the fruits of the earth. He talks no English and will give no account of himself."

For the next 20 years the hermit resided in his cave on some land belonging to Joseph Burr. There is no record of Burr himself learning very much about his tenant, but this hardy farmer never allowed his farmhands to clear that portion of the land or disturb the hermit in any way.

One who finally did get some facts out of him was Surgeon Albigence Waldo of Connecticut, who conversed with him in Latin and German, although he found the hermit also spoke Italian and Spanish. It later was learned that he spoke French as well. By the time of his conversation with Surgeon Waldo, he had survived some 20 years on wild berries, water, bread, and whatever other food neighbors brought him.

The hermit's home was a cave that he had dug out under a large oak uprooted by a storm. So shallow that it just allowed him to sit up, it was covered over with boards and bark, to provide him with both blanket and roof. The cave was lined with old clothes and rags given him by neighbors. This provided him with his sole additional source of warmth; he never lit or even approached a fire, regardless of how extreme the cold weather was.

The hermit described his small cell as his "grave," informing Surgeon Waldo that God had ordered him in a dream to live in that fashion. He was a man of deep religious convictions. He had a number of Latin books as well as others, and each day he knelt before a certain tree to pray. He wore a crucifix around his neck;

he would kiss the hand of any visitor and then his crucifix. He accepted all gifts except money, but he seldom left his wooded area unless completely out of food, when he went begging from door to door. Whatever he was handed, he accepted with gratitude and blessed the giver. Only once was he subjected to any cruelty. That happened when he was still wearing a long beard, which he did up under his chin. A group of boys fell on him and cut it off. Thereafter he kept his beard trimmed short.

After Surgeon Waldo's visit, the hermit talked to others who could understand him. He explained that God had informed him that if he remained in such a penitential state until he was 80 he could come out purified and live in general society.

With the outbreak of revolutionary fighting, the hermit was subjected to fierce firepower when an engagement took place in his area in 1777. The hermit simply remained underground as musket balls whistled above him.

Neighbors were much relieved when they found he had survived the battle, but the hermit's days were numbered; he was not to reach the age of 80. On January 19, 1778, a neighbor trudged through the snow to bring him food, and he found the hermit prostrate and feverish. He refused the neighbor's offer to come to his home, however, and the following morning a number of neighbors found the old man dead, crucifix in his hand. He was buried in the Friends' burial ground at Mount Holly.

Only after his death was the hermit identified. There was a welter of wrong accounts, some of which dubbed him Francis Furgler. Actually his name was Francis Adam Joseph Phyle. He had revealed this in 1756, through an interpreter, to Colonel Charles Read. Read, a member of the Supreme Court, had respected Phyle's desire to lose himself and his identity.

In 1756, though, he had explained to the colonel that he'd been born in Lucerne, Switzerland; he had joined the French Army and seen duty in Canada. After killing an opponent in a duel, he deserted the army and took to wandering in New York and New Jersey, searching for a place of penitence for his awful sin. A 102-page pamphlet entitled *The Hermit Or an account of Francis Adam Joseph Phyle* appeared in 1788. It proved so popular it went through a second printing.

Wilkinson, Jemima (1752?–1819)

"PUBLICK UNIVERSAL FRIEND"

Jemima Wilkinson was born into a family of 12 children some time in the 1750s. Her parents were Quakers who had been expelled from the local meeting for refusing to use the "plain language." But even that inherited strain could hardly account for Jemima being such a difficult child and, as the saying went, "taking rebellion with her mother's milk."

She was easily the beauty of the family, which apparently convinced her she should do no housework and instead spend her time reading poetry or throwing tantrums. A traveling evangelist converted her to religion, and she thereafter spent most of her waking hours reading the Bible and searching for spiritual peace. That search eventually led her to the arms of a British major who later "left her to fight Yankees but lost her address."

In 1776, this sad experience and the fearful signs of war caused Jemima to suffer increasing ill health. She took to bed, and a doctor insisted he could do nothing for her, that her problems were of the brain. Jemima started having visions, which she revealed to a trembling family. Finally, she fell into a trance and was pronounced dead.

Her "corpse" was placed in a closed coffin and carried to church where, during the service, there was a loud banging on the coffin lid. The worshipers rushed to open it—and up popped Jemima.

It was the sort of disquieting occurrence that could result in almost anything, and it certainly produced a metamorphosis in Jemima. The next day she herself preached a funeral sermon for the old Jemima. She had been up to Heaven during her brief demise, she said; God had sent her back to earth, as the reincarnation of Christ, to prepare the Chosen Few for the Second Coming, which would take place during her lifetime.

Jemima took to the circuit, seeking converts. A tall, imposing woman, she often wore kilts, a broad hat, and her shirt buttons closed under her chin in the manner of male dress. She gained a fiercely loyal following in her native Rhode Island and Connecticut. She demanded of her growing congregation of "Universal Friends" a strict celibacy.

Jemima took her campaign into Massachusetts and Pennsylvania as well, and by 1790 she had established herself in a religious settlement with some 260 followers in the Finger Lakes region of western New York, near what is currently Dresden. On one occasion, irritated by the comments of some skeptics, she announced she would demonstrate her divine power by walking on water as Jesus had done. A platform was built by her devoted followers on the shore of Seneca Lake, and they strewed white handkerchiefs for her to tread upon.

Jemima arrived at the proper dramatic moment. Alighting from her handsome carriage, she strode to the platform, from which she delivered a stirring sermon. Then she dabbed her foot in the water and gazed directly at the assembled group and asked, "Do ye have faith? Do ye believe that I can do this thing?"

"We believe!" the crowd chorused.

"It is good," the prophetess announced. "If ye have faith ye need no other evidence," she said, and with that, she departed with a flourish, amidst wild applause.

Jemima's followers built her an impressive house, a superior structure worthy of an aristocrat, with nine fireplaces. Her boudoir had the comforts and feminine amenities not usually supplied to a religious leader, and she demanded and got her meals, even if frugal, served her on the finest china and linen.

The Duc de Liancourt once described dining at Jemima's house. He told how she and her constant companion, Rachel Miller, dined privately in a separate room. After they had finished, the guests received their meal. Jemima then addressed the company through the open door.

The community prospered over the years, and Jemima achieved peace with the local Indians who apparently regarded her as some sort of "witch doctor."

Many of the Universal Friends practiced the celibacy required of them, but many ribald tales are told of Jemima, admittedly some by skeptics, of her less than total adherence to her own strictures. One concerns Mrs. William Potter, the wife of one of Jemima's wealthiest converts, apprehending her husband in the Wilkinson private quarters. She was rather unimpressed by Jemima's explanation that she was merely ministering to one of her lambs.

"Minister to your lambs all you want," she said, "but in the future leave my old ram alone."

One explanation for Jemima's hold on her flock was the fact that she maintained her beauty to an extent not measured by the years. At 40 she looked no more than 30, and when she was in her sixties, few believed she was even near 50. Of course, she led a pampered existence totally unlike the frontier harshness demanded of other women.

Jemima died on July 1, 1819, and following her instructions, she was not buried; the devout awaited her second arising. No doubt Jemima herself was taking no chances on a premature burial. However, as her body started to decompose, the faith of many of the Universal Friends faltered. The ranks thinned but some remained, sure that Jemima would eventually show up with an explanation. The movement lasted another 55 years when the last true believer died.

Bishop, Sarah (c.1753–1810)

THE ATROCITY HERMITESS

It would be difficult indeed for the world to experience a war that did not suffer from predictable atrocities. For young girls the fate is an obvious one. For Sarah Bishop of Long Island, N.Y., about 27 years old in the middle of the American Revolution, that suffering was to lead to her isolation from society, years later gaining for her the sobriquet of the "Atrocity Hermitess."

In the argot of the time it was noted, "Her father's house was burnt by the British, and she was cruelly treated by a British officer." Sarah herself attested to that fact in later years, when she occasionally talked to strangers about why she took up the solitary life. The English, entranced as always by the acts of an eccentric, studied her case with deep interest; an early 19th century publication in that country explained her motivation for withdrawal from life by reporting that "she was often heard to say that she had no dread of any animal on earth but man."

Dispossessed of home and virtue, Sarah Bishop left Long Island and ended up trudging the hills around Ridgefield, Conn., finally taking her abode in a cave located in a perpendicular descent of rock just across from the New York state line. The country, which is still wild today, was even thicker then, and offered shelter for deer, bear, and foxes. Like Albert Large (q.v.), the Pennsylvania

"Wolf Man," she feared no wild beasts and, according to a contemporary account, they "were so accustomed to see her, that they were not afraid of her presence." Indeed, they could count on her sharing the remains of her rations.

Ridgefield over the years got occasional glimpses of the hermitess; she appeared in town once in a while to attend Sunday church services. Seldom did she speak a word to anyone, quickly returning to her solitary refuge.

She had cleared a section of woods, a rich half-acre, and there cultivated all the provisions she required. She grew corn, cucumbers, potatoes, and beans. Peach trees and wild grapes abounded nearby, and close to her cave was a fine spring which she shared with the wild beasts.

As she aged into her fifties, she was not a graceful sight. Her clothes were a mass of rags done up in patchwork, and her uncombed gray hair fell around her face and below her shoulders. Her cave was not kept secret from the curious for long. The presence of strangers frightened her so that generally she retreated to her cave, barricading its opening with tree stumps she had removed from the land. At times, however, she could be coaxed to talk by those who gained her confidence. Some people even entered her cave, which consisted of a single room devoid of all furnishings. Her bed was made of rags on a rock ledge. She had no utensils but an old pewter basin and a gourd shell. Only in the stormiest and coldest of weather did she indulge herself with a fire; when the heavy snows hit, she hibernated for weeks at a time, surviving on vegetables, roots, nuts, and berries she had gathered in the woods.

Visitors to her cave in 1804 were quoted in a Poughkeepsie, New York, newspaper as saying, "We conversed with her for some time, found her to be of sound mind, a religious turn of thought, and entirely happy in her situation; of this she has given repeated proofs by refusing to quit this dreary abode. She keeps a Bible with her, and says she takes much satisfaction, and spent much time in reading it."

There is no evidence of anyone ever persecuting or harassing Sarah Bishop. Though it may be hard to prove, there seems to have been a greater tolerance of "touched" people in the early years of this nation. Her withdrawal from life may not have been approved of, but there existed a general attitude of letting "a body lead a body's own life." The Atrocity Hermitess was accepted for what she had been and what she became—right up until the time of her death in 1810.

Rapp, Johann Georg (1757–1847)

GOD'S PARTNER

Born in Württemberg, Germany, Johann Georg Rapp was a Lutheran minister who found that all the established churches of his day were, by his exacting standards, defective in their teachings and practice. He believed for example that God was both male and female, while Christ was without sex organs. Then too he insisted that the Second Coming of Christ was due in 1829, and that it was the duty of the churches to prepare the people for this great event.

The authorities soon had had enough of his preachings and threw him in jail. In 1803 the flamboyant Rapp gathered up hundreds of Württemberg farmers and led them to the New World, where he said they could practice their beliefs. These included gathering a great fortune to present to the Lord upon His return; they would then enjoy the privilege of ruling with Him.

They settled near Pittsburgh, Pennsylvania, and christened their new home Harmony. Later Rapp led them further inland to Indiana, but in time he decided his flock labored and worshiped better in Pennsylvania; they subsequently returned to a new Harmony (later called Ambridge).

Rapp's flock addressed him as Father; complete with robe, flowing beard, and shaggy hair, he looked as though he had just stepped out of the Bible. He firmly believed in keeping close tabs on his followers. He had a maze of tunnels, trapdoors, secret passages, and sliding walls constructed, which allowed him to pop into his church unexpectedly, shaking up the congregation.

So great was his hold over these otherwise hardheaded farmers that his every command was obeyed without a murmur of dissent. All his claims were accepted as gospel. Rapp offered the faithful pictures of footprints in limestone rock and explained they belonged to the angel Gabriel who had brought Rapp his heavenly instructions.

Rapp's most striking instructions concerned the matter of sex. He insisted that his followers suffer no distraction of the flesh, that they should practice celibacy. After all, since the community was involved in the creation of a fortune, it would find a lot of extra mouths to feed a needless burden. A visitor to New Harmony once wrote that the women seemed to have been deliberately "made as ugly as possible" in appearance, apparently to still potential romantic fires in the men.

Rapp never got along with his son John, and the rumor was that Father Rapp himself castrated John for his sexual sins. John Rapp was said to have died as a result of infection from this act. The Rappites denied this was the case and insisted John had died of a chest injury in a work accident.

The Rappite community was totally self-sufficient, a fact attested to by the presence of even such an establishment as the Golden Rule Distillery. The settlers also had a vinegar factory, a piggery, a soap-boiling house, a sawmill, and silk factories. They maintained a cutlery shop in Beaver Falls where 200 Chinese laborers worked for them. The Rappites raised their own fruit and vegetables, and had community tailors and shoemakers who were responsible for keeping the members well clothed.

Unlike other errant prophets of the approaching millennium, Father Rapp suffered no loss of face when Christ did not appear in 1829. He simply announced that matters had been "postponed."

By the time Rapp died in 1847, the community had close to $500,000 in gold and silver; over the next half decade, they invested heavily in oil, pipelines, and railroads. But by the turn of the century, the Harmonists disbanded. No doubt this was partly due to the fact that Rapp's edict of celibacy left them with a lack of members and likely leaders.

Bowles, William Augustus (1763–1805)

THE ADVENTURER CRANK

Was William Augustus Bowles a great American adventurer or a crank, a misfit or a spy? The matter has long been debated, but there is no doubt that his actions were bizarre enough to earn him the enmity at various times of all groups with whom he came in contact.

Born in 1763, the son of an English schoolmaster in Maryland, he so outraged his family by his erratic behavior that he thought it

Some chiefs of the Southeastern Indian tribes found the lavishly plumed garb of misfit-gone-native William Augustus Bowles too flamboyant to match.

best to run away at the age of 13. Going to Philadelphia, he managed to get accepted into the British Army. Amazingly, he was soon awarded a commission and sent to the British post at Pensacola, Florida. Running true to form, he failed completely to carry out his military assignments and was dismissed from the service.

This hardly fazed Bowles and, free spirit that he was, he went "native," living with the Creek Indians and taking a tribal maiden for his wife. The Indians regarded Bowles as a superior intellect, but this attitude would inevitably change.

At the time, the Creeks as well as other Indians in the area became involved in the colonial struggles of Spain, France, and Great Britain. Bowles, probably because of his antipathy for the British Army, instigated attacks by the Creeks on settlers in Georgia. Then, apparently tiring of this tack, he led the Indians in aid of the British after the Spanish had taken Pensacola in 1781. As a result, he was reinstated in the British Army. All this had occurred before he was 18 years old.

After the British were ejected from the American colonies, Bowles became an actor of sorts in New York City, this position allowing him outlets for his frequent flashes of temper. Outwearing the tolerance of the New York acting profession, he decided to decamp with a troupe to the Bahamas; but he soon tired of this, turning up again in Georgia, where he rejoined the Creeks in the wilderness.

It is not clear whether his Indian wife accompanied him in his sojourns in the white man's world, but her presence among the Creeks did not help him very much there. The Indians, especially the great half-breed chieftain McGillivray, concluded that Bowles was rather softheaded, the same opinion drawn by his family, the British, and others. Perhaps what upset McGillivray most was Bowles' penchant for wearing the lavishly plumed theatrical garb of his late profession.

McGillivray finally drove him from the tribe, but Bowles returned after the chieftain's death in 1793. He convinced the Creeks to make warring raids on the Spanish; later he had them again attack settlers in Georgia. Bowles himself, looking like an overdressed cock-of-the-walk, led the attack. In 1795 Bowles was captured by the Spanish and ended up in a far-off Manilan prison in the Philippines. When Bowles promised to resettle in Europe and behave himself, he was released . . . and he headed right back for Creek country.

Over the next several years Bowles repeatedly demonstrated that his word was hardly his bond, breaking promises to everyone for, what seemed, the mere deviltry of it. All this time the suspicion wouldn't die that there was cunning behind Bowles' madness, that he was in fact a secret agent in the service of the British, a charge that deeply grieved the British Foreign Ministry.

In his last years Bowles strutted about calling himself "Ambassador of the United Nations of Creeks and Cherokees," a claim that not all the aforementioned Indians accepted at this time. In 1804 he was betrayed, quite likely by Indians, to the Spanish, who shipped him off to confinement in Morro Castle, Havana. He offered to go straight to Europe, but his jailers seemed unimpressed.

When the peripatetic misfit died in prison on December 23, 1805, it was rather difficult to determine where the relief was most pronounced—among the Americans, British, Spanish, or Indians.

Robert the Hermit (c. 1769–1832)

THE BITTER RECLUSE

One of the most famous of New England's recluses, Robert the Hermit could tell a tale that had all the makings of a tragic epic. It explains why New Englanders referred to him as the "bitterest hermit in America." During the last 17 years of his life Robert was virtually devoid of any interest in humanity. Occasionally, when a person happened upon him, Robert looked through the passerby as he might a pane of glass. There was a rare exception, however. He made the acquaintance of a now-unknown author, which resulted in a 36-page pamphlet telling his life story, explaining why he wanted no intercourse with his readers.

He was a bitter man, having been buffeted by the fates; few who knew his story saw fit, during the hermit's last years, to challenge his right to his feelings. Indeed, concerned parents threatened their young with strict punishment if they ever threw rocks at Robert's abode. Some New England abolitionists saw in his story the evils of slavery, which would not be as movingly portrayed again until the 1850s, with Eliza's sad plight in *Uncle Tom's Cabin*.

ROBERT THE HERMIT

The story of Robert the Hermit, who was known to New Englanders as the "bitterest hermit in America," was embraced by abolitionists to portray the evils of slavery.

Robert was born in Princeton, New Jersey, around 1769 or 1770. His mother was of African descent and in bondage, and his father was "a pure white, blooded Englishman," a man of considerable eminence. His master moved to Georgetown, D.C., when Robert was four years old, after which time Robert knew no more of his mother.

For a time in his early teens Robert was apprenticed to a shoemaker, but eventually he was returned to his master's estate, where he worked as a gardener until he was 20. By that time Robert had met Alley Pennington, a black freewoman, who agreed to marry him if he could gain his freedom. But his master had no interest in losing his investment in Robert without reward; finally the young bonded black got a supposed good friend, James Bevens, to lend him £50 so he could buy his freedom.

Robert pledged to eventually pay off his bond, plus interest, through his labors, and he was able to marry Alley. Within three years the couple had two children and Robert had managed to pay off a large portion of his bond. However, he neglected to obtain receipts, considering Bevens an honest and true friend.

Late one evening as Robert and his family sat at the dinner table, Bevens and another man descended on their cabin, seized Robert and hauled him in shackles to a schooner bound for Charleston. There Robert was sold into slavery once again.

After a few weeks Robert escaped from his new owner and managed to smuggle himself aboard a sloop bound for Philadelphia. Doing without food and water, he made it to Philadelphia undiscovered. There he met a Quaker to whom he revealed his plight. The man gave him some money and promised to bring him more aid the following day. However, people in Robert's lodging suspected him of being an escaped slave and reported him.

Robert was jailed and finally returned to his Charleston master. Deciding Robert was incorrigible, his owner had him auctioned off again. This time Robert was bought by a Dr. Peter Fersue, for whom he labored eighteen months until escaping, this time by secreting himself in an empty cask on a Boston-bound vessel. After five days in hiding, hunger and thirst forced him from his hiding place. Fortunately, the captain was a Quaker who offered him food and drink and, on landing, turned him free on the docks.

Robert dared not try to get back to the Washington area to his family for fear of being retaken. Instead he signed aboard a ship for India. When he returned, he shipped out a second time; for a total of nine years he was a deckhand on ships traveling all over the world.

When on shore he generally stayed with a Salem woman who had three daughters. Despairing of ever seeing his wife and children again, he finally married one of the girls. He rented a small house for his wife, her mother, and her sisters; he sailed off again, returning to find he was a father.

After that he shipped out for China, a voyage that took 18 months. This was too long a time for his young wife who refused to accept him back.

Disconsolate, he moved out and took a berth with a shipping line operating out of New York. Nine more years passed—a full 20 since he had been ripped away from his beloved Alley and their two children. Finally, he shipped to Baltimore and then headed for Georgetown in search of his long-lost family. All he found were rumors that Alley had died of despair shortly after he was taken. The children, left alone and helpless, soon suffered the same fate as their mother. Bevens had long since gone West.

Robert moved to Rhode Island, where he built a hut on the tip of Fox Point. "I then felt but little desire to live," Robert says. "There was nothing then remaining to attach me to this world—and it was at that moment I formed a determination to retire from it, to become a recluse, and mingle thereafter as little as possible with human society."

Later on, some rowdy youths forced him to seek out a yet more isolated hut near the Washington Bridge. Once a week or so he wandered into Providence for a few necessities and talk to one or two acquaintances. Most persons, however, he totally ignored. With the publication of Robert the Hermit's story in 1829 he aroused a good deal of sympathy, and parents took care that their young left him in peace.

Still Robert the Hermit remained embittered with society and the fate it had saddled upon him.

He died April 1, 1832. An obituary in the *Providence Journal* read:

> In Seekonk, yesterday morning, at his Hermitage, near Washington Bridge, Robert, generally known as Robert the Hermit, aged three score years and ten. He lived a solitary life, rejecting the society of man and communing alone with his God. Funeral this afternoon at one o'clock, from his late residence.

The funeral was well attended.

Randolph, John (1773–1833)

THE FLUTE-VOICED SAGE OF ROANOKE

It has become a matter of near folklore to depict members of Congress, especially Southern ones, in past eras, in bizarre terms. In true life, the strangest of them all was Virginian John Randolph of Roanoke; he insisted upon this full appellation after he fought a duel of sorts with a kinsman also named John Randolph. John Randolph of Roanoke dubbed his relative Possum John Randolph, to indicate he only pretended to be an aristocrat.

Randolph of Roanoke had a disease-ridden, liquor-soaked body and one of the strangest gnawing consciences. He was sometimes called "Viper John" because of the way he lashed out at his political enemies. On the political spectrum of today there is left, center, and right; far beyond that was John Randolph of Roanoke. He had a record of opposing almost all legislation. Flamingly aristocratic in outlook, he championed states' rights with a passion possibly unmatched even by the fire-eating secessionists of a later day.

He was well educated. In time he inherited the family estate, which was rather appropriately named Bizarre, in Prince Edwards County, and he settled down to life as a landed Virginia gentleman. He was catapulted on to the national political scene when the country was arguing the Alien and Sedition acts. The Virginia legislature denounced them. Patrick Henry backed the president's right to exclude foreigners without trial. Randolph opposed him. On the strength of that performance, Randolph was elected to Congress in 1798.

He was six feet tall. The ravages of an adolescent illness left him the mere skeleton of a man. He was furthermore saddled with a voice that was high-pitched and flute-like. His opponents were to disparage him as "the flute-voiced sage of Roanoke," casting aspersions on his manhood. The same illness that had rendered him beardless had, according to some, caused him to be impotent as well.

In 1803 Randolph fluttered political circles with his announcement that he had fathered an illegitimate child. Since there had been not a whisper of this before, it seemed that he was merely fantasizing, trying to demonstrate his manliness. Still, he warned anyone casting aspersions on him or his babe—where he or she was

JOHN RANDOLPH OF ROANOKE

A contemporary silhouette shows John Randolph of Roanoke at his estate, appropriately named "Bizarre." He was elected to the House of Representatives, where his bibulous oratory intoxicated Congress as never before or since.

no one knew—that they would meet him on the field of honor. It was no idle threat. Randolph was an expert duelist and answered thusly many who mocked him.

In 1810, for no discernible reason, Randolph abandoned the comforts of Bizarre to live full time in Roanoke. Here, on an estate with hundreds of slaves, he lived in a log house in a dense woods. Some saw him as doing so to harken back to his roots, since Randolph traced his heritage back to Pocahontas.

When he was sober and feeling well, Randolph could be a gentle, caring person, but many biographers questioned his sanity and saw it worsen with each passing year. Others insisted his problem was merely drink; still others blamed it on the consumption that racked his frail frame. Seldom did he have two consecutive days of robust health. Others insisted he was always just plain mad. Eccentric, morose, he had a private life marked by constant changes and queer decisions made when he was drunk and outbursts of generosity when he was sober.

He often rode a horse until it was near death, and he punished slaves fiercely; not always physically abusive, he would nonetheless reduce them to tears by his savage tongue. Randolph often seemed to delight in upsetting others, especially preachers of the gospel. He once asked the Reverend Mr. Clayton to say grace at his table, and no sooner had the parson begun when Randolph interrupted him. "Stop, sir, if that is the way you are going to pray, go into the garden or garret." On another occasion he asked the parson's prayer, then halted him. "Stop, sir, if you pray after that manner God Almighty will damn us both."

Randolph was never the average matron's idea of the ideal houseguest. He was fond of coming to visit with horses, dogs, and guns; wherever he stayed his canine pack came along and, as one account put it, "they were suffered to poke their noses into everything and to go where they pleased from kitchen to parlor."

For years Congress suffered his vicious oratory in silence, regarding his as an unbalanced mind that could become unpredictable at any moment. In 1826 Henry Clay became so incensed at Randolph's barbs that a duel ensued. Neither participant was hurt.

Except during times of illness, Randolph's bibulous oratory continued to haunt Congress; his bony fingers, wagging head, and odd mannerisms gave an aura of unreality to congressional debate. Despite the claims of recent political commentators, such a strange style was never seen again.

Some say Randolph lived out the last few years before his death in 1833 in total madness, but it was not so. On his deathbed he threw aside all past hatreds and ordered his slaves freed and provided for financially. However, the laws of Virginia were most strict about any subsequent provisions for freed slaves. They required that a declaration be made in the presence of a white witness, and that witness had to remain with him until the moment of death, to insure that there was no change of mind. John Randolph saw to the effective carrying out of that requirement by ordering his loyal slave John to bolt the door to his room and keep the doctor present until he expired.

When Randolph took his time about dying, the doctor protested he had to call on other patients, but Randolph refused to let him leave until the doctor sent word to have a younger doctor and another friend replace him. When this was done, Randolph dismissed the doctor with a bony wave of the hand and said, "Very well, the young gentlemen will remain with me."

Chapman, John (c.1774–c.1847)

JOHNNY APPLESEED

John Chapman stepped into legend as Johnny Appleseed when, in 1797, he appeared on the Pennsylvania frontier burning with a benevolent monomania to plant apple orchards wherever he went. Since that time he has been extolled in story and verse; his tale has so intermingled fact with legend that it is often impossible to tell one from the other. Some have called him touched, others said saintly, but it no longer matters; he is one of America's greatest folk heroes.

He was born somewhere near Springfield, Massachusetts, sometime between 1768 and 1775 (with most estimates holding to the last two years of that span). What set him off on his zeal to cover the land with apple trees? It has been said he showed a love for apples from the moment of birth. The midwife who was taking care of Johnny and his mother, according to one tale, insisted that when she picked him up, she carried him to a window where there was an apple tree blazing with blossoms. "You'll never believe the way he carried on," she said. "Why he humped and gurgled and stuck out his little white paws as if he wanted to pick all those blossoms! And he was only 40 minutes old, too!"

Let us maintain our equilibrium and consider that story apocryphal. And what of another—that as a child he cried incessantly in his crib until he was handed a branch of apple blossoms, whereupon his squalls immediately turned to coos? In any case there is no doubt that Johnny did become mighty attached to apples. As to why he left New England in his twenties, we have it from some biographers that his motives—like that of many another footloose wanderer or, for that matter, a hermit—concerned a maiden in Clinton, Connecticut, who refused to marry him. Suffering, Chapman hit the road for his greater calling. Johnny lost a wife and folklore gained a legend, as he made his unique contribution to American pomology.

Johnny did not exactly cut a suave figure. Small and wiry, he was a restless man with "long dark hair, a scanty beard that was never shaved, and keen black eyes that sparkled with a peculiar brightness." Winter and summer he usually went barefoot, but at times when it was extremely cold he wore whatever footwear he

JOHNNY APPLESEED.

In this 19th century sketch of Johnny Appleseed, the artist probably rendered him a bit too dapper.

could find or fashion, such as rude sandals or perhaps a discarded boot on one foot and an old brogan or moccasin on the other.

Latter-day artists usually picture him wearing overalls or dungarees, but his usual garb was not quite such high fashion, consisting often of a coffee sack with holes cut for legs and arms. In lieu of a cap he wore a tin pan—utilitarian certainly since he also cooked his food in it.

After Pennsylvania, we meet our modest hero in the Territory of Ohio in 1801, with a horse load of apple seeds, which he planted in various places on and about the borders of Licking Creek. By 1806 Johnny was a regular along the Ohio River, with two canoe loads of apple seeds lashed together. Everywhere he was accorded respect. After all, there was little reason to chase off a character offering to plant apple trees on your land. And Chapman—now universally called Johnny Appleseed—promised to return regularly to make sure to cultivate the trees springing from his seeds. After some years, whole orchards sprang up everywhere—all along the shores of Lake Erie, French Creek, Walnut Creek, Elk Creek, along the Grand River, the Tuscarawas, the Mohican, the Muskingum, plus literally hundreds more lakes, creeks, and rivers.

At times Johnny sold his seeds to settlers heading west, but very often they had no money for such extravagances, and so he gave them the seeds without charge. Many people were touched by the tender charity of this gentle man and tried to help him. He was welcome in virtually any cabin along the Ohio. Once during a frigid November he was traveling barefoot through the mud and snow in Ohio when a settler insisted on giving him a pair of shoes, declaring it was sinful for a human being to be "foot naked" in such weather. About a week later the settler ran across Johnny and found him without shoes. Understandably angry, he demanded to know what had become of them. John explained he had met up with a family, all barefoot, emigrating west, and since they seemed to have greater need for clothes than him, he had given them his shoes.

The Indians too never bothered Johnny Appleseed. Some said it was because they never attacked a person they regarded as mentally afflicted, but it was just as likely that they held him in high esteem. Along with his seeds he carried Bibles, distributing them to settlers and Indians alike. Johnny was Swedenborgian in his religious inclinations, and the Indians seldom doubted his claims that he had frequent conversations with spirits and angels. (He explained he could not take a wife because he had been promised two angel spouses in the Hereafter if he abstained from matrimony on earth.)

The Indians' respect for him extended also to his fortitude for enduring pain. They were awed by his method for treating the cuts and sores resulting from his barefoot wanderings, watching with respect as he seared wounds with red-hot irons without whimpering in pain. Since Johnny was also a vegetarian, claiming he could not kill any living creature, he was further honored (if not emulated) by the Indians, who resented what they regarded as the wholesale slaughter of game by the settlers.

During the War of 1812, when the white settlers were butchered by Indians allied with the British, Johnny Appleseed was allowed to continue his wanderings unmolested by the roving bands of hostiles who met him. On several occasions this impunity gave Johnny the opportunity to ride through the countryside warning the settlers of approaching danger.

However such activities were all secondary to his spreading of apple seeds. Although he himself never went beyond Indiana, his seeds eventually spread much further. By 1838 it was estimated that the seeds he had planted himself had been growing into trees bearing fruit over an area of 100,000 square miles. Beyond that, he continually proselytized the virtues of the apple. Nothing pained him more than someone saying apples disagreed with them. "Apples," he lectured, "never, from the beginning of time disagreed with anybody. They were in all the great countries of the earth; they were in the Hanging Gardens of Babylon that were one of the Seven Wonders." And woe unto them who brought up the trouble in the Garden of Eden.

"That's wrong!" Johnny cried. "I don't know who started that story, but he was a bad man. Look in the Good Book, and you'll see that all it says is, they ate of 'the fruit of the tree.' Now that could be anything—a peach, a plum, a persimmon, a lemon—anything, in short, except an apple. Be sure the Lord wouldn't keep anyone from eating an apple. How many times is the apple spoken of in the Good Book in a favorable way? Eleven times, that's how many."

We know how Johnny Appleseed died, but there is some dispute as to the date, which may have been 1845 or 1847. After traveling some 20 miles one summer day, he entered the house of a settler in Allen County, Indiana. As usual, he was graciously welcomed. He did not eat with the family but accepted some bread and milk which he consumed sitting on the doorstep where he would watch the setting sun. Later, after offering the family his "news right fresh from heaven" by reading them the Beatitudes, he declined special sleeping accommodations and stretched out on the bare floor. The next morning this gentle eccentric was dead.

Dow, Lorenzo (1777–1834)

"THE ECCENTRIC COSMOPOLITE"

The opening of the 19th century has been described as a period of renewed religious fervor, spawning as it did a whole army of amateur John the Baptists who, self-ordained, ventured forth to spread their own form of piety. It was they who started the colorful American custom of the camp meeting, whereby an open field or a city street corner became pulpit enough to harangue a God-fearing public.

Foremost among these was a horseback evangelist, Lorenzo Dow. A tall, almost fearsomely disheveled Connecticut Yankee, Dow was brought up frugally, with five brothers and sisters, by parents who had educated them all themselves, Dow said, "both in religion and common learning." Dow caught the exhorter bug when he was only 17, after being influenced by an itinerant preacher. He thought to attain the rights of ministry quickly but that being denied him, he simply hit the preaching trail without any special sanction. His first preaching foray took him 4,000 miles over eight months, during which time he lectured as often as 15 times a week. Dow learned the backwoods evangelist art well. His typical method was to assemble his listeners in the local schoolhouse, push a table and his pulpit across the door, thus physically blocking any intended exit by bored listeners.

Actually few were bored. Dow ranted on at a hysterical pitch— Crazy Dow he came to be called—and indeed people came as much to be entertained as to get the word of God. Dow had a lot of things going against him. He was uncouth of person and appearance (ac-

By age 39, Lorenzi "Crazy" Dow had literally captivated congregations here and abroad.

cording to many contemporary reports, he enjoyed no intimate contact with soap and water), and his voice was harsh and his actions stern. Eloquent he was not, but he demonstrated a kinship for vulgar life and readily adapted to such tastes, weaknesses, and prejudices. He had no trouble spellbinding audiences even in his youthful days; he always appeared older than he was.

The words flowed from him in a fiery torrent, a fact in his favor in an era when a preacher's mettle was determined by how long he could talk and how violent his gestures could be. What he said mattered rather less than his delivery. Dow told stories artfully, and he could clinch any ecclesiastical point with an anecdote, whether confirmed by Scripture or not. Dow realized many of his listeners were cut of the same cloth as himself, and for them an illustration counted far more than logic. He was above all dependable. He would pass through an area and either stand on a tree stump or post a sign, saying, "Crazy Dow will preach from this stump six months from today, at 2 o'clock, P.M." He would too.

In 1796 he became connected with the Methodist ministry but was suspended after only three months. He was reinstated two years later, despite the general opposition of church ministers. They had reason enough to oppose him. Look at the way Crazy Dow unsettled the minds of their flocks and "seduced" virtually their entire congregations. And so it may safely be said that American clergymen in general were not unhappy when Dow ventured off to Ireland to preach—against the wishes of his superiors, however.

After 18 months of shaking up that country, Dow returned to the United States and invaded Georgia. He returned to New York and attracted large crowds in the hinterlands; he then trekked south again, his exhortations, threats of hell, and hope of paradise brought in many converts. He visited Indian tribes and became the first to preach a Protestant sermon in Alabama. He pushed northward into the Carolinas (where he was convicted of libel), Tennessee, and Virginia.

In 1804 Dow married, taking Peggy Holcomb as a bride on the firm understanding that she would not oppose his wanderings. The day after the wedding, Dow left for a swing to Mississippi. After that Peggy traveled with her husband, including a great sermon trip to England. He became known as the "eccentric cosmopolite." Peggy undoubtedly managed to miss a great many of his ranting sermons, but, as one profiler has stated, "her fidelity to him is at least worth a nomination for a martyr's crown."

Peggy died in 1820, and three months later Crazy Dow married Lucy Dolbeare of Montville, Connecticut. Thereafter, Dow, approaching 50, preached less often, instead becoming a compulsive pamphleteer. On his farm in Connecticut, he compounded medicines to cure biliousness, quarreled constantly with neighbors, railed on about Whigs, anti–Masons, Catholics, and even Methodists who, he said, were being tarred by popery. Sometimes things got so bad that Dow could not resist charging forth on the preaching trail again.

He died in 1834, but stories of his eccentricities kept his memory alive for decades. It was estimated that some 40,000 boys were named Lorenzo in honor of Crazy Dow, among them Lorenzo Dow (1825–1899), the famed inventor and businessman.

Wilbur, David (1778?–1848)

THE PUMPKIN SCRATCHER

David Wilbur was a disturbing engima to the residents of Westerly, Rhode Island. Everyone agreed he was quite mad—many called him the Wild Man—and yet there was the feeling that he might be wiser than they thought, wiser perhaps than themselves. Such can be a discomforting feeling, one that might cause resentment and persecution of the madman in question, but nothing like that was experienced by Wilbur. He was tolerated.

Wilbur was born in Westerly some time around 1778 and lived with his father until the latter's death, apparently about the time David was 20. After that Wilbur deserted the family home and Westerly, and he took to the forests, living almost completely on nature. He was virtually uneducated, and in time he developed a near universal fear of all humankind, adults and children.

Sometimes he would be seen at night sitting near a road, studying the stars in the sky. By day he watched the clouds and frequently held a wet finger in the air to check the winds. He was called by many "the Astronomer," and from a distance a passerby might call out a question about the coming weather. It was the only subject Wilbur ever answered, and his predictions were highly accurate, presumably at least the equal of 20th-century weathermen. Weather forecasting was important to Rhode Island folk, farmers and seafarers, and Wilbur's knack made him an eccentric worth knowing.

In the summer he lived chiefly on wild berries and fruits, and he slept in a swamp by the side of a large rock, using an old door as a sort of roof and a bunch of flax for a pillow. He stored up grain and nuts for the winter months, also eating roots and such game as he could trap. On rare occasions he took shelter in someone's shed or barn but almost never accepted invitations to enter a house. He preferred almost always to keep his distance from people, but he had further oddness to his behavior, which puzzled Rhode Islanders. It was evident whenever he was in an area, even though he was not seen. He had a singular penchant for scratching numbers and strange signs and figures on pumpkins in the field. What these markings indicated was never determined, although it appears that several residents tried to figure out Wilbur's "secret messages."

Was it some meteorological intelligence? One may presume that, had Wilbur etched his designs on more lasting objects such as the rock and sandstone used by ancient humanity, a Wilbur cult today would exist, trying to fathom the mysteries of his communications long after his death in 1848.

If, that is, communications they were.

Perhaps Wilbur was telling us something about the forces of Nature. Then again he might have meant nothing at all. One of Wilbur's profilers, Richardson Wright, has ascribed to him the sage observation, "There is a joy in being mad that only madmen know."

Symmes, John Cleves (1780–1829)

THE HOLLOW EARTHER

In 1818 Captain John Cleves Symmes, U.S. Infantry retired, a hero in the War of 1812, issued an astonishing circular. Entitled "To All the World," it was especially distributed to all members of Congress and to scientists both in this country and Europe. Accompanying

Although John Symmes managed to garner a few "practical" followers with his hollow earth theory—most notably politicians of the John Quincy Adams administration—his radical ideas were espoused primarily in lampoons and fiction.

the circular was a medical report signed by eminent physicians attesting to Symmes' sanity. Alas, it was not very convincing.

Symmes said that after many years of study he had concluded that the earth was a hollow sphere whose interior was inhabited and could be penetrated through a large hole at the North Pole. He wrote, "I ask one hundred brave companions, well equipped, to start from Siberia in the fall season, with reindeer and sledges, on the ice of the frozen sea; I engage we find a warm and rich land, stocked with thrifty vegetables and animals, if not men, on reaching one degree northward of latitude 82."

According to his theory, which was to be ridiculed as "Symmes' hole," the earth was really a group of hollow, concentric spheres through which the sea flowed at both polar openings (4,000 miles in diameter at the North Pole and 6,000 miles at the South Pole); plant and animal life surely had to thrive in the concave interior as well as on the convex surface of the next sphere, Symmes theorized. His expedition, he said, would have no trouble at all sailing over a curved rim and down the inner side of the earth.

Symmes appealed to all the nations of the planet to join in financing his expedition—and he got not a single contribution. The more ridicule was heaped on him, the more determined Symmes became, and the more he developed "facts" to prove his theory. The twilight that lit the Arctic regions, he said, was caused by the sun's rays bouncing through the hollow earth from the South Pole.

For a decade Symmes spanned the states, giving speeches in support of his theory and trying to raise funds; in time he gained a few supporters, including a Kentucky congressman who was later the U.S. vice president, Richard M. Johnson (*q.v.*). In 1822 Symmes' petition for support for an expedition was quietly tabled, but the following year another try by Johnson to place "Old Glory on those interior planets" actually garnered 25 votes in the House, not nearly enough but it kept Symmes' hopes alive. Indeed, a Symmes convert, John J. Reynolds, persuaded the secretaries of the Navy and Treasury under President John Quincy Adams to prepare three vessels for a voyage to the inside of the earth. When Andrew Jackson took over in 1829, he summarily canceled the enterprise.

By that same year Symmes' health collapsed from the strain of his efforts, and he died in Hamilton, Ohio, where he made his home. A monument raised to him by his son, Americus Vespucius Symmes, bore a stone medal of his version of a hollow earth.

Needless to say, Symmes' bizarre theory, which challenged most of the standard teachings of science, including Newton's theory of gravity, was too good to die easily. Symmes' leading convert, James McBride, championed the cause in a book entitled *Symmes' Theory of Concentric Spheres*, and Americus Symmes edited his father's collected works in 1878. There is little doubt that Edgar Allan Poe leaned on Symmes' theory for his unfinished *Narrative of Arthur Gordon Pym* and a short story, "Ms. Found in a Bottle." Jules Verne's *Journey to the Center of the Earth* is another likely fictional candidate indebted to Symmes.

By the 20th century, Arctic and Antarctic explorers pretty much disposed of the hollow-earth theory. Holes of 4,000 and 6,000 miles would be pretty hard to miss. Still, some hollow earthers remain to this day. Adolf Hitler was known to believe in the concept. During World War II he insisted radar experts spying on the British submarine fleet use calculations based on the hollow-earth theory. That line of investigation led nowhere, but confirmed hollow earthers are convinced that Hitler and some of his closest aides escaped at the end of the war by submarine to a base under the icecap at the South Pole.

Johnson, Richard M. (1780–1850)

THE SOMETIME VICE PRESIDENT

It is a matter of custom in politics to describe the vice president of the United States as being "a heartbeat away from the presidency." In no case was that quite as terrifying a prospect as in the late 1830s, when Richard M. Johnson served under Martin Van Buren. One can only wonder what history would have said had Richard Johnson been catapulted by fate into the highest office in the land.

There were many who cautioned that Johnson would have been more logically consigned to a prison cell or a lunatic asylum than the White House. Johnson had long served as a congressman from Kentucky, and he was noted for his erratic behavior and weird ideas. When Captain John Cleves Symmes (*q.v.*) came along with his hollow-earth theory, Johnson became his prime advocate in Congress, despite the crackpot nature of Symmes' beliefs. But then crackpot beliefs and behavior were long a hallmark of Johnson's career.

How then did Johnson rise to the level of vice president (some observers in fact credited him with putting the vice into the vice presidency)? Andrew Jackson had dictated the choice of Van Buren as his successor. He also decided that Johnson, a loyal Jacksonite, deserved second spot, especially because he was an authentic Indian fighter who often claimed credit for killing the feared Indian chief Tecumseh.

The sins and wild disclosures about present-day political Washington pale when compared to the doings of Johnson. He was known to have had sexual flings with the wives of at least four senators and congressmen, and the suspicion existed of at least three more. Johnson's casual attitude toward sex was again a lifetime affair. He'd had a love affair with Julia Chinn, a handsome mulatto slave he had inherited from his father. Johnson established the woman in his home, a wife all but in name, and had two daughters, Adaline and Imogene, by her.

To his credit, and to the chagrin of many southern members of the Democratic Party, Johnson raised them as if they were legal children, had them educated, and expected society to accept them as equals. Opponents railed that Johnson had a "connection with a jet-black, thick-lipped, odoriferous negro wench, by whom he has reared a family of children whom he had endeavoured to force upon society as equals." Both girls were light-skinned, and eventually they married white men and were accorded large tracts of their father's property as marriage gifts.

Julia died in 1833 from cholera, and Johnson later took two other slaves as mistresses, but despite this and the advice of many of his closest aides, Jackson determined to put Johnson on the ticket with Van Buren.

Such open miscegenation offended many southerners, but when Johnson just as openly declared open season on Washington wives, the protests reached epic proportions. Van Buren may well have suffered politically as much from Johnson's behavior as from the Panic of 1839. Then, with the nation wallowing in a depression, Johnson inexplicably announced he was taking an "extended leave"—with pay—while he went back to Kentucky to devote all his time to running a hotel and tavern he owned in the resort area of White Sulphur Spring.

One guest who went to "Col. Johnson's Watering establishment" complained in a letter to a member of the Van Buren cabinet that the vice president "seems to enjoy the business of Tavern-Keeping ... even giving his personal superintendance to the chicken and egg purchasing and water-melon selling department." The letter writer went on to complain that Johnson had also taken up with "a young Delilah of about the complection of Shakespeares swarthy Othello," who was to be the vice president's new "wife."

By 1840 there were other complaints about Johnson, and some persons begged Jackson, still the dictator of his party, to get the 59-year-old "old gentleman" to change his slovenly and ill-kempt appearance, at least to wash a bit more often. Even Jackson reached the conclusion that Johnson would be a drag on the Democratic ticket.

The outraged Democrats, who renominated Van Buren without opposition, refused at their convention to renominate Johnson. Amazingly they left the vice presidential slot vacant. This did not deter Johnson from running as an independent.

The fast-rising Whigs nominated the old Indian fighter William Henry Harrison for president, with John Tyler as vice president. While the slogan "Tippecanoe and Tyler Too" swept the nation, Johnson countered that while Harrison may well have defeated Tecumseh at the Tippecanoe River in 1811, it was Johnson who had actually killed the Indian chief—in 1813 at the Battle of the Thames—which probably was not the case. In any event Johnson coined his own slogan:

Rumpsey dumpsey, Rumpsey dumpsey,
Colonel Johnson killed Tecumsey.

That alone could have sunk the Democrats, and both Van
Buren and Johnson were defeated. If Johnson was rejected by the
nation's voters, he was not forgotten by those of his home state. In
1841 he returned to Congress from his home district. In 1844
Johnson actually went to the Democratic convention in Baltimore,
seeking the presidency. Badly beaten, he retired to his estate in
White Sulphur Spring. In 1850 Johnson was elected to the Kentucky House of Representatives but did not serve. A Louisville
newspaper informed its readers: "Col. R. M. Johnson is laboring
under an attack of dementia, which renders him totally unfit for
business." Johnson died shortly thereafter, of a paralytic stroke at
the age of 70.

Miller, William (1782–1849)

PROPHET OF DOOM

In the Apocrypha, the end of the world was generally held to be
predicted to occur in 1,000 years, with different theories as to what
constituted a "year." The Last Judgment was expected by many in
999, but it did not happen. Since then, prophets of doom and
Apocalypse have frequently if inaccurately predicted the end of the
world. No man in America created more havoc predicting the Second Coming of Christ than did a former atheist turned fire-and-
brimstoner named William Miller. A New York farmer, Miller—by
diligent, if mysterious, biblical research in the Books of Daniel and
Revelation—determined the end of the world would occur on April
3, 1843.

The fanatical Miller had an overpowering personality and not
only gathered a devoted cult around him but even convinced the
New York Herald to take him seriously; it printed his prediction of
the Great Fire that would envelop the earth. He was convinced that
Napoleon had been visited on humanity as the Anti-Christ herald-

Latter-day Nostradamus William Miller tirelessly predicted dates for Armageddon—four in all between April 1843 and October, 1844. Undaunted Millerites, though tired of waiting together for the fire-and-brimstone Judgment Day, still meet in smaller congregations today.

ing the onrushing Last Judgment. Miller arrived at his conclusion in 1831; he found confirmation of his premise in a shower of shooting stars in 1833; a great comet, the brightest of the century, gave conclusive confirmation in March 1843.

Miller published a fire-and-brimstone newspaper called *The Midnight Cry* and listed other omens of the impending fateful day. Supposedly, birds were falling dead in midflight, crosses were appearing in the sky, and strange rings were noticed around the sun. The Millerite believers soon totaled an estimated half million, and the *Herald* deserves honorable mention for the developing mania that led to bizarre and tragic consequences. Miller himself gave more than 300 sermons over the last fateful six months, leaving his audiences wailing.

The Millerites concluded that the dead would pass through the ordeal of "The End" to Heaven before those still alive. So some of the more fanatical members murdered relatives and committed suicide before Judgment Day arrived. On the appointed day, thousands of Millerites jammed the New England (the stronghold of the movement) hilltops. Some waited nude to meet their maker, while others wore white "ascension robes" sold by Miller. Cynics wondered if Miller had discovered some way to take his money with him; he was so concerned about raking in thousands of dollars prior to the great "Going Up." Miller had little patience for such criticism. He said he was merely doing God's work, providing the recommended attire for the devout to meet their Maker.

Nothing much happened on April 3. In one valley in Vermont an eerie sound echoed across the land, and thousands of Millerites alternately prayed and screamed until it was discovered that the local village idiot was blowing a large horn. One true believer suffered a broken arm when he tried to fly up to Heaven with the aid of turkey wings attached to his shoulders.

What became known as the Great Disappointment set in among the Millerites, but their peerless leader was not too chagrined. He had, he said, suspected something was wrong with his figures. The real date was July 7, 1843.

Amazingly, on that date there was a complete, enthusiastic re-run of the big event. Ascension robes once more sold like hotcakes, farmers ignored their ready-to-be harvested crops, jobs were resigned, and whole herds of animals were butchered for bountiful last suppers. Whole families gathered in family graves to await the inevitable.

Again nothing happened.

Miller insisted he'd get it right yet and put off the big date to March 21, 1844. By this time quite a few folks had some doubts about the fanatical Miller, but he dismissed them as having been nonbelievers all along. Some believers who had previously waited in open coffins for the end thought it enough, this time, to sit atop gravestones. At the appointed hour a tremendous thunderstorm broke out and the Millerites danced for joy in ecstasy. This was really it! However as suddenly as the downpour started, it let up, leaving the Millerites' spirits most dampened.

Miller remained his unflappable self and came up with another likely date, October 22, 1844. His still-loyal followers once more trekked up the hilltops to await what this time had to be a sure thing. One farmer even dressed all his cows in ascension robes supplied by Miller because "it's a very long trip and the kids will want milk."

They missed out on the Millennium once more. By this time many Millerites had had enough, and the movement split into several groups, of which the Seventh-Day Adventists are today the largest. Miller kept on preaching his version of the end of the world and insisted the time was soon. He lived until 1849 and, if ridiculed by some, he nevertheless lived out his days with a comfortable income from sales of his ascension robes.

Gates, Theophilus (1787–1846)

THE BATTLE AXE OF SEX

For some reason, the fathers of modern sexology are considered to be Krafft-Ebing, now generally discredited, and the still celebrated Havelock Ellis. No one seems to give much credit to Americans John Humphrey Noyes (q.v.) and Theophilus Gates; yet both these men sought much earlier, and perhaps in their own lascivious ways to bring joy to unhappily married women and their henpecked husbands. Perhaps it is that they clothed their teachings in religious mumbo jumbo that disqualifies them from consideration as important early sexologists. But both men sought to liberate their followers from the rigid restraints of sexual attitudes and biases. And, after a fashion, they succeeded in their endeavors rather admirably.

Of the two, Theophilus Gates proceeded with far more openness and thumbing of the nose at convention. Noyes was to express his frustration over that, by accusing Theophilus of stealing his ideas. The dispute left the public most confused. As one profiler of the pair noted, "Plagiarism in free love was a new charge."

Theophilus was born in Hartland, Connecticut, to a family rich in revolutionary fighters and enthusiastic churchmen. His father, however, suffered from mental imbalance, and the boy himself experienced a considerable number of visions and hallucinations. He began to "dread pleasures as an offense to God."

Hardly an auspicious start for an advocate of free love, but Theophilus had to have his ideas born on the crucible of life. He achieved that by wandering through the South and undergoing more religious experiences. In the end he engaged the Devil in a fierce battle in the woods of Virginia and, happily, he routed him. Theophilus made his way to the home of the nearest preacher and related his terrible torment. That Sunday Theophilus preached to the congregation and told how the angels had helped him in his ordeal with the Devil.

It was the beginning of a long preaching career that would take many turns, not stopping until death itself stilled him. Sometimes he worked as an itinerant schoolteacher, but he often published pamphlets on religion that sold quite well. It seemed the more Theophilus wrote on sexual matters, the better his tracts seemed to sell. And it is on such success that sexual apostles are born; thereafter there was no stopping Theophilus.

By 1820, he was publishing a magazine called *The Reformer,* in Philadelphia; devoted to religious matters, it called for the repeal of various blue laws. Theophilus did well enough financially with the magazine for more than a decade, until higher printing costs did him in. He then joined another young up-and-coming apostle of free love, Noyes, who was putting out a magazine called *The Perfectionist.* Noyes' idea of perfection was a state of affairs where any man and any woman could copulate with whomever they wished.

Theophilus agreed with that concept in general but not in detail, and he was soon back on his own, putting out an inflammatory sheet called *Battle-Axe and Weapons of War,* taking the name from Jeremiah 51:6. The editorial viewpoint was that no wife should lack a loving husband, and no husband should lack a sexually attentive wife. It was perhaps the first publication to give godly attributes to the orgasm.

Gates sold his *Battle-Axe* on street corners, at five cents a copy, and Noyes promptly rushed out a new magazine, *The Witness,* to compete. He accused Theophilus of stealing his sexual thunder.

Theophilus soon found he had a burgeoning sect on his hands. He stressed such ideas as that babies should not be brought into the world unless parents were eager and prepared to receive them; this idea of a *planned* parenthood would still meet violent opposition more than a half century later. He called also for the sharing of all worldly goods and loving feelings. His new movement was named "Onanism," but the name didn't catch on; the public preferred to call the followers Battle Axes, and its leader became known as Theophilus the Battle Axe.

His first convert was one Hannah Williamson, who was, not surprisingly perhaps, a streetwalker, but one with what was described as "aspiring piety." Hannah took to Theophilus' erotic faith with alacrity. She certainly had no problem with the proposition that if a female Battle Axe determined that a gentleman Battle Axe was unhappily married, she could conveniently have a dream in which God would order her to go to that brother and declare she's just got the word. The pair might continue that arrangement for a day or two, a week, a month, or years. Hannah and her sister Lydia turned out to be dedicated practitioners of his procedure, so much so that they each regularly had to announce they were expecting another Christ to be born.

Theophilus and the Williamson sisters established a community near Pottstown, Pennsylvania, where the rules of this form of promiscuity could take place. He called his refuge Free Love Valley. The original contingent of Battle Axes numbered 45 and were to grow considerably, since the Dutch farmers of the area proved highly susceptible to the new sect's tenets. A former God-fearing farmer sat at his dinner table when a young female appeared and announced she was his new divinely selected mate. The farmer immediately shuttled his wife down to the end of the table and installed his new mate next to him. Presumably night arrangements followed a similar pattern.

Authorities tried fining people for adultery, but they were dealing with an epidemic of promiscuous sex. Theophilus was also a nudist and would have his male and female followers disrobe and march in a single line down the street of the community to a pool where they bathed together.

Even when Theophilus overstepped himself and did something foolish for a true apostle his flock kept the faith. Once, he anticipated the Wright brothers and determined to fly. He fastened wings made out of light shingles to his arms and went soaring off a roof—straight to the ground. He needed a month for his recovery. But the flock remained convinced Theophilus would fly sooner or later.

Meanwhile, they had other matters to occupy their time. Scandalous tales spread throughout the countryside about what sexual doings went·on in the very aisles of the sect's church.

There is no telling how big Free Love Valley might have become had Theophilus stayed around, but he died suddenly on October 13, 1846. Within a year the Battle Axes started fading away. It took a powerful personality to hold together a movement built on such a facile expression of piety.

It may be recorded that some Battle Axes hurried off for Oneida, New York, where at that very moment John Noyes,

Theophilus' hot-blooded rival, was launching his own free-love community.

Palmer, Joseph (1788–1875)

BATTLER FOR THE BEARD

The wearing of beards in America did not become popular until the middle of the 19th century, and one man who took to whiskers earlier, Joseph Palmer, became one of the most hated eccentrics of his day. As such, he was subjected to persecution so incredible that it boggles the mind. Palmer may well have been the first man in the nation to wear a beard, and it was no ordinary one; it reached the flowing proportions of a biblical patriarch's.

When Palmer, a Massachusetts farmer, moved to the thriving city of Fitchburg in 1830, the protestations of the townsfolk were overwhelming for the next decade. Neighbors snubbed him, tradespeople either sneered at him or refused to serve him, women crossed the street when he approached, fearing an attack from such a "degenerate," and men and boys stoned him or hurled missiles through the window of his house. The local minister, Reverend George Trask, sermonized to his flock; "Let us join in prayers for the vain Mr. Palmer. He admires only his own reflection in the glass."

In the worst attack Palmer was subjected to, he was ambushed by four men armed with scissors and razor. They hurled him to the ground and attempted to forcibly shave him, but Palmer, a powerfully built man, managed to work his arm free and pull out a pocketknife. He slashed away at his persecutors, cutting two of them in their legs and putting them all to flight. Palmer was arrested on a charge of "unprovoked assault" and fined. He refused to pay and was clapped in jail in Worcester.

Palmer's jailers urged other prisoners, dangling a promise of reduced sentences for them, to debeard Palmer, but the stubborn farmer proved strong enough to beat off all assaults; on two separate occasions he decked his would-be barbers. Palmer's fate became known to the press and soon such champions of individual rights as Ralph Waldo Emerson, Henry Thoreau, and Bronson Alcott led protests against his imprisonment, citing a man's inalienable right to choose his own appearance.

After a year Palmer had proved an embarrassment to the authorities, and his jailers tried to set him free. Palmer refused to leave unless officials publicly acknowledged his right to a beard. Finally, the jailers picked him up in his chair and set him out in the street, barring him from access to his cell.

Palmer went home, beard flowing in triumph. He lived until 1875, long enough to see beards become commonplace in the 1850s and Abraham Lincoln become the first of several presidents to sport whiskers. Palmer's gravestone is well preserved today in Evergreen Cemetery in Leominster, Massachusetts. The inscription on it well describes the irrationality not of Palmer but of his community as a whole. "Persecuted for wearing the beard."

Graham, Sylvester (1794–1851)

THE APOSTLE OF EATING MORALITY

Today the graham cracker is a monumental tribute to one of America's most eccentric reformers, Presbyterian minister Sylvester Graham, who preached moderation in so many human pleasures. A confirmed opponent of the eating of meat, white bread, fats, spicy foods, and demon rum, as well condemning ejaculation among other things, Graham was a firm believer in bowel-movement regularity, hard mattresses, cheery dispositions at the dinner table, and bathing at least three times a week.

So impassioned was Graham in all his crusades that he fired up both supporters and detractors, so much so that they fought pitched battles in many American cities. Graham himself was the object of lynching attempts on more than one occasion. As a young fire-and-brimstone sermonizer still in his twenties, Graham took to the lecture circuit around the country, warning of the evils of drink. He soon expanded his platform to include prescribing a special

In his crusade to curb the dietary excesses of Americans, Sylvester Graham stirred up not only the Graham cracker, but also the ire of America's bakers.

vegetable diet to cure alcoholism, among other things. Fats and meats, he explained, produced unwholesome sexual desires, and such spices as mustard and catsup could bring on insanity. Besides, he added, a single pound of rice offered more nutrition than two and one-half pounds of the best meat, and three pounds of potatoes equalled two pounds of meat.

However, the greatest eating sin of all, he insisted, was the consuming of white bread. He accused the bakers of America of adulterating their white bread with pipe clay, chalk, and plaster of Paris. He insisted that only the use of homemade unsifted whole-wheat flour (which became known as graham bread) could purge the poisoned bodies of the American citizenry. Graham boarding houses sprang up in the 1830s in a number of eastern cities. There, his supporters munched on special whole-wheat wafers, the original graham cracker.

Graham was driven off many a speaker's rostrum by bakers, butchers, and, it was said, many a husband who wanted their wives to continue serving them meat and white bread. But over the next two decades, Graham garnered many important supporters, including James Russell Lowell, Amelia Jenks Bloomer, Joseph Smith (head of the Mormon Church), Bronson Alcott (father of Louisa May Alcott, author of *Little Women*), and newspaper publisher Horace Greeley.

Graham's closest call came in 1847, when his charges against Boston bakers brought them into the streets in an angry demonstration. They surrounded the hotel where Graham was staying and finally broke through police lines, determined to string up their tormentor. The lynch mob, armed with several ropes, was finally routed by a contingent of loyal Grahamites who poured clouds of slaked lime out of upper-story hotel windows, putting the choking attackers to flight.

Such events deterred Graham not the slightest, and he continued his attacks on white bread and meat, steadily increasing his diatribes against what he considered a dangerous side effect of poor diet—sexual excess. Rich foods, overly spiced dishes, and the consumption of flesh led to ruinous sexual desires, he warned goggle-eyed audiences. In his famous "A Lecture to Young Men on Chastity, Intended Also for the Serious Consideration of Parents and Guardians," he warned that couples who overdid sexual activities would be smitten with such minor ailments as "languor, lassitude, muscular relaxation, general debility and heaviness, depression of spirits, loss of appetite, indigestion, faintness and sinking at the pit of the stomach, increased susceptibilities of the skin and lungs to all the atmospheric changes, feebleness of circulation, chilliness, headache, melancholy." That was only the beginning, he warned. After these trifles there followed "hypochondria, hysterics, feebleness of all the senses, impaired vision, loss of sight, weakness of the lungs, nervous cough, pulmonary consumption, disorders of the genital organs, spinal diseases, weakness of the brain, loss of memory, epilepsy, insanity, apoplexy, abortions, premature births, and extreme feebleness, morbid predispositions, and an early death of offspring." He undoubtedly caused endless soul-searching and torment in many a marital bedroom by his further claim that each ejaculation a man had shortened his life expectancy.

Instead of all this, Graham strongly urged his listeners to follow the moral road, which included a vegetarian diet and daily bowel movements in place of sexual excesses. While Graham may have been far afield on some of his "scientific" claims, it must be said that much of his advice later gained acceptance, including the virtues of whole wheat, exercise, moderate eating, and sleeping with an open window. Grahamism did not die with Graham in 1851. It later gained almost fanatical adherents, including John Harvey Kellogg, the breakfast cereal champion, and Thomas Edison. Only the most obstreperous anti-Grahamites ever seemed to make much of the fact that Graham himself lived only into his fifties.

Lick, James (1796–1876)

THE FOLLY-BUILDER

Few men have been as driven to seek a fortune as California pioneer James Lick. His motive was vengeance. Having once achieved the status of millionaire (perhaps the first in California) he lost all interest in the trappings of comfort that went with the territory.

Born in Lebanon County, Pennsylvania, on August 25, 1796, Lick (in Pennsylvania Dutch, Lük) was enmeshed in a scandal at the age of 22: he had gotten the daughter of a wealthy flour-mill owner pregnant. Lick did what he considered the honorable thing: he offered to marry the girl. The mill owner was more chagrined at the thought of having a penniless son-in-law than of being the grandfather of a bastard. He is supposed to have arrogantly and brusquely dismissed the young man by declaring, "When you own a mill as large and as costly as mine, you can have my daughter's hand, but not before."

Lick left Pennsylvania immediately, promising angrily that some day he would own a mill that would make "this one look like a pigsty"; this was taken in the area as little more than childish pique. But the young man proved to be a hardy enough entrepreneur. In South America over the years he became a wealthy piano maker, being successful in turn in Argentina, Chile, and Peru. In 1848 Lick sold out all his holdings for the then kingly sum of $30,000 and headed for California.

It was a move of classic good timing. He arrived in California in January 1849, and the discovery of gold did not become a matter of wide knowledge for several more months. In the meantime Lick bought up between $6,000 and $7,000 worth of San Francisco real estate. By the following year those land purchases had made him the richest man in the booming town.

While others sought gold, Lick stuck to land speculation, put off as he was by the hard work involved in being a prospector. He bought acre upon acre in the Santa Clara valley, and soon he had the most impressive estate in all of California. He became known as a millionaire eccentric, wearing tattered old clothes and living in a dilapidated wooden shack. His bed consisted of a mattress atop the gutted frame of an ancient grand piano. Despite his wealth, he drove about in an old wagon "held together by spit," according to one old account, searching for cattle, horse, and other animal bones, horns, and hoofs, which he buried in his farmlands to enrich the soil. In one of his more bizarre acts, he hired workmen to plant trees upside down, their roots facing skyward. To his neighbors, this was a sign that Lick had really passed into the world of the daft. To Lick, it was a way to test his new workers' willingness to follow his orders without dispute. That was not a matter of small consequence to him; he certainly had many daft orders to give.

As outrageous as many of his acts were, Lick continued to gain in wealth because of the steady rise in land values. In 1871 the *San Francisco Morning Call* published what became famous as its *"Mucho Dinero"* list of the town's leading citizens. Lick's net worth was estimated at $3 million, which was probably an understatement. By then, this miserly collector of funds was dispensing much money. He set up the Lick Trust to heap benefactions on the state. His funds were to assist the California Academy of Sciences and the Mechanics Institute Library. Perhaps his greatest memorial was to be the University of California's astronomical center atop Mount Hamilton, the Lick Observatory. He also built the Lick House, the most elegant hotel in San Francisco until it was eclipsed by the fabulous Palace Hotel.

However, in his day he became much more famed for yet another edifice, Lick's Folly. He built an elegant three-story redwood and brick flour mill on the Guadalupe River. As the name indicates, it was unlike any other flour mill in the world. Sacks of flour lay stacked in an interior of fine mahogany and Spanish cedar. The floors were done in hardwood parquet. It was not so much a mill or a warehouse, folks observed, as a palace.

Lick had built this lavish monstrosity in the 1860s for only one reason—to fulfill his youthful oath and make an autocratic father back in Pennsylvania see his error in rejecting Lick. Lick had photographs made of his grand mill and sent them back to the mill owner who had scorned him. Since he might not have been still living, Lick made sure others back in Lebanon County also got the proof. Having had his vengeance, Lick lost interest in the mill and, by the end of the decade, he all but abandoned it. To some, the name Lick's Folly was most appropriate, but to the eccentric millionaire it was money well spent. Lick died in 1876. In tribute to the good works his money did, rather than to his irrationalities, he was buried in the base of a giant telescope in the Lick Observatory.

Johns, James (1797–1874)

THE COMPULSIVE JOURNALIST

Today there are publishers who advertise for book manuscripts to publish. They reject nothing, finding anything submitted a near literary classic. The catch is that the writer must subsidize the printing of the book. Such "vanity" publishers point with pride to the rare book that actually achieves some sales, and there will never be a dearth of eager authors to supply them with writings and cash.

It is doubtful that James Johns of the Green Mountain country of Vermont would be among such eager writers. As far as Johns, the son of a Revolutionary War soldier, was concerned there was not a publisher or printer extant worthy of printing his noble words. Indeed, when he was 31, he published a little volume called *Green Mountain Muse*. It sold virtually nary a copy. Like other writers before him and many since, he blamed its failure on the publisher-printer.

Johns vowed he would thereafter have nothing to do with printers, who were only capable of diverting his journey to the peak of literary achievement. Fortunately he had other publishing methods at his disposal. Since 1810 he had published a newspaper, the *Vermont Autograph and Remarker,* which chronicled as a good gazette should the important happenings of the community of Huntington—weather, births, deaths, and accidents. Johns as he got older even showed a penchant for investigative journalism, railing about what he regarded to be instances of political corruption. How Johns had the time for much of this is a mystery, considering that he published his newspaper five times a week.

It was a beautiful paper, with lettering far superior to what that rascal of a printer had done on his book. To the casual viewer it seemed to offer a remarkably clean typeface. Only on closer inspection could it be discerned that the *Autograph and Remarker* was entirely hand lettered. It took Johns almost half a day to pen-print an entire copy, which he then posted in the center of town for the residents to read. Occasionally he printed out a second edition, for someone who wanted a souvenir copy of special importance to him. Johns kept up this amazing output for 63 years, stubbornly refusing ever to switch to a printing press, even though he finally compromised with technology and obtained one for other reasons.

While he occupied himself weekly on his paper he also wrote and pen-printed a forty-four page book, *A brief sketch or outline of the History of the town of Huntington.* Needless to say, demand exceeded supply.

In 1857 Johns, wanting to expand his book production finally bought a printing press and issued broadside after broadside of poems. He also printed another 22-page pamphlet entitled *A brief record of the various fatal accidents which have happened from the first*

Few writers out of mistrust of conventional publisher/printers have ever demonstrated the zeal or calligraphic skill of James Johns, who, in order to maintain complete control of his work, hand-lettered his own newspaper for five-day-a-week publication.

settlement of the town of Huntington to the present time. Needless to say, it is the definitive work.

Having made the break to the printing press, Johns was able to increase his production enormously, and thus he was able to issue such works as *Green Mountain Tradition, Remarkable Circumstances,* and *The Book of Funny Anecdotes.*

Though he had bowed, to a limited extent, to Mr. Gutenberg's printing press, he continued to pen-print his major love, the *Autograph and Remarker.* It may be noted that Johns never married; it would be difficult to envision any woman being content with a man whose hands were constantly inked, as penman Johns' hands must have been.

It was probably a small sacrifice for Johns to make. He was wedded to his art, his Green Mountains, and the doings of its people. He did not lay down his pen until August 1873, just eight months before his death. At least 500 of his writings, of varying lengths, remain preserved, and this sweet singer of the pen stands out, whatever his eccentricities, as one of the most prolific American writers.

McDowall, John (?–1838)

THE WHOREFINDER GENERAL

The trouble with the Reverend John McDowall, to whom sex and vice in 19th-century New York became an obsession, was that no one, apparently not even the good parson himself, could decide if he was a reformer or a pornographer. In 1830 the elderly McDowall descended on such vice areas as the Five Points and Paradise Square, announcing he intended to bring morality and the word of God to their corrupted denizens. The Reverend McDowall became the friend of prostitutes, pimps, sundry thieves, and other criminals. He entered whorehouses, ostensibly to lecture the inmates, but there were those of the scarlet profession who noted he had a way of chucking them under the chin that had little to do with reformation.

Still, McDowall had a good record of getting women to leave the houses and enter one of his Magdalen Refuges. These refuges were established by his Female Benevolent Society, for which he enjoyed considerable success at raising money from reform-minded citizens. But the reverend would soon drench the ex-prostitutes with such a heavy portion of prayers and exhortations that almost all would shortly flee, returning to the comfortable depravity from whence they came.

McDowall was nonetheless celebrated as the front-line fighter against evil, and he was invited to the best homes to lecture on the awful conditions he had found in the vice dens. He would insist that "modesty and purity forbid a minute detail." But as a matter of fact, if any of his listeners really wanted the lowdown, they had only to buy his *McDowall's Journal*. This forerunner of the United States' later gutter and yellow press subscribed to the theory that readers not only wanted exposés and proper lamentation about depravity— they also wanted all the terrible details.

McDowall's Journal was one lamentation after another, and its amount of detail clearly bordered on the pornographic. A latter-day analyst might well see the good parson as an individual much obsessed, to the point of near-personal involvement, with the unsavory behavior he uncovered. He was particularly upset—titillated, according to his critics—by the number of dusky island maidens whom he discovered being shuttled into New York to work as prostitutes.

Many a solid citizen called for the suppression of the parson's publication as itself a corrupter of morals. McDowall was outraged, regarding his work as noble and vital. "There are 20,000 harlots loose in the city," he stormed. Among his detractors, he won for himself the sobriquet of the "Whorefinder General," after Matthew Hopkins, the infamous English pretended discoverer of witches and so-called "Witchfinder General." Cynics pointed out that if there were that many prostitutes in New York, and if they handled only three customers a day, it would mean that one out of every two adult males was patronizing a prostitute three times a week; this would be an enormous drain on the city's financial well-being, to say nothing of the impact on health services.

Still, *McDowall's Journal* kept up a drumbeat of the parson's claims and published a complete list of brothels in the city—which of course served as an excellent guidebook and was facetiously referred to as the Whorehouse Directory.

McDowall also must be given credit for staging New York's first "sex fair," an exhibition of pornography in a local church. In it he displayed the various obscene materials he had readily obtained, from books all the way to naughty pastries. Clergymen streamed in to see the special showing, and they expressed the proper outrage and regret. It was said that some of the porn-parson's financial angels were also accorded a special private peek.

As the reverend's behavior and devotion to the perverse became more pronounced, many other religious leaders attacked him for his bizarre devotion to duty. Finally he was indicted by a grand jury for subverting the morals of the city. He was also accused of misusing funds contributed to his supposedly nonprofit publication. He avoided conviction by quitting his publishing pursuits and being defrocked. He died in obscurity a few years later, still insisting to the few who paid him any mind that he had saved the morals of the city.

Harper, Richard (?–c.1839)

CHICAGO'S OLD VAGRANT

The record on Chicago's first town character, Richard Harper, is not a clear one. He is presented as being, in the early part of the 19th century, the town's first thief—meaning obviously the first to be caught. Before that, according to various historians, he was the town's first vagrant. One such historian informs us he was an unfortunate wanderer laid low by frontier whiskey so that he apparently remained in a supine position for several decades, begging money for drinks and resorting to sneak thievery when the need arose. As to his background, one 19th-century profiler insists that he was a ne'er-do-well from Maryland who never did a day's labor in his life. Yet another makes Harper out to have been originally an Easterner of considerable respectability and education doing penance for some unknown sin.

Whatever Harper's distant past, his presence in the Chicago of founder Jean Baptiste Pointe du Sable's time, when it was known to the Indians as *Shi-kai-o* or "place of the wild onions," is better recorded. He was the town fool, someone to tease or mistreat savagely, or he might even be offered an empty whiskey jug to drink.

In 1833 Chicago got around to constructing its first jail, made of "logs firmly bolted together," and the vagrant Harper was incarcerated therein as its first prisoner. The charge was theft but the particulars are no longer in evidence. Thereafter, Harper was frequently in deep trouble because of a state vagrancy law. Finally, late that year, the authorities apparently got tired of scraping him off the sidewalk and incarcerating him; instead they exercised their rights under the statute to auction him off as a manservant.

A considerable segment of public opinion was rather upset at a white man being put up for sale in this manner, but such outrage did not carry over to anyone's purse. The only bidder for Harper was George White, the black town crier, who bought himself a servant for the impressive sum of 25 cents. White led his property away at the end of a chain.

According to historian John J. Flinn, who was nearly contemporaneous with Harper but whose reports need not always be taken at face value, the vagrant escaped from White that very night and "never was seen in these parts again."

Actually, "Harper, Richard, called 'Old Vagrant,' " appears in the city's first directory in 1839, indicating that he was still around then. The only logical surmise is that town crier White was induced to free his slave, there being those in the community apparently who had coughed up enough cash—who knows, perhaps as much as a dollar—to buy Harper's freedom. Clearly, the choice between having an eccentric vagrant littering the scenery and a white man in servitude to a black was not much of a close call.

Henry, George W. (1801–1888)

THE HOLY SHOUTER

Throughout the history of man, religion has taken many forms, utilizing some violent manifestations of the spirit to pay homage to the Deity. Early in the 19th century, a New Yorker from Oneida, George W. Henry, was himself converted and sanctified at religious camp meetings, thereafter becoming a circuit preacher. However, even in the company of such stalwarts of that stripe as John Wesley, Peter Cartwright, Benjamin Abbott, and J. B. Finley, Mr. Henry stands out most singularly.

He was known at camp meetings in America as Henry the Holy Shouter. The title hardly does him justice, for he believed in far more than shouting in his practice of theology. In what must stand as a unique theological classic, Henry espoused his beliefs in a 1859 book, the title of which covers a number of his tenets—*Shouting:*

Circuit preacher George Henry, the Holy Shouter, posed with his son for the frontispiece of his definitive work on that unique method of worship. "Great shouts, issuing forth from deep in the abdomen," he advised, "made Heaven take notice."

Genuine and Spurious in All Ages of the Church. . . . Giving a History of the Outward Demonstrations of the Spirit, such as Laughing, Screaming, Shouting, Leaping, Jerking and Falling under the Power.

Presumably, Henry offered his manuscript to a number of commercial publishers, but all of them rejected it. Undeterred, he printed and bound it himself, burnishing the edges of each volume with fine gold.

We have no record of the book's sales, but the feeling endures that Henry did yeoman work hawking his wares. Henry was the champion of hearty, devout laughter and indeed revelled in the giggles, snickers, and uproarious reactions of his congregations. Indeed, his own conversion had come at a camp meeting one night when he awoke to find his mouth "filled with loud laughter." In fact, Henry's laughter roused the entire encampment and "saints" gathered around the door of his tent. The word "glory" rolled from his mouth, as he put it, "like hot bomb-shells from a mortar."

When Henry got hundreds of shouters praising God at once, the tumult was indeed tremendous. Great shouts erupting deep from the abdomen, he averred, made Heaven take notice. However, Henry was not to be fooled by false shouters among the truly converted. "Men may pass counterfeit money on ignorant men," he declared, "but it is not so easy to deceive a sanctified ear in regard to a genuine shout. . . . There is as much difference between the true and counterfeit shout and song as between the sounds of a maniac dancing to the music of his own chains and the sweet music that enraptures the saints in heaven."

As much as Henry loved shouts, he most certainly enjoyed a good jerk as well. At his camp meetings, he noted, "most usually, persons taken with jerks, to obtain relief, as they said, would rise up and dance. Some would run, but could not get away. Some would resist; on such the jerks were very severe. . . . I have seen more than five hundred persons jerking at one time in my large congregations."

Mr. Henry did not think highly of worshipers who insisted on wearing their finest raiment. "To see those proud young gentlemen and young ladies, dressed in their silks, jewelry and prunella, from top to toe, take the jerks would often excite my risibilities. The first jerk or so you would see their fine bonnets, caps and combs fly; and so sudden would be the jerking of the head, that their long loose hair would crack almost as loud as a wagoner's whip." Mr. Henry was clearly a holy man of the people.

Henry exhorted his followers with other tomes besides those given to the holiness of shouting and other wild reactions. He authored such works as *Trials and Triumphs or Travels in Egypt, Twilight or Beulah; Wedlock and Padlock, Temporal and Spiritual;* and the *Camp Meeting Hymn Book.* Later in life George Henry went blind but that did nothing to still his abdominal Hallelujahs and Amens. Religion has not seen—or heard—his likes since.

Large, Albert (c.1805–?)

THE HERMIT AMIDST THE WOLVES

An unrequited affair of the heart caused Albert Large to trek off into the Pennsylvania woods to become a 19th-century "wolf man." He was, at the time, in his thirties and, to the residents of Bucks County, a bit queer. He'd been that way since early youth. The effort to keep him in school was truly a lost cause. Sent off to the little red schoolhouse, he followed his feet on other paths, straying into the woods away from the cares and worries of book learning. His mother died and was replaced by a stepmother who cared little what he did save that, as he got older, she undoubtedly wished he would leave the family fireside.

Albert himself got to thinking that way when, in his thirties, he set his sights on a girl living down the valley. A beauty she was, so it would be hard to imagine what she could see in Albert. Rejected time and again, Albert finally concluded he was unwanted by her, his own family, almost everybody. So Albert left.

There was in Bucks County a certain hilltop popularly called Wolf's Rock because it was known that she-wolves found it a safe area for their litters. Humans, even hunters, generally avoided the area. Albert however had often trekked over the hill in quest of solitude, and now that he wanted to make the condition permanent, he set up housekeeping there.

The wolves? There is no evidence they wanted any more to do with him than had their human counterparts.

Albert cleaned out a small cave and proceeded to fix it up for housekeeping. It sported a kitchen, with a crevice for a chimney, and a separate, boarded-off bedroom, just in case wolves slipped into the cave at night.

Albert was not a true cave dweller. By day, he shut off his cave with a large rock and trekked through the woods. By night, he slipped down into the valley and raided hen roosts, stealing other provisions. He even stole jugs of liquor. Albert was not the sort to be without the human comforts, even if he had forsaken human company.

Albert proved a good provider and, when winter set in, he could hole up in his cave for weeks on end, gorging on stolen food and slugging down stolen liquor.

Remarkably, Albert managed to stay out of sight for more than 20 years. Indeed, his family and neighbors had searched for him when he was first missed. They scoured the countryside but never found his cave up in Wolf's Rock. In time, he was presumed dead.

So it was electrifying news when on April 9, 1858, some hunters followed wolf tracks up to Albert's cave, to encounter the love-sick Hermit of Wolf's Rock, as he was subsequently called. To the folks of the valley, it was as if Albert Large had returned from the dead. He became something of a folk hero, queer perhaps, but a man of some accomplishment, having conquered the wilds for two whole decades.

Of course, in time, some thought was given to the 20 years of farm and town depredation. There was no way to gauge how many people had falsely suspected their neighbors of stealing from them. This was no concern to Albert Large however. He soon vanished into the woods again. Wolves, he discovered anew, were better company than humans.

Pierce, Jane Means (1806–1863)

THE PRESIDENT'S PHANTOM LADY

No American First Lady, not even Mary Todd Lincoln, matched the bizarre behavior of Mrs. Franklin Pierce, the wife of the fourteenth U.S. president. She did not even appear at the inauguration of her husband, and for half of his term she never appeared in public. She locked herself away in her bedroom, and it was said that about the

Nicknamed "The Shadow in the
White House," First Lady Jane
Means Pierce locked herself away in
her bedroom as much to avoid her
husband as to escape society and
politics. (Library of Congress)

only time she ventured down to the first floor of the White House
was to take meals. Newspapers irate at her behavior nicknamed her
"The Shadow in the White House."

Pierce was most sympathetic toward his wife, despite the political embarrassment she caused him. He knew their marriage had
been a tragic one, and he undoubtedly felt guilt for the misery he
caused her. They had had three children, none of whom lived to
be 12 years old. One died in infancy, another at the age of four.
The most tragic death of all occurred in January 1853, two months
before Pierce took office. The Pierces and their 11-year-old son,
Benny, were involved in a railroad accident: the child's head was
sliced in two. Jane Pierce shrieked until the president-elect threw a
shawl over the dead child and led her away.

Jane blamed Pierce and his political career for the boy's death,
and she had other complaints about her husband. Even after he
won the Democratic nomination for the presidency as a "dark
horse" at the convention on the forty-ninth ballot, she pressed him
not to campaign actively in the election because of her hatred
for politics. When he won, she took that as a betrayal, just as she
had felt betrayed previously by Pierce's well-known bouts with
alcoholism.

Compounding the blame she heaped on her husband were her
own feelings of guilt for not having been more attentive to her son

while he was alive. She often stayed up late into the night writing letters to Benny, begging forgiveness for not having been affectionate enough toward him.

Finally, in 1855, Jane Pierce attended her first social function in the White House, a New Year's Day reception. What should have been a joyous event became a disaster; her wan expression and mourning clothes cast a pall over the proceedings. Jane never emerged from her gloom, wearing mourning her last two years in the White House and indeed right up to the time of her death in 1863.

Patch, Sam (c.1807–1829)

"THE GREAT DESCENDER"

Sam Patch, who comes down to us as a great American folk hero, was the product of a strange mania that hit this nation in the first quarter of the 19th century. It was jumping. Manhood was expressed by sailors jumping over the sides of their ships, farmers jumping fences, store clerks bolting their counters.

Some historians have suggested that this era, especially after the War of 1812, was one in which brash men of modest circumstances were advancing in the young country that was also just starting to flex its muscles. The jumpers were expressing this desire to get ahead. And Sam Patch was destined to become the Jumping Hero of the nation.

Does a daredevil qualify as an eccentric? This question can be debated in general but not in the specific when it comes to Sam Patch. In later years as the mythmakers took over, Patch was transmitted into the "fakelore" of other mythical characters such as Paul Bunyan. He was made larger than life and pure of heart (did he not, before his last and fatal jump, ask that all his monies be sent to his mother?), intrepid, debonair. The real Sam Patch was a "wharf rat" and an ignorant loafer, a short, chunky sot who pilfered the piers. Debonair? Eyewitnesses described him as being stone drunk before he made his famed jumps.

But after all cowardice is something understood when dealing with daredeviltry. Such a failing could be excused had Sam Patch in his two-year jumping career not come to believe he was truly one of God's greatest creations. Napoleon was great, he allowed. Wellington beat Napoleon, so naturally he was greater. But neither of them could jump like Sam Patch, so he was greater than both of them.

Nathaniel Hawthorne, certainly an observer of the darker side of man's character, wrote: "How stern a moral may be drawn from the story of poor Sam Patch! Was the leaper of cataracts more mad or foolish than other men who throw away life, or misspend it in pursuit of empty fame, and seldom so triumphantly as he?"

Sam started jumping rather naturally, in line with the contemporary mania. He had tried sailoring and then became a mill hand in Rhode Island. The Slater Mill, just above the Pawtucket Falls, had a bridge nearby, and the hardier mill hands took to jumping from it into the water.

Later Sam moved on to the Hamilton Mills in Passaic, New Jersey. Here, often and loudly, he would declare he was going to dive 90 feet from a bridge into the Passaic River. The law would have no such suicidal nonsense, and he was arrested. But Sam escaped, jumping from the rocks at the foot of the bridge. Later he jumped from the bridge itself, thereby leaping into national prominence.

There was money to be made in jumping, and Sam started traveling the country demonstrating his prowess, dropping from the yardarms and bowsprits of ships; all these jumps were rather tame compared to his Rhode Island escapades and his great Passaic River dive. Had he stuck merely to them, passing the hat after begging the crowd that, if he died, the monies were to be sent to his dear mother, Sam might have lived a long time.

However Sam got to really believing in himself. What on this continent, he wondered, was worthy of his death defying? He decided it was Niagara Falls. In a classic jump from a rock atop Goat Island, he dropped down half the height of the falls.

The acclaim was thunderous. "The jump of Patch is the greatest feat of the kind ever effected by man," the *Buffalo Republican* enthused.

With press notices like that, Patch began to have his delusions of grandeur. He looked for an even greater challenge. He found it at the Genesee River in New York. He announced he would jump from the banks above the Genesee Falls "into the abyss below, a distance of 125 feet." He rejected the sane advice of those who told him he had been lucky at Niagara and that he should jump no more.

The residents of Monroe and Ontario counties poured out for the great jump. Coach and schooner excursions were organized. In any bar in the area one could place a bet on the outcome—Sam Patch or the falls, which one would win?

At the appointed hour Sam climbed up to the platform. Some thought he staggered and lacked his usual verve. Some said he was reeling drunk. Others said he had had but a single glass of brandy, to steel himself against the November cold. Sam made a brief and rambling speech. He talked of Napoleon and Wellington. Had they ever jumped the Genesee Falls? That was left for Sam Patch.

Sam's bravado may not have lasted his lifetime however. His jump lacked its usual precision. Before he was halfway down, his arms began to flail. It was as though he were trying to climb the air. Had he sobered enough during those last split seconds to realize that this was more than mere tomfoolery?

His body hit the water, his arms and legs hopelessly extended. It didn't come back to the surface. In fact, Sam's body was not found until the following March 17, near Lake Ontario.

But if Sam died in a sad display of madness, there were scores of poets and rhymesters ready to pay him tribute in verse. Legends grew around him. His deeds grew. He achieved household currency "before you could say Sam Patch."

Poems appeared about the "Great Descender." He was compared to Columbus, Newton, Galileo, Nelson, and Franklin. William Dean Howells had one of his characters express shock when his wife proved to be ignorant of Patch. "Isabel," he cried, "your ignorance of all that an American woman should be proud of distresses me."

Yet perhaps it was the children of Patch's day who more correctly gauged the real Sam Patch. They played to a jingle that went:

> Poor Samuel Patch—a man once world renounded,
> Much loved the water, and by it was drownded.
> He sought for fame, and as he reached to pluck it,
> He lost his ballast, and then kicked the buck-it.

Sam was 22 when he died. No money, it appears, was sent to his mother.

Pratt, Daniel (1809–1887)

THE GREAT AMERICAN TRAVELER

One of the most famous and popular vagrants of the 19th century, Daniel Pratt was a deluded soul who was dubbed by the press "the great American Traveler." He covered well over 200,000 miles in his wanderings from Maine to remote army posts in the Dakotas, visiting 27 states and 16 Indian tribes. As his fame spread, he could rely on the kindness of strangers, white and red, to offer him food and shelter. He was clearly demented, but those taking him in could count on being regaled with wild tales of his misadventures; he was particularly welcomed on college campuses. Madman perhaps; a challenge to the intellect nevertheless.

Born in the Prattville district of Chelsea, Massachusetts, he belonged to a lesser branch of the family that gave the district its name. In his youth he worked as a carpenter's helper, until he suddenly disappeared. When he turned up again a dozen years later, he talked nonsense and was called by residents "maggot-brained" and "brainsick." He spoke of roaming the country going nowhere, and soon he was on his way there again. Over the years Pratt trekked by foot from Massachusetts to Washington, D.C., 17 times and witnessed the inauguration of five presidents. These were not happy journeys for him; his chief delusion was that he had been elected president but was constantly deprived of his office by scheming politicians.

Often his recourse was to tour New England college campuses, denouncing the political system and urging the future graduates to change it and, in the process, give him his due by placing him in the White House. Regularly, almost as sure as a holiday, Pratt turned up spring and fall on the campuses of such institutions as Yale, Dartmouth, and Brown, arriving in town and putting up in a cheap hotel. In his frock coat and dingy stovepipe hat he looked very much the retired professor as he took up his station under the campus elms, there awaiting a call to a hastily organized lecture. The students, attending in the hundreds, were always taken by his oratorical style which, although he said little that made sense, was filled with remarkable word-creations and a stunning mastery of the non sequitur. Among his favorite topics, all guaranteed to produce handsome returns in the collections that followed, were "The Four Kingdoms," "The Harmony of the Human Mind," "The

Solar System," and perhaps most dazzling of all, "The Vocabula-boratory of the World's History."

College authorities did not think highly of Pratt's visits and on several occasions tried to eject him from the campus. However a "Praetorian Guard" of students generally protected him from the philistines and more than once sent the disciplinary officers fleeing. At Dartmouth once a group of appreciative students and faculty conferred on him the honorary degree of C.O.D., for Cash On Delivery. A jest of course; yet here was a lunatic worthy of the recognition and esteem no other babbler could achieve.

In his last years Pratt confined his wanderings to Boston, still demanding his presidency but willing to be pacified by citizens referring to him as "General."

Smith, "Windwagon" Thomas (c.1810–?)

THE DRY OCEAN SAILOR

Exactly when Tom Smith, a New England sailor, first came up with the notion that the prairies of the Midwest were neither prairies nor plains but really "dry oceans" is not apparent. It seemed to the folks in Nickport, Massachusetts, that he was always talking that way, which was especially odd since he had never seen the prairies. Nonetheless, Tom was sure of one thing: a smart seadog could sail that country. He could design a wagon, four times, no *ten* times the size of the standard covered wagon, and transport it across the plains at breakneck speed—so fast that it would easily run over any horses trying to pull it.

For quite a spell Tom Smith, and his "windwagon," was all talk. But one day early in 1853 Tom announced down at Sharp's General Store that he was a-goin' west. The men around the cracker barrel were duly impressed. Windwagon Thomas was after all a man of action. The jokes about Tom ceased, and even the *Nickport News*, announcing the event, reported Windwagon Thomas' plans with a degree of awe. "Tom Smith plans to leave Nickport next week to go to Baltimore. From Baltimore, he aims to go Out West on the National Road. Good Luck, Tom."

Later that year Windwagon Thomas arrived in Westport, Missouri, with his Yankee scheme for navigating the prairies with wind power. Westport—long since swallowed up by Kansas City—was at the time the launching site for many of the wagon trains moving westward, via the Oregon Trail to the Northwest and the Santa Fe Trail toward the Southwest. Westport capitalized on the prairie schooner business, both the freight business to Santa Fe and the emigrant traffic.

Windwagon Thomas was quite a spellbinder and, even if the Missouri folk had a certain reserve about accepting the words of a Yankee slicker, his spiel seemed to make sense. Why couldn't man use the powerful prairie winds to drive his wagons? Lord knew, those winds could blow a body about. Perhaps they might have reconsidered if they knew Smith's reputation as a "wild talker" back in Massachusetts.

Still, folks weren't about to buy a boat in a poke by any means, and they demanded to be shown. Windwagon Thomas was eager to oblige. He mounted a sail on a small wagon and negotiated the 300-mile round trip from Westport to Council Grove without benefit of horsepower. He explained he was improvising and not getting the proper speed out of his land craft and would not until a special windwagon was built with the proper nautical appurtenances.

"That windwagon will fly over the plains," he bragged. His wagon would cut through the prairie dirt like a hot knife through butter, outrunning all beasts of burden and, of course, pursuing Indian ponies as well.

To the businessmen of Westport, the demonstration and Smith's promises about a superior wagon made hard business sense. The Overland Navigation Company was formed, including among its directors Windwagon Thomas; Dr. J. W. Parker, the town's leading physician; Benjamin Newsom, the Indian agent; Henry Sager; Thomas M. Adams; and J. J. Mastin, a brilliant young lawyer.

The building of the windwagon was the biggest show to hit Westport in years and, as it grew, folks started feeling like the Trojans when the Greeks constructed that famous wooden horse. What folks didn't know was that Westport was getting its own Trojan Horse.

The mammoth wagon was somewhat similar to the Conestoga prairie schooner, but it looked more like a rude ship. About 25 feet long, seven feet in beam, it was equipped with huge wheels, 12 feet in diameter; the hubs alone were as big as barrels. The huge sail and mast rose a full 20 feet over the wagon. The local blacksmith fashioned an anchor for it, and the ropemaker constructed a special ladder for access to and from it. And this, Windwagon Thomas informed his investors, was only a small model of the land craft they would build later, one that could transport several families and all their possessions at the same time. The oxen would not be able to keep up, so they too would be loaded aboard the super models. Windwagon Thomas got a wild glaze in his eyes as he spoke, but then so too did the Overland directors. The profit potential for the windwagon was staggering.

Westport did itself up proud for the great launching ceremony. Unfortunately President Franklin Pierce, Secretary of State William Marcy, and Secretary of the Navy James Dobbin (Windwagon Thomas thought it appropriate that he especially be invited) were unable to attend because of pressing affairs of state. Still, in the crowd were some governors, congressmen, and important folks from as far away as Council Groves. They set off a mighty cheer as a team of 20 oxen hauled the windwagon to the open plain. It was an inspiring sight—painted in red, white, and blue stripes, with a great white sail and a cigar-store Indian figurehead.

The maiden voyage aboard the windwagon, much to the disappointment of the visiting politicians, was restricted to investors, who scampered gleefully up a special gangplank. Only Doc Parker did not come aboard. He mounted a saddle mule loaded down with medical supplies, "just in case."

Then Windwagon Thomas took his position on deck, made sail, and took the helm. The craft soared over the plain, over small hills and through gullies. The speed amazed the windwagon's passengers, but Thomas hadn't even opened it up yet. "Now I'll really let her take the wind," he cried, swigging from a bottle in triumph. He put the helm over, and the windwagon rounded smartly. But suddenly the wind caught her and, despite all of Thomas' efforts, she went cockeyed in reverse. Doc Parker, who had disappeared on the horizon moments before, came sharply back in view. He had to whip his ass fiercely to get the beast out of the way of the free-running craft.

Aboard the windwagon, the stockholders were cursing Thomas—those that hadn't become wagon-sick, that is. There was nothing Windwagon Thomas could do: the steering gear had locked, and so the craft sailed round and round in a mile-wide circle. When the windwagon slowed a bit in the slackening wind, the stockholders started going overboard, welcoming the risk of bodily injury to escape the careening craft. Determined to remain with his ship and go down, if need be, with colors flying, Windwagon Thomas held to the deck until the windwagon ground to a stop against a stake-and-ride fence on Turkey Creek.

After that, there was not much to be said. Some of the investors, many of whom were suffering from injuries, talked of prosecuting Windwagon Thomas, but it was doubtful he had any assets— aside from the windwagon itself, and nobody wanted that.

Thomas actually tried to talk folks into giving the windwagon another chance. They turned their backs on him. The next morning Windwagon Thomas mounted his craft, cursing the cowardice of the "landlubbers," and sailed away.

The records of the white man offer no further mention of Windwagon Thomas, but Western historian Stanley Vestal, a man whose respect for Indians gained him access to their lore, in later years learned of the Indians' hearsay concerning Windwagon. He wrote:

Somewhere north of the Santa Fe Trail (the Arkansas River) a white man travelling in such a vehicle encountered a camp of Arapahoes. The flag the Indians mention was evidently the sail, though the red men had no notion that it had anything to do with the movement of the craft. In that camp was a visiting Sioux, or perhaps a Cheyenne, from whom our cloudy story comes. Apparently, the Indians found Thomas stalled, or should we say becalmed? That would account for their boast that they did not run. But the windwagon did run later, after they had made friends with its navigator. Whither he sailed, or what became of him, my informant could not tell.

Noyes, John Humphrey (1811–1886)

THE METICULOUS FREE LOVER

John Humphrey Noyes is often credited with being the first expo-nent of "free love" in America. He was not, but he did coin the phrase and pursued its goals with the passion of a Galileo exploring the skies. With Noyes sex was an obsession, requiring orderly rules to permit disorderly activities.

He was the first to formalize mate-swapping, giving it the high-flown name of "complex marriage." Even though he came up with certain rules that later won praise from sex experts such as Have-lock Ellis, there is no doubt that Noyes was a sex nut. In the Oneida Community he formed in New York, 300 of his followers consid-ered themselves married to one another. Exclusive attachments were not permitted, although anyone had the right to refuse inter-course if he or she wished. A special committee kept a large ledger in which it was recorded who was sleeping with whom, and when, etc. One character who wouldn't take no from a certain woman was chastised, on Noyes' orders, by being heaved out of a window into a snowbank—to cool his ardor.

The firstborn of a religious couple in Brattleboro, Vermont, Noyes was studying theology at the Yale Theological Seminary when he made the stunning discovery that he was free of all sin. This was possible, he determined, because the Second Coming of Christ had occurred in 70 A.D. He started preaching about the perfectability of man, which led to being expelled from school and stripped of his preacher's license.

Noyes kept right on preaching his gospel anyway, including his very permissive ideas on sex. With his red hair and freckles, he was not a handsome man, but his message seemed to have made him popular in some circles.

It also lost him a potential bride, Abigail Merwin, eight years his senior, who was much taken with him but was finally convinced by her parents that Noyes was a bit touched. When she married another, Noyes was shattered. He went off to New York City, where he preached his doctrine for a few years in the slums. He slept in hallways, telling vagrants and bums that they had perfection within them and were therefore entitled to the love of all good women. His listeners agreed with his precepts but somehow nothing much came of it. In 1838, contrary to his view that a man should not engage in an official marriage, he wed Harriet Holton, a woman of considerable means, and they settled in Putney, Vermont.

There Noyes devoted his mind to the intricacies of his new gospel, especially on such matters as ejaculation. He came to the conclusion that "it is as foolish and cruel to expend one's seed on a wife merely for the sake of getting rid of it, as it would be to fire a gun at one's best friend merely for the sake of unloading it." From this major deduction Noyes came up with the idea of male continence. Harriet liked that, having had four stillbirths out of five up until then. So did many men Noyes talked to. Even more so did many women, perhaps because Noyes' philosophy held the female orgasm in great esteem, an idea not to be reborn in America until after the time of Kinsey.

Mary Cragin, a female much taken with the teachings of "The Honorable John," as Noyes encouraged folks to call him, came to him with a straightaway proposition that Noyes did not want to refuse. Noyes went to his wife and Mary's husband, spelling out his idea of a four-way marriage. It was agreed, and mate-swapping came to Putney. In all, 35 persons were ready for this new life-style, although the rest of the Vermont community certainly was not. In 1847 Noyes was arrested for adultery. He jumped bail and fled to Oneida, New York, where his wife, Mary, Mary's spouse, and a few dozen converts soon joined him.

In time the Oneida Community grew to be 300 strong. They lived communally, sharing everything in their conception of a "Bible Communism." Being able to feed themselves mainly by trapping animals, the Oneidians soon began to concentrate on making goods to sell to the outside world; chiefly they sold canned fruits and vegetables, animal traps, straw hats, mop sticks, and the silverware that they would become famous for. The salesmen who went forth to thus raise funds were enthusiastically welcomed back by the women who treated them to communal Turkish baths and other rewards.

The sexual rules of the Honorable John applied rigidly to those who remained home. Older women were required to teach the young men the concept of male continence, while virgin girls, many in their early teens, were introduced to complex marriage by old men acting as "first husbands," a role Noyes played with considerable ardor himself.

It was estimated that Noyes took hundreds of lovers in his lifetime. He sired at least nine of 58 children born under his "stirpiculture" program whereby the most well-endowed men were chosen to sire children.

There were many other rules, nonsexual in character, that applied to the community, but Noyes and his eccentric sexual theories were the glue that held things together. Trouble invaded this paradise in 1877, when jealous males started complaining that Noyes was monopolizing most of the pretty young girls. They finally went so far as to charge him with statutory rape. Noyes was forced to flee to Canada, where he lived to the age of 74 with his wife, sisters, and a small group of followers, mostly women.

Back in Oneida, his experiment in sexual freedom and communistic possession of property failed to survive a year without its prophet. The members voted to incorporate and establish private ownership. There was no more sharing of wives. Indeed, it got so that it was very difficult for an Oneidian to as much as borrow a hammer from a neighbor.

Marshall, James Wilson (1812–1885)

THE MAN WHO OWNED CALIFORNIA'S GOLD

James Marshall's place in history was secured on January 24, 1848; while working as a carpenter for John A. Sutter, Marshall noticed some bright metal beneath a mill he was building at Coloma, California. It turned out to be gold, and the great California Gold Rush was on. It was, to Marshall's eternal frustration, virtually the last bit of the yellow metal he would ever find.

Both he and Sutter became famous—and both became poor. The two men in on the ground floor went broke while others made fortunes. For a time Marshall made money selling lumber to feed the gold towns and camps that sprang up all around. His lumber sold for $500 per 1,000 board feet, but the stand of timber was soon depleted, and he spent the money almost as fast as he had made it.

In desperation Marshall took to mining, and he was always welcomed as a hero at the mining camps. Other gold hunters viewed him as eternally lucky and staked out claims near wherever he prospected. Sometimes they struck it rich and sometimes not, but Marshall never did. Occasionally Marshall misdirected prospectors to what he regarded as the most unlikely spots, only to suffer the agony of seeing them hit pay dirt.

The thought of his ill fortune festered on Marshall's mind until he was driven to the point of delusion. He developed the idea that everyone was cheating him out of his gold, that in fact all the gold in California belonged to him.

He became the crank of the mining camps, altering miner's claim boundaries—literally a hanging offense for all but the hero who found California's gold. However, Marshall continued his ill-tempered acts, and finally he was driven out of one camp after another, warned not to return unless he wished a tar-and-feathering or an even worse fate at the end of a noose.

Also weighing heavily on Marshall was the fact that Sutter often won the honors as the discoverer of gold, and when the latter went broke he was awarded a state pension of $250 a month. Marshall snarled out an angry autobiography and finally won himself what he considered an unjust pension of only $100 a month. Still he managed for six years to live comfortably, but then the legislature neglected to renew his special grant, and Marshall became an indigent, living in a rude shack within sight of his historic find.

He rejected intercourse with persons trying to befriend him and was often seen walking alone, talking to himself. He died in 1885 and was buried at Coloma. Four years after his death the Society of the Native Sons topped his mean grave with a statue of a bronze figure of the Discoverer of Gold. Ironically, the funds expended for the monument would have eliminated the want and suffering he endured during the last eight years of his life.

Lee Ah Bow (c.1814–1912)

"DEVIL APPO"

Lee Ah Bow, one of the most controversial Chinese people ever to settle in New York City, is often described by careless historians as the first member of his race in that city. In fact, he arrived no earlier than 1847, at least seven years after the first Chinese settled on Mott Street. Lee Ah Bow was imported to the West Coast by American slavers who sold him in California. How he eventually made his way to New York remains a mystery.

In any event he came and soon wound up a regular in the police records—recorded, in the strange ways of the white man, as Quimby Appo; probably, as the latter-day crime reporter Meyer Berger theorized, for no other reason than that the New York police have always shown a weakness on names.

Lee Ah Bow was an odd sort, as one must be to have served four terms in the New York prison called the Tombs, for murder, as well serving several other stretches on lesser charges. Yet the prevailing public attitude was that Lee Ah Bow was to be tolerated, that his murderous ways with a knife, for example, often had a great deal of justification, and far from being a homicidal madman, he deserved to be elevated to the level of a sort of homicidal eccentric.

Lee Ah Bow was a muscular little man with great strength and a short temper, but prison guards always made allowances for his nasty behavior, delighted to have such an oddity to exhibit to visitors. Hardly anyone in New York had till then seen a Chinese, and certainly not a dangerous one. Missionary ladies vied energetically—sometimes, it was said, almost to the point of violence— against each other for the honor of converting Lee Ah Bow to their respective faiths. Lee Ah Bow was delighted by the competition and switched religions constantly, depending on who had last tempted him with a good cigar or a succulent roast chicken. These white ladies, he appears to have concluded, must all have been quite mad.

Lee Ah Bow got into his first serious trouble in 1859. He was living at the time with one Catherine Fitzpatrick, about whom he had a number of complaints, the most offensive of which, to the Chinese husband, was that she couldn't cook; but she also often arrived home drunk. When Catherine came in suffering from beer hiccups, the angry little Chinese upbraided her, and she promptly shoved him up against the hot coal stove. Lee Ah Bow screamed but his inamorata did not let him off the red iron. In desperation he bit her and she screamed. A neighbor, Mary Fletcher, rushed in, decided it was a case of a celestial going amok and wrestled him perilously close to the blazing coal stove again. Lee Ah Bow stuck her with a knife and fled. Another neighbor, a decidedly bulky woman, tried to inhibit his flight by turning her back on him on the stairway. Lee Ah Bow cleared a path by jabbing his weapon into her rump—not fatally.

Lee Ah Bow was eventually caught, convicted of murder, and sentenced to hang. Clearly, he had been ill represented legally, considering the extenuating circumstances, which Lee Ah Bow readily exhibited in his death cell by showing off his burn scars.

The missionaries got the death sentence commuted, and Lee Ah Bow was released after doing only a few years. Not long afterward, Lee Ah Bow used his knife on a Miss Lizzie Williams, his Bowery landlady, but she too had a bad reputation, being known to rifle her boarders' possessions. A lawyer hired by the missionary ladies made mincemeat of the murder charge, and Lee Ah Bow was released after doing only a brief stint in the Tombs.

In the early 1870s Lee Ah Bow, somewhat under the influence, did in a laborer named John Linkowski by caving in his head with a cobblestone. It was an open question as to who started the argument and who dug the cobblestone out of the street, but Linkowski was noted as a man who hated the Chinese "heathens." As a compromise, Lee Ah Bow was given three years.

By now the newspapers were referring to him as "Devil Appo" and "The Chinese Devilman." Lee Ah Bow was showing a bit of an antisocial streak. He would constantly gnash his teeth and try to bite the hands of trusties serving him food through his cell bars. The missionary ladies were undeterred. Lee Ah Bow, they felt, had a right to be upset by the way the white man's law was treating him. Besides, he was most polite to them whenever they visited him, especially when they brought him the Good Book—and some food and other presents.

In 1875 Lee Ah Bow took a knife to Cork Mag, a Bowery streetwalker, but the law did nothing about it. Cork Mag recovered, and it seemed she was at fault; she had tried to lure Lee Ah Bow from his new Christian ways. However, in 1876 Lee Ah Bow lost a game of draughts to a derelict named John Kelly. When Kelly laughed triumphantly, Lee Ah Bow naturally resorted to his trusty knife with fatal results.

By this time Coroner Woltman felt the city had had enough of the Chinese's fatal moodiness and he declared he thought Lee Ah Bow, whatever his difficulties with grasping Western ways in the past, had definitely become unhinged. A number of alienists agreed and Lee Ah Bow was transferred from the Tombs to the state institution for the insane at Matteawan. Not everyone could disagree with Rebecca Salome Foster, one of the most famous "angels" doing welfare work at the Tombs, when she opined that it was the white man who had driven Lee Ah Bow over the edge.

In any event, with the passing years Lee Ah Bow's madness became more pronounced. When the Hudson River night boat played its searchlight on the prison, Lee Ah Bow would beat on the bars of his cell and scream, "Here comes my diamond." An asylum report reads: "He believes that he has grand hotels, palaces, servants, and horses outside the asylum; that he is King of the World and Omnipotent; the Second God; commands the Wind and the Sun; that Tom Sharkey and General Coxey are his military staff and that he must suffer for Ireland." Clearly, Lee Ah Bow had his finger on most of the ills of the world.

When he died in 1912 he was believed to have been 98 years of age. His body was unclaimed and he was buried on the asylum grounds.

Monk, Maria (1817–1849)

THE JOAN-OF-ARC OF THE KNOW-NOTHINGS

When in January 1836 a young, earnest-looking, beautiful girl of 19 arrived in New York City in the company of a Canadian clergyman, the Reverend W. K. Hoyt, religious passions in America were to be stirred up to the equal perhaps of the Salem witchcraft madness of a century and a half earlier. The girl's name was Maria Monk, and she was as compulsive and as nasty a little fibber as Salem's Ann Putnam. Maria comes down to us as one of the greatest religious hoaxers in our history.

She may well have been induced to such activities by the promise of fame and fortune, but above all she was a pathological liar.

Her mother, who was to denounce her daughter's vicious anti-Catholic crusade, declared in an affidavit that her daughter at the age of seven had jammed a slate pencil through her head. This, Mrs. Monk stated, caused Maria to have frequent headaches and led her to constantly tell whopping lies. She had gone into service as a housemaid but had lost several positions because she made up terrific tales that drove her employers to distraction.

These facts would come out later; but in the 1830s young Maria became the focal point for American Protestants ready to accept the worst possible facts about the awfulness of popery. Maria was indeed to have a powerful impact on the emotional outlet that later became known as Know-Nothingism.

Reverend Hoyt freely informed all who would listen that he had saved poor Maria from a "life of Sin" in the famous, or as he and Maria told it, the infamous Hotel Dieu nunnery in Montreal. That was not quite accurate. Maria herself later stated their first meeting had occurred at a street corner where certain amorous and monetary discussions were carried out in centuries-old fashion.

Still, Maria spun out a wild tale of her years as a novice and nun at the Hotel Dieu, and Reverend Hoyt enthusiastically transcribed them, adding an embellishment here and there to further his view of the divine line.

In New York the clergyman raised funds that allowed for the publication of the girl's story under the title of *The Awful Disclosures of Maria Monk*, as scurrilous a book as ever published in North America. According to Maria's shocking charges, the remote cellars of the nunnery were little different than sex clubs of today, except of course that all the swingers were Catholic ecclesiastics. She said the sisters were visited nightly by priests from a neighboring monastery who reached the cellars through convenient subterranean passages. According to Maria, through the years some nuns who had pledged their love to Jesus alone had resisted the amorous and often abusive advances of the priests, and their bones were strewn in graves in deep basement recesses.

Maria had traveled to New York with a tiny tot in her arms whose birth, she averred, traced to those nocturnal visits from the clerics. Later, journalistic and Canadian governmental investigations produced rather strong evidence that poor Maria simply had trouble discerning between variously garbed gentlemen. She had been involved, although not in the nunnery, with a black-garbed Montreal policeman.

However, even when such disclosures surfaced, the "true believers" were not dissuaded, so ingrained was the will to believe the worst of Catholicism. Maria and Reverend Hoyt gained Dr. W. C. Brownlee, and the organization he headed, the Society for the Diffusion of Christian Knowledge, as sponsors of their book. Dr. Brownlee was pastor of the Collegiate Dutch Reformed Church. He embraced *The Awful Disclosures* since it confirmed his own opinions expressed in his militantly anti-Catholic bestseller, *Popery.*

Naturally, he viewed Maria as little short of an angel, and he gave her refuge in his own house under the ministrations of his wife. This was to lead to the first split between Maria and the Reverend Mr. Hoyt, who denounced her as a "damned jilting jade."

It could well be that the differences between Hoyt and Brownlee were contentious over the matter of money rather than Maria herself. Almost instantly her book sold 20,000 copies, an incredible sale for the era. Grist for antipapists were her awesome charges that one nun's punishment for a minor infraction was to be stretched out on a mattress, another mattress flung over her, and then to be stomped on by a priest and several nuns "until there were as many on the bed [mattress] as could find room, and all did what they could do, not only to smother but to bruise her. Some stood and jumped upon the poor girl with their feet: and others, in different ways seemed to seek how they might beat the breath out of her body." This went on for about 15 or 20 minutes, until the priests and the nuns tired themselves out. "They then began to laugh. . . ."

Certainly avid Protestants nodded in agreement when the authoress assured them "speedy death can be no great calamity to thouse who lead the lives of nuns." Maria also issued a challenge that she would go to the Hotel Dieu "with some impartial ladies and gentlemen, that they may compare my account with the interior parts of the building, and if they do not find my description true, then discard me as an impostor."

The challenge was not taken up, but in time Maria's continued wild tales planted doubts among even her firmest adherents. In Montreal, Maria's mother denounced her daughter as worthless and denied she had ever entered a nunnery. She said the Reverend Mr. Hoyt had offered her $500 in 1835 to state her daughter had entered a nunnery, but she had refused. Eventually even Dr. Brownlee decided Maria was an incorrigible liar, a conclusion perhaps reinforced when she decamped with his young clergyman protégé, John J. L. Slocum, who became what was called Maria's "next friend."

For a minister of the gospel, Slocum proved to be a tough-minded businessman. Late in 1836 he sued Harpers', the publishers of the book, for Maria's share of the royalties, all of which had found their way into the coffers of the Society for the Diffusion of Christian Knowledge.

When the case came to trial, it proved a disaster for Slocum and Maria. Her entire story was exposed as a fraud. It was shown that she had served several terms in reformatories, and that she had started telling her "escape from a nunnery" as a way to earn a little extra money from street-corner clients. It turned out that Maria's tale, even with its embellishments by Hoyt, had not been enough for members of the Society for the Diffusion of Christian Knowledge; a Theodore Dwight had been engaged to put in some added chilling details. Dwight was knowledgeable in Spanish, Italian, German, and French, and he dug up all he could find of bizarre charges made in Europe about convents and torture, and he added them to Maria's text.

The *New York Herald* ordered Maria's followers: "Ye withering fingers of scorn, unskin yourselves at once." And the *Commercial Advertiser* announced: "MARIA MONK IS AN IMPOSTOR, AND HER BOOK AND ALL ITS ESSENTIAL FEATURES ARE CALUMNIES."

While Dr. Brownlee disowned Maria, her book perversely continued to sell very well. In August 1837, Maria, who however had still got no monies for all her imposturing, turned up at the home of a Philadelphia clergyman, a Dr. Sleigh, who was a friend of Dr. Brownlee and apparently just as gullible. After swearing him to secrecy, Maria informed him that she had been kidnapped by a group of priests and held captive in a nearby convent. She had been able to get away, she said, only by conspiring with a priest to marry him.

The result of all this was a sequel, *Further Disclosures of Maria Monk*. Sales, needless to say, were enormous. But if Maria maintained the ability to hoodwink supposedly learned men, she had no defenses of her own. Slocum welcomed her back to New York and conned her into signing over to him a number of rights to both her books. He immediately took off for London where he garnered a sizable fortune for himself marketing the foreign rights to the book.

Once more Maria received not a penny. Dr. Sleigh meanwhile figured out that Maria was rather abnormal, and he issued a pamphlet attacking her. Maria had by this time run out of believers. She was soon on the Bowery, given over completely to drinking, whoring, and telling anyone who would listen how she had been raped the other night by a holy father or two. The record shows that in 1849 she was convicted of pickpocketing. When she died in jail a short time later, she was not even accorded an obituary by any of the newspapers. Indeed her true identity did not become known for some time.

However, Maria's hallucinations and lies have outlived her. *The Awful Disclosures of Maria Monk* is still available—in all 300,000 copies have been sold—and there are still those today who accept Maria's ravings as the true word.

O'Sullivan, Dennis (1818–1907)

THE BUM WHO DINED AT THE ASTOR

Dennis O'Sullivan was the only Bowery bum to dine regularly at New York's Astor Hotel with the president of the United States. Whenever Ulysses S. Grant visited New York, he would invite his old friend, O'Sullivan, to join him in that hostelry's hallowed dining room. This incongruous scene is perhaps best matched in fiction in *The Prince and the Pauper.* Presidential aides were dispatched to the lower Manhattan to find O'Sullivan, which was not always an easy task.

Grant and O'Sullivan went back a long time, well before the Civil War, when the former ran a shop in St. Louis, Missouri. O'Sullivan became a close friend of Grant, whose military career at the time hardly looked promising.

At the beginning of the Civil War, O'Sullivan cast his lot with the Confederacy and was assigned to General Robert E. Lee's staff. Later he was taken prisoner by the Union Army. After his capture, O'Sullivan switched and became an ardent supporter of the North. He was permitted to join the Union Army. Captured by the Confederates, he was sent to Andersonville prison where he finished out the war.

Unlike most other returning veterans, O'Sullivan's life did not improve over the postwar period. He started on a long slide that ended with him living in the "Flea Bag," as New York's chief lodging house was called because of its unsanitary conditions. O'Sullivan lived in the Flea Bag by choice. During Grant's presidential years, he was said to have declined Grant's many offers to help him. He would however trek uptown to see the president and dine in the elegant surroundings of the Astor. It was quite a moment for the man whose Bowery friends called him the "Penny Plug," because he could never afford to buy more than a penny plug of tobacco.

The dinners were heartwarming events for both men, and O'-Sullivan never forgot courtesy and always addressed Grant as "Mr. President." After the meal and some recollections of the good old days, O'Sullivan bade farewell and shuffled off by foot for his home far down on Park Row.

He died in 1907 at the age of 89.

Norton, Joshua A. (1819–1880)

NORTON I, EMPEROR OF THE UNITED STATES

English-born Joshua Norton migrated to San Francisco in 1849 and became a highly successful real-estate broker and speculator. However, within 10 years, he saw his quarter-million-dollar fortune dissipated in bad deals, and he was relegated to working in a Chinese rice factory, living in a seedy rooming house. His turn of fortune affected his mind, and he told anyone who listened that only an emperor with full imperial powers could save the country. Finally one day in September 1859, he delivered the following announcement to the *San Francisco Bulletin*:

> At the peremptory request and desire of a large majority of the citizens of these United States, I, Joshua Norton, . . . declare and proclaim myself Emperor of these United States; and in virtue of the authority thereby in me vested, do hereby order and direct the representatives of the different states of the Union to assemble in Musical Hall, of this city, on the first day of February next, then and there to make such alterations in the existing laws of the Union as may ameliorate the evils under which the country is laboring and thereby cause confidence to exist, both at home and abroad, both in our stability and in our integrity.

San Franciscans took to their hearts
mad Joshua Norton, who, in 1859,
proclaimed himself Norton I,
Emperor of the United States.

He signed the communication as "Norton I, Emperor of the United States and Protector of Mexico."

The newspaper gleefully printed the decree without comment, and Norton's fame was instant. He was accepted by San Franciscans with grace as their new-found eccentric, the citizens having a zeal for such types as is more commonly ascribed to the English.

Norton I promptly consolidated his power by dissolving both political parties and the Republic, but he soon made it clear he intended to be a benign ruler. For 21 years Norton I was perhaps the city's best-known citizen. He wore a blue military uniform with gold-plated epaulets given to him by U.S. Army officers of the post of the Presidio; he wore also a beaver hat bearing a feather and a rosette. He always carried an umbrella and a cane. When his outfit turned shabby, the city's Board of Supervisors, with much ceremony, appropriated money for a new one. Emperor Norton in turn elevated all the supervisors to noble rank.

As emperor he attended all public functions and never missed a session of the state senate, where a chair was reserved for him.

All transportation lines granted him free passes, and newspapers published without charge all his royal decrees. Norton I ate in whatever restaurant, hotel dining room, lunchroom, or saloon that struck his fancy, without paying, and exercised his royal prerogative of chewing out the waiter if the service was not up to his standards or the food not properly done.

The emperor never wanted for cash, since he always carried 50-cent bonds with him to sell to his subjects. At times he would visit a bank seeking to negotiate a loan of several million dollars, but he would leave satisfied, having signed a royal note for four or six bits. Additionally, there was not a merchant in the city who would refuse his 50-cent checks. For his part, Norton I judiciously spread the checks around widely; he believed strongly in equitable taxation.

When Norton died in 1880, the *San Francisco Chronicle* headlined the event: "LE ROI EST MORT." He was given a lavish funeral, one of the largest ever held in San Francisco, with 10,000 mourners lining the funeral route. A millionaires' club picked up the tab.

Corbett, Boston (1822–?)

THE MAN WHO KILLED JOHN WILKES BOOTH

In the various conspiracy theories regarding the murder of Abraham Lincoln, which all go far beyond the vengeance plot by John Wilkes Booth and a handful of sympathizers, Boston Corbett is a central figure. A sergeant in the Union Army in 1865, Corbett, contrary to orders, shot and killed Booth, who was trapped in a burning tobacco barn in Virginia. Conspiracy addicts saw this, not as the act of a twisted mind, but the move of a dutiful assassin following the orders of higher-ups, especially Secretary of War Edwin Stanton.

It is difficult to imagine a character as unstable as Corbett being a dependable cog in any coherent conspiracy. He believed he took orders directly from the Almighty. Thus he marched to a different drummer, gorily so, one might add. In 1858 Corbett, a

Overruling the orders of his superiors were the orders Boston Corbett received from the Almighty to shoot the sinful—among them John Wilkes Booth. (National Archives)

hatmaker in his premilitary days, was accosted by a pair of street-walkers. It is unclear whether he succumbed to their blandishments or simply feared in the future that he might. A conversation with the Creator showed him the way to salvation: Corbett castrated himself, thus foiling lust's temptations.

At the onset of the Civil War, Corbett enlisted in the Union Army. According to his military comrades, he was an odd soldier indeed, given to suddenly erupting in religious hymns or else spending hours staring at lights in the sky, which others developed eyestrain trying to see. In combat, however, Corbett proved to be a fighting machine. In the engagement at Culpeper Courthouse, he was said to have held more than two dozen Confederates at bay single-handedly before finally being taken prisoner. Five grueling months at the Confederate prison at Andersonville probably did little to improve his rationality, and when he was involved in a prisoner exchange, one must assume the Rebels felt they had struck a good bargain indeed.

Corbett was assigned to one of the many detachments searching for Booth, after the assassination of Lincoln in April 1865. On April 26, Union troopers, including Corbett, under the command of Lieutenant Baker, cornered Booth and David Herold in a tobacco-curing barn near Fort Royal, Virginia. Herold, castigated by Booth, surrendered, but the assassin refused to leave the barn unless the troopers pulled back 100 yards, saying that then "I will come out and fight you."

Baker rejected the offer and, ordering his men not to shoot Booth under any circumstances, had the structure set on fire.

Boston Corbett decided such orders could not apply to him as "the Avenger of Blood," as he was later to call himself. The troopers could see a dark figure hobbling about inside the barn. Suddenly, there was a shot—some say by Booth himself, but most, including Corbett, say it was by the wild-eyed sergeant. Soldiers rushed into the barn and pulled Booth outside, where he soon died. Boston Corbett rejoiced, unconcerned that he had broken discipline.

After testifying at the assassination trial, Corbett took to the public appearance circuit, billing himself as the Avenger of Blood. However, his lectures proved less than a total success; he often digressed from the stated subject, the pursuit of Booth, to impart to his audience caustic messages and insults from God.

In the 1880s he was pensioned off by the Kansas legislature, which named him a doorkeeper. Corbett soon came to see these politicians as rogues disobeying the will of God. One spring day in 1886 he fired two revolvers into the crowded assembly. Somehow, no fatalities resulted and Corbett was hauled off to the Topeka Asylum for the Insane.

It did not take long for Corbett to escape from the asylum, leaving behind a letter addressed to the American public, complaining of their ingratitude for the services he had rendered.

Nothing more was ever heard of him.

Bourglay, Jules (c.1824–1889)

THE OLD LEATHER MAN

In the late 1880s he was the East's most famous wanderer, endlessly trudging a penitential 360-mile circle of rural Connecticut and New York areas. He completed the circuit every 34 days—doing better than 10 miles per day—year in and year out for some 32 years. Clad head to toe in leather, which he had fashioned into wearing apparel, he was a truly bizarre sight as he made his virtually word-

Jules Bourglay, the Old Leather Man, wandered the East in a full suit of leather clothes—his protest of a long lost love.

less trek, an apparent act of penance for a business failure. His round-visored hat, his coat, and his trousers were laced together from such discarded leather as bootlegs and heavy soles; all fragments were held in place with thongs at one-inch intervals. The trousers were stuffed into high leather boots with wooden soles. Over this outfit he wore his patchwork leather coat, wide-pocketed and loose, which hung to his knees.

He wore this outfit winter and summer. In the warmer months, the outfit literally creaked like a harness. He refused any offers of other clothing, but he did accept pieces of leather, which he would then fasten to thongs, to save for when he had repair work to do.

He is still remembered in this century. Boy and girl scouts have long been taken on annual Leather-Man hikes, visiting caves where he rested, being told the Leather Man's story around a campfire.

For many years his identity was unknown; he was, for a time, called the French Leather Man, because he spoke that language fluently while only speaking a few words of English. In time, however, it was learned that his name was Jules Bourglay or Bourlay.

His history, pieced together from small snatches he revealed to a few listeners, was that he had as a youth fallen in love with a French girl, Marguerite Laron, whose father was a wealthy leather merchant in Lyons. Although Jules had an excellent liberal education, he was considered by Papa Laron to have come from too low a station for marriage into his family. However, the merchant finally agreed to take him into the business, to let him prove himself. If successful, he would be given new consideration as a potential son-in-law.

Jules grasped the business quickly, and Mr. Laron was soon satisfied enough to allow him to handle the firm's investments. Seeking to impress his potential father-in-law, Jules invested heavily in leather, only to be caught in a sudden drop in the market. The company was almost destroyed.

Jules' life fell apart. Laron dismissed him and forbade the marriage. The young man's mind became affected, and he wandered through the streets of Lyons, cursing himself for his foolhardy business acts. His mind became deranged, and he was eventually confined to a monastery. He escaped after some months and eventually made his way to America.

There, he took up vagrancy as his penance for his ruin. In a period of a little over a month, he traveled his fixed route between the Connecticut and Hudson rivers. The northernmost point was Harwinton, Connecticut, from which he headed southeast through Burlington, Forestville, Southington, and other towns. After traversing a corner of Middletown, he followed the Connecticut River to its mouth at Saybrook. Then his path turned west through Westbrook and several other communities to Guilford. He skirted the city of New Haven and again emerged at the coast at Milford, then on he moved through Stratford, northern Bridgeport, Fairfield, and Westport. Eventually he reached Wilton and crossed into New York, passing Croton Falls to Ossining and veering north to Peekskill. After hitting Shrub Oak and Brewster, he reentered Connecticut near Ball Pond and moved through a number of towns again, the last of which were Watertown, Thomaston, and Plymouth. He completed the circuit at Harwinton.

The *Hartford Globe* and other newspapers published maps showing his itinerary, and it became important local news whenever the Leather Man fell behind schedule. Probably thousands of school compositions have been written about him. Writer Lawrence Treat did a mystery story about him, titling it "The Leather Man"; picture postcards of the Leather Man still grace many family albums.

He slept in caves or built lean-tos of brush against an overhanging rock. There are in Connecticut any number of his resting points known today as the Leather Man's Cave; and it is still possible to find railroad ties bound together in some obscure copse, the last traces of one of Jules' rude huts.

The Leather Man's insistence on wearing nothing but leather probably was a bitter mockery of his own past, but he never displayed any signs of violence or anger. Even when youngsters dogged his trail, he tended merely to ignore them. Childish minds eventually developed a certain respect for him, and he was never subjected to teasing or rock throwing. A contemporary account notes: "He never begged for food, but as the years went by, he picked one or two homes in each village where he could go unmolested for food and tobacco. He never entered a house, never returned if he was questioned, never took any money or worked for what he got."

The Leather Man also never appropriated fruit or vegetables from the gardens he passed. He would knock on a kitchen door where he knew by tacit understanding that food would always be provided. When the door opened, Jules would put his finger to his mouth and mumble, "Piece to eat," exhausting much of what he knew in English. He sat on a bench by the door until the food was set down by him. He could never be induced to enter the house. Whatever he didn't eat, he stuffed in his pockets and moved on.

Usually he ignored efforts of people to communicate with him, although from time to time he would mention a bit out of his past; hence came the tale of his fall from grace in France. Naturally this tale had its variations. There was a version that made him a veteran of the Napoleonic Wars, who had been trying to blot out the horror of his remembrances ever since. Another had him as the sole survivor of a burglary gang that had ravaged Connecticut. The *New York Times* once published an account that came partly from "words told a Yale professor who got him to talk." It went:

> When a young man he fell in love with a girl employed in a leather manufactory near Marseilles and owned by her father. The father opposed the match. The girl rejected the proposals of a dishonorable alliance with the son made by the parents. The girl disappeared. The young man became convinced there had been foul play and eventually that the girl had been murdered through the machinations of his parents. He then left home and his country and never let his friends hear from him. Frequent publications of his regular route and punctual appearance at designated points came to the attention of his brothers. His identity was absolutely established.

He would not quit his vagrant life that he followed so persistently as a sort of expiation for the crime he believed his father had [committed] or had someone else commit.

Most locals disputed that version as the uninformed prattle of outsiders. They preferred their own Lyons story.

The blizzard of 1888 doomed the Leather Man. He was then about 65 years old, and more than three decades of wandering had taken its toll. Caught in the snow near Hartford, he suffered frostbite in his extremities. He was taken to a hospital but he escaped a few hours later. It was announced that the Leather Man was also suffering from an advanced case of cancer. People all along his route watched for him. By intuition, the Leather Man altered his travel pattern. In March 1889, a New York farmer spotted him and invited him to spend the night in his barn, but the Leather Man, gaunt and white, pressed on through the snows. He made it to one of his rock shelters near Briarcliff, New York, on the farm of George Dell. There, on March 24, 1889, his lifeless body was found.

He was buried in Sparta Cemetery, on Route 9 between Briarcliff and Ossining. His grave was marked by an iron bar stuck in the ground. His suit was for many years exhibited in the Eden Musée in New York, while the leather bag was given to the Connecticut Historical Society.

The Leather Man remained a popular figure, even in death. Indeed he was given no rest from his wanderings. The *New York Daily News* once headlined a story: "Saw The Leather Man's Ghost." It reported that a farmer named Clematis Sorrel had come across the Leather Man gathering dry sticks, apparently for a fire in his cave. "Mr. Sorrel is not a drinking man," the story added.

Johnston, John (1826?–1900)

"OLE LIVER-EATING" JOHNSTON

One of the more storied characters of the Old West, John Johnston has been immortalized in a number of Hollywood westerns. However, the movies have tended to make him a bit more wholesome than he really was. Always, Johnston is portrayed as a vengeance-seeking buckaroo who, in his vendetta against Indians, did something awful, such as collect their scalps or some such thing. In real life, Johnston did nothing of the kind. What he really did was kill Crow Indians, an estimated 250 to 300 in his lifetime, and cut them open to feast on their livers. Hence, he was known as "Liver-Eating" Johnston.

A normal enough trapper and trader in the 1840s, Johnston, who sometimes allowed that he was born in New Jersey in 1826— although he could have been at least 10 years older—was trading and trapping along the Shoshone River in what is now Wyoming. He took himself a "bride," a beautiful Chinook Indian. One day while Johnston was away from their cabin, Crow Indians attacked and killed his wife who was then about six months pregnant.

The tragedy, not surprisingly, unhinged Johnston, and he began exacting vengeance by killing Crow Indians. Other westerners did not find this surprising, and they would indeed have understood if he had also lifted his victims' scalps for good measure. Instead, he feasted on their livers. No one knew any explanation for this odd behavior. It didn't seem to represent any sort of strange "medicine" in Indian lore. But other whites tolerated his behavior, simply providing him with the appropriate sobriquet.

In 1861 Abaroka Dapiek, or Crow Killer as Johnston was called by the Indians, was captured by some Blackfeet who figured he would bring a good supply of ponies from the Crow Indians, but Johnston escaped by killing his guard. Because he figured he would have trouble scouring up food on the run, he cut off one of the Indian's legs to provide his ration. Thus, no matter how one looked at it, Liver-Eating Johnston was quite a cannibal. Still, none of this hurt Johnston's career, and he served with the Union during the Civil War as a scout, afterward holding several lawman posts. Of course, whenever he saw a Crow, he would revert back to his liver-eating propensities. Those historically minded souls who kept track of such matters put his total kills in the mid- to high-200s.

In the 1880s, when Johnston was getting along in years, he made peace with the Crow Indians. True, he was slowing up by then and perhaps some Crows might have gotten him first, but the Indians figured it was best to make peace. They ensured Johnston's friendship by taking him into the tribe as blood brother of one of the chiefs. Thus, Johnston finished out his years quietly as a peace officer and army scout. He died in his bed in California in 1900. In 1969, after a popular campaign, Johnston's body was moved from a California veterans cemetery to a burial site along the banks of the Shoshone River in Wyoming. It was fitting, most felt. A man should finish up where he did most of his life's eating.

Train, George Francis (1829–1904)

THE CHAMPION CRANK

Although orphaned at the age of three and receiving only a mini-
mum of formal education, George Francis Train garnered a fortune of some $30 million in shipping and real estate by the age of
30. He then spent the rest of his life going from riches to rags as
the self-proclaimed Champion Crank of America.

He wrote some ten books (not particularly renowned for their
lucidity), made two celebrated trips around the world, took part in
many countries' political disputes (for which he served a total of 15

**Riches-to-rags, raconteur-to-recluse, George Francis Train is perhaps the most colorful
unsuccessful presidential candidate in U.S. history. (Library of Congress)**

sentences, including almost facing a firing squad for joining the French Communards in their revolt against the Third Republic), and helped promote the Union Pacific Railroad through the notorious Credit Mobilier scheme. Train escaped much public censure for that scandal, already being regarded as an irresponsible eccentric or, as abolitionist William Lloyd Garrison once described him, "a crack-brained harlequin and semi-lunatic."

While doing time in a Dublin jail cell for involvement in the Irish emancipation movement, Train decided he was just what the United States needed for president. "I am," he announced, "that wonderful, eccentric, independent, extra-ordinary genius and political reformer of America, who is sweeping off all the politicians before him like a hurricane, your modest, diffident, unassuming friend, the future President of America—George Francis Train." It was not an offer the British could refuse; they released him posthaste and packed him on a clipper for the States.

Train made over 1,000 speeches in quest of the presidency. He had little trouble financing his campaign, hitting on the novel idea of charging admission to his political lectures, an engaging bit of lunacy that entranced the voting public. When the votes were counted in 1872 however, Train came in last, even behind prohibitionist James Black and free-love feminist Victoria Woodhull. However, thanks to his speeches for pay, his campaign ended up an impressive $90,000 in the black.

In the midst of the campaign, Train took time out to make a lightning-fast trip around the world, a voyage that was to so impress science-fiction writer Jules Verne that he used it as a model for Phileas Fogg's exploits in *Around the World in Eighty Days*.

In 1873 Train came to the aid of his former rival Victoria Woodhull and her sister Tennessee Claflin, when they were arrested for publicizing the scandalous details of the Reverend Henry Ward Beecher's adulterous affair with Elizabeth Tilton. Train issued a newspaper of his own, called *The Train Ligne*, and published several columns of sexy quotations from the Old Testament. He declared, "Every verse I used was worse than anything published by these women."

The bluenoses of the day agreed. They had him arrested and charged with obscenity. For this offense and irrational acts in his political campaign, Train was labeled insane and found not responsible for his deeds. Set free, Train protested his treatment by leaving the jail unclad save for an umbrella.

In the aftermath of the legal proceedings, virtually all of his vast holdings in real estate were left tied up. Train became embittered toward mankind, although he continued to do things that held the public in awe. In 1890 he once more circled the globe, this time to put female journalist Nellie Bly in her place: she had established a circumnavigational record of 72 days, six hours, and 11 minutes. Train's new mark—he kept the time meticulously—was 67 days, 13 hours, three minutes, and three seconds.

During the next 14 years of his life, Train's behavior turned more bizarre. He refused to speak to or shake hands with old acquaintances, simply shaking hands with himself in acknowledgement of them. Then he more or less stopped talking to adult men and women, and he lost all interest in living well or in money in general, although he could probably have rewon his fortune.

He lived out his days in a $3-a-week room in the Mills Hotel in New York City and preferred to spend his time telling stories to children. Two years before he died in January 1904, he deigned to dictate his autobiography. It took him 35 hours.

Helper, Hinton Rowan (1829–1909)

THE BIGOTED ABOLITIONIST

Ironically, one of the most virulent—and certainly one of the most explosive—antislavery books in U.S. history was written by an anti-black eccentric, Hinton Rowan Helper. Helper was more than a bit deranged, a condition that worsened steadily through the years.

A North Carolinian who answered unsuccessfully the call of the California Gold Rush in 1850, Helper turned to writing. He made very little splash with his works until he wrote *The Impending Crisis of the South: How to Meet It*. Sometimes described, while yet in his twenties, as a tall, bleak man, Helper developed an odd thesis that mixed hardheaded reality with bigotry. His book, which in its day produced a far greater sensation than *Uncle Tom's Cabin*, caused men to be hanged for mere possession of it, as well as book burnings, court trials, and fisticuffs on the floor of the U.S. House of Representatives.

Helper insisted that slavery was a political and economic hindrance that had brought and would continue to bring financial and moral ruin to the white South; it had to be abolished. However, he could not be accused of being soft on blacks, favoring as he did their complete expulsion from the country. Hopes for the achievement of that end, as much as the destruction of slavery, led him to advocate armed revolt by the slaves. The appearance of the book made Helper one of the most hated men in the South (for safety's sake he had moved to New York before publication). Most Southern states banned the book and subjected owners of it to stiff jail terms. Many persons were punished, and many more were the victims of vicious beatings. In Arkansas alone three men were lynched for the mere possession of copies.

In the North ardent abolitionists preferred to ignore the racial hatreds Helper espoused and, in 1859, a fund was raised for the printing of 100,000 copies of it for use by the Republicans in the elections of the following year. The book caused physical turmoil and, at one point, a near-riot in the House of Representatives. Republican John Sherman's endorsement of *Crisis* led to his defeat for speaker of the House, arousing secessionist sentiments among Southern members to fever pitch, becoming a powerful contributing cause of the Civil War.

In 1861 Abraham Lincoln appointed Helper consul at Buenos Aires, Argentina, which had the effect of removing him from the domestic political scene. After the war Helper returned to the U.S. and took up his old campaign, which, with slavery eliminated, focused completely on near-psychotic antiblack positions. In three books, *Nojoque, Negroes in Negroland,* and *Noonday Exigencies,* he furiously denounced blacks as being a continued menace to the South and to white labor. He declared specifically that his purpose was "to write the negro out of America . . . and out of existence."

As he traveled about the country, he would ask, upon entering a hotel or restaurant, if any blacks were employed there. If so, he marched out and sought other accommodations. Helper did this for the rest of his life, but as his odd behavior increased, a new monomania occupied his time. He saw himself as "the new Christopher Columbus" and tirelessly promoted the idea of building a railroad from Hudson Bay to the Strait of Magellan. He wrote thousands of letters, petitioned Congress, and made personal appeals to hundreds of financiers and other giants of industry. He never could produce any convincing need for the project other than his own desire to be recognized as another Columbus.

He had garnered a considerable fortune from *Crisis,* but his last years were spent in bitter privation as he sacrificed family, fortune, and comfort for his dream. Bitter and despondent, he committed suicide in a seedy Washington hotel in 1909. Obituaries spoke of him as a man with a touch of genius akin to madness.

Allen, John (c.1830–?)

"WICKEDEST MAN IN NEW YORK"

In his own way, spunky little John Allen, a dance-house (i.e., brothel) operator in New York City in the mid–19th century could be decribed as the Jekyll and Hyde of sex. The press of his day labeled him the "Wickedest Man in New York." His brothel may have made him deserving of the sobriquet, but there was more about Allen that singled him out for contempt. It was his background. He was a former seminary student whose pious family included three clergyman brothers, in whose steps he refused to follow, preferring the ways and rewards of the flesh.

Nevertheless, if Allen eschewed the religious road, he compulsively continued to spread the gospel in his own peculiar way. Allen's establishment sported a holy aura never found in any other pesthole of vice in America. Before the place opened for business each afternoon, Allen gathered his harlots in the saloon section and read to them, as well as to the musicians, bouncers, and bartenders, selections from the Scriptures. This would be followed by a hymn-singing session at which the most popular song was "There is Rest for the Weary," a comforting thought for the girls.

Customers and patrons who accompanied the girls to the special cubicles in back found the sparsely furnished rooms supplied with numerous religious tracts and a Bible. Allen would reward regular clients with gifts of the New Testament.

Needless to say, the press and police were bewildered by Allen's incongruous behavior. In that, they were probably no worse off than Mrs. Allen, a hardened biddy who feared the possibility of her husband turning his back on business and returning to the cloth. That never happened. Just when it seemed about to happen (especially when he threw his establishment open to evangelists), Allen

John Allen, the Jekyll and Hyde of the New York sex scene, conducted daily prayer meetings for the staff of his highly successful dance hall-brothel.

would be arrested on some charge—robbing a patron, suspicion of murder—and the threat would fade.

Eventually though, business declined precipitously at John Allen's Dance House; the criminal elements felt they just couldn't trust a religious eccentric. The establishment was shuttered, and Allen and his wife faded away. Naturally, the story spread that he did, after all, go back to the church, becoming a respected and trusted preacher in some distant community. Another story had it that he was off in the wilds of mid-America, still playing the flesh trade.

More likely, Allen did neither. Being torn as always by the twin drives of piety and greed, he probably just retired on the huge fortune he had acquired.

Black Bart (Charles E. Bolton) (1830–?)

THE OUTLAW PO-8

Is it a contradiction in terms to describe a man as both as eccentric and one of the most successful outlaws in the Old West? The answer is no, as it applies to Black Bart. In fact, the eccentric manner in which he went about his tasks accounted in large measure for his success. Bart has been aptly described by biographers as a great walker. There were not many stagecoach robbers who operated sans horse, and many a posse that pursued Black Bart went off in the fruitless following of horse-hoof tracks, ignoring, if they even noticed, any human footprints.

In short, Black Bart was a bizarre square peg who got away with exploits not even a Jesse James would have dared pull—all because of the sheer unconventionality of his acts. A bandit, everyone knew, was to be a shoot-'em-up hell-raiser who would as soon kill a man as look at him. Black Bart was cut from different wood. True, he often carried a shotgun (when he didn't just fake a weapon with a stick from a manzanita bush), but he would never dream of loading it. And, true to his own code, he never took any money or valuables from stagecoach driver or passengers. The Wells Fargo box was all he wanted before sending the coach on its way. On the spot, Bart would smash open the treasure box, wrap its gold in his pack, and trek off. In a short time the law would be at the scene of the crime. They would ride off hard following likely horse tracks. Bart was shrewd enough to pick spots with fresh hoofprints, to oblige the law as much as he could.

If this modus operandi was not unconventional enough, Bart had a way of taunting the authorities and Wells Fargo with his "po8try," as he called it, leaving his unique verses at the scene of the crime. A typical one read:

> Here I lay me down to sleep
> To wait the coming morrow,
> Perhaps success, perhaps defeat
> And everlasting sorrow
>
> I've labored long and hard for bred [sic]
> For honor and for riches
> But on my corns too long you've tred
> You fine-haired Sons of Bitches

> Let come what will, I'll try it on
> My condition can't be worse
> And if there's money in that box
> 'Tis munny [sic] in my purse.
> Black Bart, the Po-8.

And another:

> This is my way to get money and bread,
> When I have a chance why should I refuse it.
> I'll not need either when I'm dead,
> And I only tax those who are able to lose it.
>
> So blame me not for what I've done,
> I don't deserve your curses;
> And if for some cause I must be hung,
> let it be for my verses.

By most reliable count, Black Bart pulled 27 successful holdups in California from 1874 to 1883. Only once did a stagecoach get away; the fact that Bart's weapon was unloaded was excuse enough for failure. Bart's operation was simple. Wearing a duster and a flour-sack mask over his head, he would bound out of the bush onto the trail and shout to the stage driver, "Throw down your box or die."

Occasionally, a driver hesitated obeying, and Bart would yell to his confederates in the bushes to start shooting unless the order was followed. The driver would see five or six rifles in the shadows and invariably did as he was told. Actually the rifles would be nothing more than broomstick handles or stripped branches. Bart then scooped up his loot, deposited his doggerel for the law . . .

> I'll start out to-morrow
> With another empty sack.
> From Wells Fargo I will borrow
> But I'll never pay it back.

. . . and started walking.

Biographers have presented various theories regarding his background and history. The files of the Pinkertons indicate he was born in Jefferson County, New York, and that he went West when he was 10 years old. Other sources say he was born in Norfolk,

England, and was brought to the St. Lawrence River's Thousand Islands area as a child. He served in the Union Army under the name of either Boles or Bolton, one of which was apparently his real name.

In either case he was in California in the early 1870s, either laboring as a miner or as a schoolteacher in the Northern Mines area. We are indebted to grass-roots historian G. E. Dane for the information that, in any event, he loved a practical joke, and "it's only one step from that to crime."

Indeed, Black Bart may well have started his robbery career as a prank. According to this legend, he was on his way home from school as night was falling when he heard the stage bucking the grade. He tied a handkerchief over his face and thought to throw a scare into the driver, Johnny Shine, whom he knew well. He broke off a stick from a manzanita bush at about pistol size and pounced out at the stage, announcing a robbery.

"Throw out the box!" he yelled, and much to his surprise the driver obeyed. Bart was momentarily distracted when the box landed on the ground, and the frightened driver seized the opportunity to whip the horses and take off.

The loot, Bart found, came to a few thousand dollars in bullion and dust, and he realized that in two minutes he had made more than he could in two years of honest labor. It is arithmetic like that, says our legend, which can lead a man astray. Black Bart was born that night.

Under the name of Charles E. Bolton, Black Bart took up a new life in San Francisco, living in distinction, even dining at a fashionable restaurant near the Hall of Justice, and being on speaking acquaintance with a number of detectives and prosecutors.

And of course the robberies followed, one after another. Bart would traipse from the scene on foot, a typical route taking him to a rail line where he'd catch a train either bound for San Francisco or going in the opposite direction, to Reno, where, after dallying a few days, he would finally head for the California city. On other occasions, though, Black Bart would set out to walk the entire way, stopping at isolated houses here and there, begging food. It was clear that Black Bart was an eccentric not entirely sure of his proper calling.

All things, at least good ones, must end and the finis to Black Bart's career came in November 1883, after a holdup that earned him almost $5,000. A rider came up during the robbery and fired at the outlaw, forcing Black Bart to leave quickly without so much as dropping his verse. He did however drop his handkerchief, and Wells Fargo detectives traced the laundry mark, F.O.X. 7, until the trail led to a man named Charles E. Bolton in San Francisco.

The *San Francisco Bulletin* reported the suspect to be "a distinguished-looking gentleman who walked erect as a soldier and carried a gold-knobbed cane." Evidence to numerous robberies were found in Bolton's room, and he finally admitted he was Black Bart. He was sentenced to 8 to 10 years in prison, but with good behavior he was released in early 1888.

A reporter at the prison gate asked him if he intended to return to crime. "I'm through with all that now," Black Bart replied.

"Are you going to write any more poetry?" another asked.

"Young man," Black Bart snapped, "didn't I tell you I wasn't going to commit any more crimes?"

What happened to Bart after that is a mystery. According to Wells Fargo detectives he sailed off to Japan. But for years the old-timers in California told a different tale. Immediately on Black Bart's release, according to them, a new wave of robberies hit the stage line. This time however the unknown bandit left no verses behind. Still Wells Fargo recognized the technique of Black Bart. They located him and offered him a deal. He was getting up in years, they said, and ought to be thinking of retiring. Black Bart saw merit in the idea, and he allowed that he might consider it if he had some steady income. So eventually Charles E. Bolton went on the company's pension list at $200 a month.

A crazy story? Perhaps, but hardly crazier than the whole career of Black Bart, the Po-8.

Walker, Dr. Mary (1832–1919)

"AMERICA'S SELF-MADE MAN"

A pioneer woman physician, Mary Walker was a flamboyant, often radical crusader for women's rights who at times even embarrassed other suffragettes by her mad acts. During the Civil War, fellow doctors refused at first to allow her to work as an army surgeon and relegated her to menial labors in the field as a "medical assistant." However, she proved her bravery under fire, and at Gettys-

A flamboyant and radical crusader for women's rights, Dr. Mary Walker managed to offend even fellow suffragettes with her odd behavior, though her apparel became standard for women half a century later. (Library of Congress)

burg and other battlefields she saved the lives of hundreds of Union soldiers. She was accorded the Congressional Medal of Honor, the first and only woman ever to win the highest of all U.S. combat awards. Late in the war she was taken prisoner by the Confederates and held for months in notorious Libby Prison, until she was exchanged "man for man" for a Southern major.

If Dr. Walker proved popular with the soldiers, she offended many important individuals with her attire. A "bloomer girl" in the early 1850s, she wore the costume introduced by Amelia Jenks Bloomer—a knee-length, dark broadcloth tunic, gathered at the waist, over some loosely fitting pantaloons.

"Why don't you wear proper clothing?" Major General William Tecumseh Sherman once demanded of her in the field. "That clothing is neither one thing nor the other." During the later stages of the war, she did partially bow to his admonition, donning the same uniform as the men. Later, by the 1870s, she wore a frock coat and trousers, and for lectures or night wear, male formal dress.

Immediately after the war, her attire was so notorious that she was arrested on several occasions for "masquerading as a man." However, she was never prosecuted, since a grateful Congress had passed a special act granting her the right to wear trousers, in recognition of her wartime services.

This did not still her critics. The newspapers referred to her as "America's Self-Made Man." One newspaper editorialized: "What must be demanded by all who have the interest of the Republic at heart is the refeminization of Dr. Walker. Her trousers must be taken from her—where and how is, of course, a matter of detail." Dr. Walker saw to it that that never happened.

She campaigned vigorously for women's rights—the right to vote and, just as important to her, the right not to wear the "vile corset" and the hoop skirt, which she said was a fashion foisted on women by "the prostitutes of Paris" and their male clients. She offended many women by citing the age-old male line that their "immoral clothes" led to seduction and rape, and that women had to accept responsibility for that. Barrenness in women, she also insisted, was caused by the tight waistlines, which injured fallopian tubes, ovaries, and uteruses.

With the passing years, she became more crotchety and strong-willed about getting her way, and she launched many odd campaigns, including a utopian colony for spinsters only. She was much upset by the "smoking mania" and the "nicotine evil," and so she carried a tightly furled umbrella with which she batted the offending cigarettes from the mouths of startled men.

In 1907, the Medal-of-Honor Board redesigned the medal and sent her a replacement. She wore both whenever she went out. Then in 1917, the board reversed itself and struck her name from the honored list, along with those of 911 others. It was ruled that the medal could only go to a member of the armed services who "in action involving actual combat with an enemy, distinguished himself conspicuously, at the risk of life, by gallantry and intrepidity above and beyond the call of duty." Infuriated, Dr. Walker refused to turn in her medals and continued to wear them to the end of her days.

Retired from medical practice for many years, in order to devote her full time to reform movements, Dr. Walker lived on fees from public appearances and lectures. At the age of 66, after much campaigning, she won a $20-a-month pension for her war services. Thereafter, despite her bouts with the Medal-of-Honor Board, she had considerable time to spend being a full-time crank. She was constantly involved in schemes that alienated her friends and neighbors in Oswego, New York, where she lived on a farm. She once tried to implicate her hired man in a New Hampshire murder, apparently looking to collect a $5,000 reward. She started plans to turn her farm into a training school for young women. Near the end of World War I, she sent a long, garbled telegram to Kaiser Wilhelm of Germany, offering the farm as a peace-conference site.

In early 1919, Dr. Walker took a nasty fall on the Capitol steps—where she was once more petitioning Congress about her metal. She died on February 19. True to her words that the government would not even get her medals back "over my dead body," she was buried with them pinned to her Prince Albert coat.

Mary Walker did not live to get her medal back, and she died just before she would have enjoyed the right to vote. And it would take another half century before her costume became ordinary wear for women.

Barter, Dick (1834–1859)

RATTLESNAKE DICK

For rather unfathomable reasons, an Englishman named Richard Barter became one of the most vicious outlaws of the West—if we judge by the dime novels of the era. These works gave such individuals as Wild Bill Hickok, Belle Starr, Deadeye Dick, Calamity Jane, and others far more notoriety than they deserved. But in the case of Dick Barter—make that Rattlesnake Dick Barter if you like your characters colorful—it is a matter of fiction run absolutely amok.

Rattlesnake Dick was the stuff satires are made of. If the West was wild and woolly, Barter was far more woolly than wild. His nickname of Rattlesnake was said to have sprung from the fact that he was so dangerous and devious; in actual fact, Dick, who came to America as a youth, got the moniker for having done a stint, during the California Gold Rush, looking for the precious metal in Rattlesnake Bar. He was unsuccessful at it and, in fact, got out of the profession partly because of his unabiding fear of rattlesnakes. Besides, he felt he could do much better stealing gold than digging for it.

The legend-makers never note that he made no money out of his prospecting and precious little as an outlaw, netting less than $20 or so on any of his "monumental" holdups.

His trouble was that, even for the West (where outlaws were not generally cut from high-I.Q. cloth), Rattlesnake Dick was a scatterbrain. But it must be admitted that even among his peers, before the dime novels, Barter enjoyed a handsome "rep" as a bad man; the only apparent reason for this was that he spoke with a distinct English accent and, as some of his contemporaries put it, "must be the smartest at evil doin's in these parts," because of it.

Barter was a real master of planning. He would spy out the fact that a stagecoach was carrying a goodly amount of gold dust, celebrate by getting drunk, and then lead three colleagues in the stage robbery—picking out the wrong coach.

But to his credit, Barter did mastermind one "big one"—the 1856 $80,000 robbery of the Yreka Mine's mule train. Despite by then having suffered considerable loss of face concerning his criminal prowess, he managed to round up a gang to help him. Barter had figured out how to rob a target long considered immune from attack by other genuine badmen.

The problem was that when the mules came down the mountains with their loads, they would become so tired by the time they were halfway down that they had to be rested for a considerable period before they could continue. That meant robbers would have the same trouble with the pack animals, and pursuers would quickly catch up with them.

Rattlesnake Dick figured out all he had to do was provide fresh mules on the mountain trail for his gang and they would get clean away. Among those who were impressed by the logic of Barter's plan were a pair of brothers, George and Cyrus Skinner. It was agreed that George would lead a number of gunmen on the actual robbery while Barter and Cy rounded up the extra mules and met them on the trail. There was a flaw in the plan, of course: the fact that Rattlesnake Dick played an important role in the caper.

Barter and Cy had more than enough money to buy the mules needed but Rattlesnake Dick insisted they have a few drinks to celebrate in advance. The more they drank, the less they had to buy pack animals. So what, Rattlesnake Dick slurred. They were big-time outlaws and getting mules was no problem for gunnies like them. And so, late the night before the big robbery, the pair was behind bars, having been caught, dead drunk, trying to steal some Army mules.

Meanwhile George Skinner and his boys executed their part of the job to perfection, spurring their animals on to the rendezvous point where no mules were waiting. Desperately, George Skinner buried most of the stolen nuggets and then rode off with his boys for the town of Folsom, still cursing that "crazy Britisher."

Wells Fargo agents caught up with the gang in Folsom and shot them all dead, even George, who was in the bed of a screaming saloon girl.

Meanwhile Rattlesnake Dick and Cy Skinner broke out of jail. It was not a particular cunning act; a guard had forgotten to lock their cell door. They went looking for the buried treasure but could not find it.

There was only one thing to do, Rattlesnake Dick observed. They had to go back to the outlaw trail. So they pulled a few stage robberies. But after one that came to $18—$9 apiece—Cy Skinner decided his late brother had been a shrewd judge of foreigners when he called the Britisher crazy.

Rattlesnake Dick was now on his own. He pulled a few lone-handed, and unproductive, holdups. He always took care to wear a mask so he wouldn't be recognized. Of course, everyone recognized his British accent. Finally, in 1859 a pursuing posse gunned Rattlesnake Dick to death, mercifully ending a most embarrassing criminal career.

Green, Hetty (1834–1916)

THE WITCH OF WALL STREET

Henrietta Howland Robinson grew up to become the greatest American miser who ever lived. Her upbringing in a frugal New Bedford, Massachusetts, Quaker home undoubtedly helped. As a child she got an allowance of five cents a month and was much belabored if she spent so much as a penny of it instead of saving it. Such frugality seems to have had its rewards, however, for the Robinson family's thrift enabled it to accumulate millions from its shipping and whaling activities. By the time she was six years old, Hetty was sitting at her father's knee, reading the financial pages to him.

Hetty grew into a rather handsome woman, but the family emphasis on thrift left her personal habits rather on the sloppy side. She dressed in rags and wore mismatched stockings. Turned off by this, several suitors dropped their pursuit of her. Hetty was not particularly upset; she had come to the conclusion that men were nothing but fortune hunters.

Hetty's father died when she was 30, and she inherited a million dollars outright as well as the income from several millions more, with the total capital to pass to her children. She later inherited an additional million dollars from an aunt's estate. It was never determined if she was entitled to that money. There was considerable speculation that she may have used forged documents to win the inheritance. This latter inheritance presented Hetty with other problems. If she didn't have children, the money would pass on her death to others related to her aunt. So in 1867 she married 46-year-old Edward H. Green, himself a millionaire, but to protect her interests she made him sign a premarital agreement relinquishing all claims to her money.

Green was a happy-go-lucky sort who eventually went broke in the 1880s, and the couple separated. This did not have a shattering

Although buying a new dress for her daughter Sylvia's wedding to Matthew Astor Wilkes didn't kill Hetty Green (left, with her son-in-law and Sylvia), an argument over the price of milk caused the demise of Hetty Green's parsimonious life. (Library of Congress)

effect on Hetty since she had by then two children. Her offspring would grow up to become certified eccentrics in their own right—the daughter, Sylvia, turned into a recluse, and the son, Ned, after his mother's death, became a free-spending magnifico, running through $3 million a year without even trying. While Hetty said some harsh things about her husband after their parting, she apparently still regarded him with some affection—apparently providing him with some support—and when he died in 1902, she wore mourning black for the rest of her life. Happily, black showed dirt least and could go longer between washings.

From the moment Hetty inherited her first million, she devoted her every breathing moment to but two pursuits—the grasping chase of more money, and the equally satisfying nonactivity of spending none of the same. She did not see much sense wasting so much soap washing all of her long black dresses. Instead, she merely scrubbed the lower portions of the skirts. Her dresses in time took on a brown, and then a green, tint because of the long interval between scrubbings.

Once, when charged 10 cents for a bottle of medicine, the

outraged Hetty informed the druggist she would henceforth bring her own bottle and cut the cost of the prescription to five cents. She was even more frugal about newspapers, devouring all the financial news and then refolding the publication, having little Ned take it out on the street and resell it. After her husband departed, Hetty went on to prove that three—she and her children—could live as cheaply as one, and by Hetty's standards that meant cheaply indeed.

They resided in the dingiest hotels—transferring quickly and often from Hoboken, New Jersey, to New York City and back again—traveled in the cheapest conveyance possible, and ate in the simplest restaurants. There was a method to Hetty's madness, the hotel residence changes making it difficult for state officials to levy taxes on her. Her appearance of abject poverty was also important to Hetty, who feared assassination by relatives; under certain inheritances, portions of her funds reverted to them on her death. Hetty constantly promoted the fiction with them that she had gone broke.

Perhaps her most scandalous exercise of parsimony involved Ned's sledding accident. Her son dislocated his kneecap, and Hetty attempted to save on medical bills by treating the injury herself. When it did not respond, Hetty put on her most impoverished wardrobe and presented her son at Bellevue Hospital as a charity patient. Unfortunately, she was recognized, and the doctors demanded payment. Enraged, Hetty left with Ned, vowing not to give the grasping medical men a penny. Eventually, the boy's condition, which would have been easily curable with early medical treatment, worsened; amputation of the leg became necessary.

It must be said that after that Hetty did dote a bit over her son, sending him to Fordham College and later to Manhattan and Chicago for further specialization in real-estate law. When Ned was 24, Hetty packed him off to Texas to see what he could do to make money for her running some of her railroad interests there. Ned did reasonably well, but he certainly never matched Hetty's financial acumen.

By that time Hetty had gained the reputation as the Witch of Wall Street, trading with a surefooted audacity that stunned other renowned speculators. Immediately after the Civil War, Hetty bought heavily in U.S. bonds, while other financial figures avoided them; this latter attitude sent their value plummeting. But Hetty had displayed a greater understanding of financial and political realities; she believed the nation would not repudiate its debt. She also took over ailing business enterprises, especially railroads, and by making war on her competitors, returned them to profitability. One biographer called her "a sort of reverse Florence Nightingale" who, in her financial dealings, "was soon stacking the maimed and dying like cordwood as a result of her ruthless operations."

Such a callous operator as Jay Gould was appalled at the carnage she wreaked, destroying a number of his own plans. Even that arch–robber baron Collis P. Huntington—whose motto was: "What is not nailed down is mine. Whatever I can pry loose is not nailed down"—turned livid at Hetty's ruthlessness.

Such criticism didn't prick Hetty. The name of the game was making, and keeping, money. She operated out of free desk space offered her by the old Chemical National Bank—her constant threat of removing her money obtained such rent-free concessions—heated oatmeal on a radiator to feed herself, sometimes simply slicing and devouring a Spanish onion. Onions, she said, were not only healthy but most economical. Whenever Hetty was particularly morose, she would empty a safe-deposit box or two and sit on the cold marble floor, caressing the notes and certificates.

With Hetty making money hand over fist and Ned off in the wilds of middle America, denizen of the highest priced brothels whenever he could fool his mother, the housekeeping was left to daughter Sylvia. She mended clothes, cooked, washed dishes, and shopped, subject to Hetty's checking on the prices she paid for the necessities of life. Years later, Sylvia was once asked if she lived with her mother in Hoboken, and she replied, "Yes, if you call it living."

It was not a remark Sylvia would have made to her mother's face, nor would Ned have been so inclined. It was rash behavior indeed for anyone to question Hetty's penny-pinching ways. Just that sort of effrontery was to prove the death of old Hetty. In 1916, Hetty was the houseguest of some friends and, as was her wont, she proceeded to lecture her hostess for her extravagant spending. Her hostess absorbed the criticism, but the servants bridled at Hetty's words. One day the cook got drunk and told her off, an argument having ensued over Hetty's claim that skim milk would fulfill a certain recipe as well as whole milk. Hetty insisted that the cook was simply squandering her employer's funds. Right in the middle of the verbal outburst, Hetty suffered a stroke.

She never recovered, dying a short time later, with several trained nurses in attendance. Ned had hired them but made them wear street clothes. He knew that if his mother suspected they were professionals, the thought of the fees involved would have been enough to cause an immediate second stroke.

Walsh, Ellen, alias Mayfield, Ida (1838–1932)

THE FAKE SOCIALITE

She was a belle of New York in the 1860s and seventies, having married Benjamin Wood, a copperhead congressman and newspaper publisher. She was the former Ida Mayfield; she had been a New Orleans belle before she became a New York belle, the vivacious daughter of Judge Thomas Henry Mayfield of Louisiana.

She was a true beauty and Ben Wood lavished gifts on her, and when he took her to New York, where he ran the *New York Daily News,* she was socially active, danced with the Prince of Wales (who became King Edward VII), and counted Samuel J. Tilden among her personal friends. She entertained President Grover Cleveland. She was widowed in 1900. Then in 1907, she simply vanished—not before she walked into the Morton Trust Company, drew out all her money, amounting to nearly a million dollars, in cash, and stuffed it into a large brown shopping bag, never to return to the bank again.

Mrs. Wood did not resurface until 1931, when she was found living in New York's Herald Square Hotel, in what can only be described as Dickensonian squalor. She was 93, and the contents of the room, including huge stacks of yellowed newspapers, seemed that old as well. Hundreds of letters and old pictures carpeted the floor. Cardboard boxes were piled to the ceiling. All over lay half-century-old ball programs from New Orleans, as well as all sorts of inscribed portraits of famous personalities. Lying promiscuously amongst the litter were all sorts of jewelry. When police started opening some of the cardboard boxes, they found them stuffed with negotiable securities worth as much as half a million dollars. They opened a cracker box and out fell a diamond-and-emerald necklace.

Mrs. Wood was found to have a canvas pouch tied to her body. It contained fifty $10,000 bills. The courts declared Mrs. Wood incompetent and supplied legal counsel to look after her interests. The old lady was almost deaf, but she was amused by the official action. She had taken her money out of the bank in 1907, before the Panic of 1907, protecting her entire fortune. "I did quite well, you know, and it seems very strange they should call me incompetent. I made money and I kept it. So many people whom everyone considers quite competent can't do that." She may have been a recluse but she certainly knew of 1929 and, having kept her fortune in good hard cash, she had survived that as well.

Legally, it seemed there was no reason to deprive her of her money. If she wanted to live in squalor and keep her money out of banks that failed, there seemed little reason not to allow her to do so. However, the matter became a moot point early the following year, when Mrs. Wood contracted pneumonia and died.

There was, not surprisingly, much rejoicing in Louisiana, where scores of Mayfields pushed into view to claim a share of the former Ida Mayfield's fortune. Then came a bizarre twist. The courts rejected all their claims. Careful research determined that there had never been any Ida Mayfield. Actually Mrs. Wood had been born plain Ellen Walsh, and her father was an Irish immigrant peddler who had lived for a while in Malden, Massachusetts, and died in California in 1864.

Ellen took the name of Ida Mayfield to satisfy her desire to crash high society. Not even Ben Wood ever suspected the truth. She even pinned the Mayfield name on her mother, brother, and sister. Her sister became Mary E. Mayfield and her brother, Michael Walsh, changed his name to Henry Benjamin Walsh. Ellen even changed the name on her father's tombstone to Thomas H. Mayfield. And when her mother died in 1883, Ellen had her buried as "Ann Mary Crawford, widow of Thomas Henry Mayfield."

The shattered Mayfields returned to Louisiana. Eventually the Wood estate was divided by ten Walsh descendants who received $84,490.92 apiece from an eccentric ancestor they hadn't even known had ever lived.

Teed, Cyrus Reed (1839–1908)

THE INSIDE-OUT MAN

Unlike hollow-earthers Captain John Cleves Symmes (*q.v.*) and Marshall B. Gardner (*q.v.*), Cyrus Teed concocted what scientists regard as an even more preposterous variation of that theory. By Teed's standards, Symmes and Gardner were towers of sanity. Under

Teed's version of the universe the earth was indeed hollow but the difference was that *we were the people inside.*

Symmes and Gardner arrived at their conclusions by mere intellectual achievement. But Teed enjoyed some help from a heavenly character. One night in 1869, Teed was alone in his laboratory in Utica, New York, working on his previous line of endeavor—alchemy—when a beautiful girl appeared to him in a vision. She informed him of his past incarnations and told him that he was a new messiah. Rather offhandedly, she let him in on the secret of the true cosmogony.

The cosmos was not anything like the way scientist-writer Carl Sagan was to describe it a century later. No, really it was rather like an egg, with mankind living on the inner surface of the shell; the hollow inside contained the entire universe—the sun, moon, planets, comets, and stars. At the center of this open space was a huge sun, half light and half dark, and our sun was really just a reflection of it. Only because this central sun rotated did we suffer from the illusion that our sun rises and sets. The moon? A mere reflection of the earth. The planets? Reflections of "mercurial discs floating between the laminae of the metallic planes." The heavenly bodies? Focal points of light, all explained away later by Teed under his various "optical laws."

For 38 years Teed labored away with unflagging dedication to spreading the gospel of this view of the universe. It was quite a step up for this former farm youth who had served as a Civil War private. Later Teed went into practice as a doctor in Utica, New York, having graduated from the New York Eclectic Medical College. Eclecticism was a 19th-century medical movement relying mostly on herb remedies.

As a sideline to his medical practice, he dabbled in alchemy, looking for a way to make gold. He junked that enterprise when it became apparent that the heavenly forces had greater things in mind for him.

And it must be said that Teed's inside-out theory enjoyed considerable success, attracting thousands of followers. His first two works, *Illumination of Koresh: Marvelous Experience of the Great Alchemist at Utica, New York* and *The Cellular Cosmogony,* attracted a wild-eyed following. Later a number of observers, including author Carl Carmer in his *Dark Trees to the Wind,* would note that the great appeal of Teed's cult was its clear representation of a "return to the womb."

Not surprisingly, Teed's early interest in Koreshanity (*Koresh* is Hebrew for Cyrus) led to a falling off of his medical practice. Folks began calling him Utica's "mad doctor." His troubled wife left him, but Teed paid that little mind. In 1886 he shook off the dust of Utica and headed for Chicago. There he established the headquarters of his Koreshan movement, including a commune called Koreshan Unity, a magazine called *The Guiding Star* (later succeeded by *The Flaming Sword* which, along with the womb theory, was in later years to delight the Freudians), and a "College of Life."

The *Chicago Herald* in 1894 described Teed as "an undersized, smooth-shaven man of 54 whose brown, restless eyes glow and burn like live coals. . . . He exerts a strange mesmerizing influence over his converts, particularly the other sex." Indeed, approximately three out of four of his followers were women. He traveled from coast to coast spreading the word, clad in a Prince Albert coat, black trousers, flowing white silk bow tie, and wide-brimmed hat. In California alone he had 4,000 followers.

Of course he had no followers at all in the scientific community. Perhaps this was because these "humbugs," as he called them, could not in their doltishness fathom his simple explanations. Thus Teed lost them when he called planets "spheres of substance aggregated through the impact of afferent and efferent fluxions of essence," and described comets as being "composed of cruosic 'force,' caused by the condensation of substance through the dissipation of the coloric substance at the opening of the electro-magnetic circuits, which closes the conduits of solar and lunar 'energy.' "

Somehow this made his female followers swoon, and they added their amens when he announced: " . . . to know of the earth's concavity . . . is to know God, while to believe in the earth's convexity is to deny Him and all his works. All that is opposed to Koreshanity is antichrist."

In the late 1890s Teed established a new town called Estero, about 16 miles south of Fort Myers, Florida, and announced it was "The New Jerusalem." He predicted that it would eventually have eight million inhabitants and become the capital of the world.

Teed also began to prepare his followers for his physical death, promising that he would then arise and lead the faithful to Paradise. He got out a book, *The Immortal Manhood,* on this theme just in time. In 1908, at the age of 69, he got into a physical dispute with the marshal of Fort Myers and died as a result. Death occurred on December 22, and 200 members of the colony took up a constant prayer vigil over the corpse. Forty-eight hours later it started to take on a rather distinct odor. Christmas passed; the odor had become so pronounced that the county health officials ordered immediate burial. Teed's distraught followers put him in a concrete sarcophagus on Estero Island, off the Gulf Coast. They waited for the next 13 years for Teed to arise like Lazarus, but he never did. Then a tropical hurricane pounded the tomb and carried Teed away to the ocean depths. The last of Teed's followers remained until 1949, awaiting his return to New Jerusalem. Then they finally disbanded.

Winchester, Sarah Pardee (1839–1922)

THE UNFINISHED MANSION

The mansion—perhaps the most fantastic and certainly one of the most expensive structures ever erected—stands today as a museum open to the public, a still uncompleted monument to fear and guilt. Sarah Winchester, the widow of William Wirt Winchester of the Connecticut gun family, began to build her mansion in San Jose, California, in 1884; it was to become an incredible obsession, always being built and rebuilt because she was tortured with the idea that she would die if it were ever finished.

Sarah Pardee had married Winchester in 1862, when she was in her early twenties. It was a luckless marriage, childless save for an infant who died shortly after birth. Winchester himself died in 1881, and Sarah apparently developed the notion that she and her family were being punished for the sins of "the gun." Thousands of people, white and red, had died by the Winchester rifle, and she became obsessed with the belief that these victims had cursed the Winchester fortune and would haunt her the rest of her days. Spiritualists whom she consulted confirmed the theory, but, happily at last, one offered her a solution to her dilemma. She had to build a magnificent mansion to protect herself from these vengeful ghosts, one that would at the same time attract friendly spirits, including her late husband, to keep her from harm's way.

Sarah Winchester was convinced. She took her $20 million inheritance and moved west, to San Jose; in 1884, work began on Winchester House. While the widow was sure the good ghosts would take up their duties, she was not content to leave her worldly safety to the spirit world. The bad ghosts would be sure to come, she knew, and she would have to employ all the guile she could to frustrate them. She would fool them with secret passages, false doors, and stairways that would end in midair. Thus, for the next 38 years, work went on without pause at the mansion. Some carpenters did no work elsewhere for periods of upwards of two decades.

And Winchester House grew. Eventually it had blossomed into being eight stories high, containing 158 rooms. There were five fully equipped kitchens (plus four more in ready-reserve), 13 bathrooms, 48 fireplaces, five separate heating systems, and no less than 2,000 doors and 10,000 windows. Hundreds of these doors and windows opened on blank walls, all part of the scheme to confuse the ghostly invaders. Secret passages twisted for miles between the walls of the rooms, many of which would over the years be torn down and reconstructed according to some new inspiration of Mrs. Winchester. If an intruder, earthly or unearthly, got into the place, he might well go mad trying to find his way about. One stairway had 44 steps and seven turns but at the end rose less than 10 feet. The uninvited would no doubt give themselves away if they lighted the wrong fireplace. Some bore chimneys that did not reach the roof, and the smoke would quickly spread the alarm.

Although she had no architectural background, Mrs. Winchester made up her own plans or altered those of others. She had a huge bell tower constructed, inaccessible save for a torturous climb over the roof, and the bell rope fed into a concealed well that emerged only in a secret cellar. Thus the widow would be able to move to safety and ring an alarm if the spirit invasion occurred.

For 38 years—on weekends and holidays—construction work never ceased on Winchester House. Mrs. Winchester could awake each morning to the comforting sounds of workmen shouting and hammers pounding, and she would realize she had remained safe within the bizarre multi-walled structure. When she died in 1922 at the age of 83, the mansion, on which she had expended more than a quarter of her legacy, had already achieved the status of a legend. In 1973 California made Winchester House a state historical landmark.

Leese, George "Snatchem" (fl. c.1840s–1860s)

SPORTING MAN

One of the most infamous toughs of New York City in the mid–1850s, George Leese was nicknamed Snatchem because, as a member of the notorious Slaughter House gang, he was adept at stealing almost anything from almost anybody. The newspapers of the day profiled him as one of the great perils to both citizens of and visitors to the city. One reporter described him as "a beastly, obscene ruffian, with bulging, bulbous, watery-blue eyes, bloated face and coarse swaggering gait." Snatchem, with considerable pride, called himself a "rough-and-tumble-stand-up-to-be-knocked-down-son-of-a-gun," and a "kicking-in-the-head-knife-in-a-dark-room-fellow."

He was all that and more. When not engaged in violent crime, he was something of a sporting gentleman: he was an official bloodsucker at illegal, bare-knuckle prizefights in lower Manhattan. He also served as an entertainer at the notorious rat pits where shows were held of terrier dogs fighting rat packs to the death. It was the duty of both Snatchem and another character of the day, Jack the Rat, to scour the waterfront for the fattest, meanest rats to be found. Both of them entertained the audience between canine-rodent battles, biting the heads off live mice for sports who offered them dimes. For a quarter, they would perform the same grisly act upon a huge rat.

In the late 1860s it became the vogue for indefatigable men of the cloth to wander into the slums of lower Manhattan, to spread the gospel and reform the vilest human creatures. Probably more efforts were expended in vain efforts to alter the habits of Snatchem than for any other rogue. "His intelligence," wrote one chronicler of the times, "was not of a very high order, and he was easily aroused by the fiery exhortations of the preachers and the emotional appeal of the shouting and hymn-singing. He asked for prayers at every meeting, and frequently embarrassed the ministers by publicly inquiring when they would receive the barrel of water from the river Jordan, which he had been assured would wash away his sins."

The ministers in the end gave Snatchem up as a lost cause after he explained why he wanted to become an angel and go to Heaven: he wanted to bite off Gabriel's ear.

Snatchem's later fate, both here and in the Hereafter, has not been convincingly chronicled. Reports that he went to Philadelphia after the police closed down a number of his sporting-house haunts may have deserved some credibility; it was reported that a vicious street criminal was forcing victims into an alley and robbing them of their valuables by holding a live rat to their faces. Another tale had Snatchem wandering to New England where, after a rat-biting exhibition, he died of "food poisoning," but that tale was most probably apocryphal.

Coit, Lillie (1842–1929)

"5"

It has been said that no American city felt more at home with its "characters" than did San Francisco. It is perhaps doubtful that Lillie Hitchcock Coit would have become the city mascot of any other community. One might have thought San Francisco had had quite enough, with its "Emperor" Joshua Norton (q.v.), but within its bosom it had room for Lillie as well. These two were strikingly different. Norton was totally impoverished, while Lillie was very, very, *very* rich.

Lillie's accomplishments were many in her role of active eccentric, and her unconventional behavior paved the way for women to leave the home and enter the affairs of the world. If she was thought of as strange, her behavior was probably no more unusual than her more socially minded contemporary Susan B. Anthony. After all, the act of being different than society deemed correct for women—often merely by doing the same things as men—inspired the feminist movement in general. The more Lillie did that was unusual and, to some, outrageous, the more other California women felt free to strike out for their own individuality.

A stunning beauty, Lillie Hitchcock could have been the belle of San Francisco society—just as her mother had been, among the first families of Virginia—but, as some of her biographers have noted, she showed none of the snobbery that went with the territory. When she was 10, Lillie felt most comfortable sneaking down to the waterfront to chase rats with the boys or, alternately, follow the fire wagons. By the time she was in her late teens, she had become one of the "bhoys" of the volunteer fire companies and was made an honorary member of Knickerbocker Engine Company No. 5.

She often waited in the firehouse for the return of the fire-fighters and had soup or tea ready for them. She would appear at company parties wearing an evening dress with a huge fireman's belt around her waist and a shiny black fire helmet. She was the star attraction at parades, mounted on the fire engine, waving to the cheering crowd. After an arduous time fighting a fire, the firemen would be led, still grimy and tired, to one of the city's finer eateries to be treated by Lillie to a sumptuous dinner.

At all times Lillie wore a gold "5" badge, indicating her membership in the engine company, and she took to signing all her letters and legal documents as "Lillie Hitchcock 5." As popular as Lillie was, she and her pro-Confederacy mother were forced to leave San Francisco in 1862 because of harsh feelings engendered by the Civil War.

Mother and daughter went to France, but Lillie missed the city on the bay and returned home the following year, to be fully accepted by a citizenry who had missed her as much as she had missed it. Once more, Lillie Hitchcock 5 was the darling of the fire companies, and in time she was generally accepted as a sort of city-wide mascot. She married the socially prominent Benjamin Howard Coit and became Lillie Hitchcock Coit 5 thereafter. If Coit thought he could reform Lillie or channel her energies into what he regarded as more constructive pursuits, he was sorely disappointed. She took to dying her hair in what would now be called punk fashion. When her husband objected, Lillie got even by shaving her head, wearing red, black, or blonde wigs on successive days. It drove poor Coit to distraction, a condition hardly improved upon when the couple ventured out for an evening, and he found himself in the company of what had become a sightseeing attraction.

Eventually, Lillie's father, Dr. Charles M. Hitchcock, attempted to tame his daughter and save her marriage by plucking her from her bohemian life-style in San Francisco, ensconcing her in a country estate in the Napa Valley. Coit left Lillie after she proceeded to turn the retreat into a sort of little Frisco, inviting her many friends, most of whom he regarded as uncouth. Lillie's country estate also became a calling station for literary lights passing through; she played hostess to such figures as Robert Louis Stevenson and Joaquin Miller.

Still, the lure of San Francisco was too powerful for Lillie, and she returned to her beloved city to reign as mascot from a suite in the lavish Palace Hotel. She maintained her own form of rowdy grace even as she aged, but in 1904 she suffered a severe trauma when an acquaintance of hers (an old Confederate soldier) shot one of her visitors to death in Lillie's hotel sitting room. Lillie became so unnerved that she fled to Europe for refuge once again. This was a much longer trip than her previous emigration. Lillie feared to return to San Francisco while the killer still lived, although he was institutionalized. Finally, when the man died in 1924, Lillie came home. Two decades had passed. Lillie was now in her eighties, but Frisco had not forgotten her. She was received with raucous celebrations.

Lillie, still the mascot of the city, lived another five years. When she died in 1929, she was buried wearing her famed "5" badge.

She bequeathed the major portion of her substantial estate for civic improvements. An observation tower was constructed atop Telegraph Hill to honor her. Never cited as an outstanding example of civic architecture, it has been described as nothing more than a huge fire-hose nozzle.

Comstock, Anthony (1844–1915)

THE GREAT AMERICAN BLUENOSE

He conducted a lifelong crusade against vice in all its forms, including some we would not consider to be so. In fact, today very little of the "bestial matters" he sought to suppress, from contraceptives to "pornography," are illegal. Perhaps the sole legacy of Anthony Comstock, called "the great American bluenose," whose fight against "sin" often bordered on the eccentric, is the word *Comstockery*, which is defined in the *American College Dictionary* as "overzealous censorship of the fine arts and literature, often mistaking outspokenly honest works for salacious productions." Comstock's excessive attribution of sin to anything he didn't approve of indeed made Comstockery, in the words of George Bernard Shaw, "the world's standing joke at the expense of the U.S."

He was himself used and abused by others who profited from the publicity he gave them. On one occasion a California judge, before whom Comstock had dragged some department-store window dressers for putting clothes on wax dummies in full public view, exploded at him, "Mr. Comstock, I think you're nuts."

Comstock found his calling at the age of 18, when he forcefully demonstrated his hatred for demon rum by breaking into a liquor store and turning on the spigots of all the kegs. In 1873 he established the New York Society for the Suppression of Vice and remained its operating head for the last 42 years of his life. That same year, the 29-year-old Comstock pushed through a federal law banning the sale of obscene literature, including contraceptive information, through the mail. He got himself made a Post Office special agent charged with enforcing its statutes. During the presidential campaign, he met with Ulysses S. Grant in order to gain support for the law. Grant, in need of votes in the Midwest, agreed;

The life work of Anthony Comstock is little remembered but for the word "Comstockery," defined as "overzealous censorship of the fine arts and literature, often mistaking outspoken honest works for salacious productions." (Library of Congress)

as one political wag put it, perhaps he thought his support of Comstock "might kill his whisky breath" with the voters.

From then on, there was no holding Comstock back. In 1913 he would review his career proudly, informing a newspaper interviewer, ". . . I have convicted persons enough to fill a passenger train of 61 coaches, 60 coaches containing 60 passengers and the sixty-first almost full. I have destroyed 160 tons of obscene literature." Among those whose works felt his moral wrath were Margaret Sanger, for her books on birth control, and Walt Whitman, whom Comstock got the Department of the Interior to fire for publishing *Leaves of Grass*. Under the fury of Comstock's outrage, publishers censored their own works. Under the rules of Comstockery, *pregnant* became *enceinte*. But Comstock's proudest boast was that he had caused 16 persons to be so hounded that they either committed suicide or died from fear of him.

No one was safe from Comstock's wrath. New York art galleries learned that they could not display paintings of nudes. There was no difference in Comstock's mind between dirty pictures and art if both featured nudity. Many art dealers found themselves grabbed by the scruff of the neck by Comstock, heading for the nearest police station.

Comstock waged a one-man war on street hawkers of what were called French postcards. He would sidle up to the man and ask for something really dirty. Unimpressed by the hawker's initial offerings, he would insist he wanted something, as they said, "feelthy." Many a hawker, delighted to have such a live one, would take Comstock back to his abode and offer him the pick of his prize pornography. Instantly Comstock would flash his badge, and off they went. Comstock used leads from these postcard sellers to locate their suppliers. He led Post Office raids on four printing plants that supplied pornography for the entire country. More than 50 tons of plates and pictures were seized. It was said that the dirty-picture business never recovered in Comstock's lifetime.

But, just as Comstock's eccentric zeal reached legendary proportions, he became victimized by his own foolishness. The great publicist Henry Reichenbach utilized Comstock to turn an inoffensive and not particularly good painting of a naked young lady bathing in a lake into a bestseller. It was "September Morn" by Paul Chabas, and it was considered so tame that it had been rejected for a barber-shop calendar. Reichenbach had come across a New York art dealer who was stuck with 2,000 prints. Striking a commission deal with him, Reichenbach promised to promote the picture's sales. He had the dealer put the picture in the window and then, posing as a minister, telephoned Comstock to protest the filthy painting. Comstock hurried to the scene and was shocked to see several young boys congregated in front of the store window, leering at the picture. Reichenbach had paid the kids a quarter each to man their stations, and the hoax worked. When the dealer refused to take the offending picture from the window, Comstock started legal action, claiming the picture was obscene. Comstock lost the court battle, and the resulting publicity made "September Morn" the best-known painting in America in the early 20th century. It went on to sell millions of prints, thanks to Comstock.

George Bernard Shaw similarly could thank Comstock for making his play, *Mrs. Warren's Profession,* a huge success in 1905, when it was closed by police after one performance in New York's Garrick Theater. The self-appointed protector of public morals had complained to the law, calling the play "reekings." It was in return for this that Shaw coined the word *Comstockery.* The courts did not find the play to be salacious, and *Mrs. Warren's Profession* soon after mopped up.

In 1915 President Woodrow Wilson appointed Comstock the country's representative to the International Purity Congress being held in San Francisco. Although enfeebled of body, Comstock proved to be a fire-eater at the gathering, although he was to be disgraced by a local judge's description of him as "nuts" in the store-window mannequin case. Some say Comstock came home a beaten man after that. A short time later, on September 21, 1915, he died.

Sherman, Charles R. (1844–1921)

HUCKLEBERRY CHARLIE

It was often said in Watertown, New York, that Charlie Sherman was the town's most beloved liar. If every town is entitled to its "town character," Watertown people agreed proudly that Sherman made it a matter of civic responsibility to have one.

He was better known as Huckleberry Charlie, and when he died he was just short of his seventy-eighth year; that, despite the fact that he had celebrated at least several hundred birthdays. As the *Watertown Standard* reported in his obituary in 1921:

> Huckleberry Charlie Sherman's days of spellbinding are over. Watertown will miss a familiar figure. The champion huckleberry picker in the United States has passed away.
>
> The age of Charlie was 78, but everytime he came into Watertown he announced a birthday anniversary. On the strength of that he garnered many gifts from the merchants, as he made his pilgrimage about Public Square. . . .
>
> His presence here always meant innumerable speeches in which he recited that he was born in Watertown, lived at Pine Plains and was the champion huckleberry picker. He always said the Plains was good only to 'raise hell and huckleberries.'
>
> At each store he would be given an unsalable article of dress. At the end of the tour he would be decked out in the colors of the rainbow. Joseph's coat of many colors was tame beside Huckleberry's duck trousers, checked pongee coat, brilliant red necktie and a college boy's panama. Added to this Charlie was certain to have a stogie poised at the Joe Cannon angle.
>
> At county fairs he was always a visitor—his entrance was gratuitous for he was one of the midway attractions. Lucky was the vendor in front of whose stand Sherman took his position. The crowd followed him and listened avidly to the time-worn theme. Charlie talked so fast that it required three renditions of the speech to comprehend the ideas and sequences. If one remained any length of time, he would hear the third rendition.

No matter with whom Huckleberry Charlie had a confrontation, he had a way of coming out ahead. He often got conductors to let him ride the train free, pointing out his pants were checked. Once a visiting judge, before whom Charlie appeared on a charge of having imbibed too much, looked at his bizarre wardrobe with distaste and asked him if he worked. Huckleberry showed him his hands and said he didn't "have hands like that from sittin' in a cane-bottom chair." He was on his way home on the 5:10 train.

Once Huckleberry was almost convicted of spying in a military court-martial. It was the fault of the U.S. Army that it attempted to hold maneuvers involving thousands of soldiers at Pine Plains, with Charlie's home in the middle of the theoretical battle. The Blues scored a notable victory over the Reds, a situation that called for an official investigation. It turned out that Charlie had taken a liking to some of the Blues and reported the movements of the Reds to them. Some officers were very incensed, but Charlie merely shrugged, pointing out he never did much like any Reds. No more war games were staged in Huckleberry's territory.

If the communities of the area all had their own delightful tales to tell of Charlie, his wife of almost 50 years, Dell, was not always amused. At one time she petitioned the courts to have her husband confined to an institution. Doctors agreed that there was no doubt of Huckleberry's insanity, but nothing much came of it all. Public opinion was against losing Huckleberry Charlie and he remained free. Officially this was due to a squabble by various towns as to which would be required to pay for the costs of his treatment.

Dell got the message, and in time, like all those in the Watertown area, she accepted her lot with Charlie.

Dowie, John Alexander (1847–1907)

THE BLUENOSE OF ZION

A Scottish-born charlatan, John Alexander Dowie emigrated to Australia where he operated as a faith healer until he moved on, perhaps under inspiration of the law, to the United States. He tried his hand at the Columbia Exposition as Prophet Elijah III but didn't do too well. He drifted out of Chicago into the hinterlands, and in 1896 he established a brand new religious order, the Christian Apostolic Church. Having now progressed from crank to full-fledged megalomaniac, he identified himself as the messenger of the Covenant who had been prophesied by Malachi. Later he asserted he was Elijah the Restorer.

On a 10-square-mile site on Lake Michigan, 42 miles north of Chicago, he established Zion City where some 5,000 of his followers took up residence. The entire community—factories, homes, tabernacle, bank, and printing plant—was owned by Dowie.

The dour Dowie established the moral and legal rules of his fiefdom, strictly forbidding such activities as smoking, consuming alcohol, or eating pork. Also banned were such evil institutions as dance halls, theaters, and drugstores, the last hardly necessary since no doctors were allowed in Zion City.

Garbed in white robes, Dowie paraded through the town looking for other evils, such as high heels on women's shoes, and several times a day he conducted devotional services for the faithful who wee summoned by a steam whistle.

Now equipped with the title of General Overseer, Dowie exercised complete control over his followers, and his kingdom was estimated to be worth some $10 million, every penny of which belonged to Dowie. As the fame of his church spread, Dowie published newspapers in six different languages to instruct his followers in different parts of the world.

By 1903 Dowie was convinced he would soon be converting all of mankind, and he invaded New York City with a crusading army of 3,000 of the faithful aboard 10 special trains. The more sophisticated New Yorkers listened to Dowie's message and then practically laughed him out of town.

Crushed by the New York debacle and other costly ventures in different countries, Dowie, faced with a severe cash-flow drain, ordered all members of the church to deposit all their money in his bank. He then went to Mexico to investigate the possibility of establishing a branch of the church there. He signed over power of attorney to a supposedly devoted follower, Wilbur Glenn Voliva (*q.v.*). In 1905 Voliva engineered Dowie's removal from office with all the finesse of a banana-republic maneuver.

Dowie returned from Mexico critically ill but took up battle in the courts. He denied Voliva's charges that he had squandered some $2 million of church funds on such things as women and drink, and he called Voliva a madman.

Dowie died in 1907, having been officially declared insane shortly before. There were those who thought he had been mad for a great many years. But there were also many who agreed with Dowie's assertion that Voliva was rather mad himself.

Cannary, Martha Jane (c.1848–1903)

CALAMITY JANE

Few characters of the Old West have come down to us with as many exaggerations, misrepresentations, or downright lies as Martha Jane Cannary, or Canary, better known as Calamity Jane.

She has been heralded as a great shot, Indian fighter, raving beauty, and lover, and of these qualifications only the first and last have any claim to validity. She was quite a shooter when drunk— which meant she was quite a shooter. As for romantic inclinations, she was not, as often ascribed, the secret bride of Wild Bill Hickok; but she *was* quite a lady with the boys, especially during her stay at E. Coffey's celebrated "hog farm" near Fort Laramie.

In truth Calamity—she was thus nicknamed because wherever she turned up calamities were sure to follow—was one of the West's foremost eccentrics, a 19th-century bag lady, if you will, of the plains. A nomad with all her possessions in a duffel bag, she came out of Missouri farming country with her folks in 1863, and she continued on her own when both parents took sick and died in Utah around 1865. Calamity was somewhere between 13 and 17 years old, and she drifted from town to town, working for a time as a laborer on the Union Pacific.

According to her own account, Calamity also worked as a mule skinner on a cattle-driving team. She had by this time taken to wearing men's pants, smoking cigars, chewing tobacco, and drinking heavily. It is unclear how often on these various jobs she was known to be a woman or was considered one of the boys. Big-boned and muscular, she could easily pass as one of the latter.

She did precisely that in the 1870s, when she joined General Crook's campaign against the Sioux as a mule skinner. The army was under the illusion she was a man, a misconception that ended when a horrified colonel found her swimming in a stream with some of the soldiers. Calamity was sent packing. It was, as near as can be determined, the last time she attempted the masquerade. Throughout the seventies, Calamity's legend blossomed. It was in this period that she allegedly married Hickok and had a daughter by him. But if Calamity ever married anyone it was Clinton Burke, an odd-job Texan who tarried in the Black Hills at the same time as Calamity. If Calamity actually married Burke, she certainly didn't take the vows seriously and was happier as a riding mate of Hickok,

Calamity Jane endeared herself more to folklore than to the folk of the Wild West. (Library of Congress)

although certainly the latter never regarded her as anything more than an occasional and humorous member of his entourage. Calamity would flit off here and there for some cowboy work or, when things were slow, a stint in a whorehouse.

When she showed up in town, the cry would go up, "Here's Calamity!" She would swagger into a saloon and fire her six-gun, shattering a mirror now and then. The men loved it; the bartenders smiled. It was good for business.

However, Calamity only became a legend with the death of another legend, Hickok, who died in 1876 in Carl Mann's Saloon in Deadwood, Dakota Territory, shot in the brain from behind by a saddle-bum coward named Jack McCall. The way Calamity told it— and years later Hollywood preferred it that way—it was she who cornered McCall later, hiding in a butcher shop, and turned him over to the forces of justice. By the time Calamity got around to compiling her memoirs, she believed her fanciful adventures, saving army officers from Indians and the like and being dubbed with an imposing list of heroic appellations (of which the White Devil of the Yellowstone was typical).

Calamity toured with the Buffalo Bill Wild West Show and various other enterprises, and was the Famous Woman Scout of the Wild West! Heroine of a Thousand Thrilling Adventures! The Terror of Evildoers in the Black Hills! The Comrade of Buffalo Bill and Wild Bill! Well . . . not quite. She seldom held on to such jobs, getting too drunk to go on stage. Hitting a town, she was likely to head for a saloon and enter beer-guzzling contests with the boys. Calamity was bounced from one public-appearance job after another as too drunk and disorderly to perform.

If she never married Hickok, Calamity also found time later to either marry or not marry others, among them Burke, who in time passed from the scene. Later a Montana newspaper informed its readers that Calamity married at least two others, "a young man named Washburn who entered the Army, and also . . . a Lt. Summers, who apparently fathered her daughter."

No matter with whom she had a liaison at the moment, Calamity could be counted on to provide some entertainment. In 1880 she took up with Arkansas Tom, a notorious gunfighter, and they took in a performance of the Lard Players at the East Lynne Opera House in Deadwood. Calamity grew enraged at the conduct in the play of Lady Isobel, who eloped with Sir Francis. Suddenly Calamity stood up in the audience and let fly a stream of tobacco juice at the offending female. The juice splattered the actress' long pink dress, and the stage and audience was in a turmoil. The actress screamed as the lights went up. Calamity was undeterred. She flipped a gold piece on the stage and proclaimed, "That's for your damn dress."

Then she and Arkansas, upholders of morality, strode arm in arm up the aisle away from such degeneracy. It must be noted that two days later Arkansas Tom was shot to death while robbing a bank in a nearby town.

By the late 1880s, when she was probably not yet 40, Calamity drifted from town to town, seldom holding on to any job, save whoring, for much length of time. In the 1890s she did several more Wild West shows, invariably being fired for drunkenness. By now she was reduced to cadging drinks by offering bartenders a dog-eared copy of her *Autobiography* from her duffel bag.

In 1899 she was back in Deadwood, a grotesque shadow of her

former self. She had by now a seven-year-old daughter in tow. Folks felt sorry for her and held a benefit for her. Calamity forgot the child and, in a saloon that night, she guzzled the money away, heading home in the early hours of the morning, howling like a wolf.

The following year a newspaper editor who knew her in the old days found her in a bawdy house and took her into his home to recoup her health. In 1901 she was hired to appear at the Pan-American Exposition. Calamity celebrated her arrival by destroying a bar and blackening the eyes of two policemen. She was fired of course but shrugged off further efforts of aid, declaring she wished people would "leave me alone and let me go to hell my own way."

Billings, Montana, saw her the next year, but only for a short time. She was run out of town after shooting up a bar. Later that year the explorer Louis Freeman ran into her in Yellowstone. He bought her several pails of beer and was astounded at how she polished them off. He judged her to be a woman of at least 70.

Although she was nowhere near that, her hard-living years were catching up with her. Enfeebled of body and mind, she was most often tired of the fabricated role she had played for so many years. Still, early in the summer of 1903, she visited Wild Bill's grave in Deadwood and posed for a famous photo. She was able to peddle a goodly number of copies of her autobiography.

In early August, she lay dying of pneumonia in a hotel in Terry, a town not far from Deadwood. On August 2, her eyes fluttered open, and she asked the date. "It's the 27th anniversary of Bill's death," she said. "Bury me next to Bill."

Alas, Calamity lingered until August 3 before dying, but that didn't matter. They buried her as she requested and recorded the date as August 2. The West believed in doing right by its characters.

Goodall, Nick (1849?–1884)

NICK THE FIDDLER

It is said that the greatest violinist of the 19th century, superior perhaps to Niccolò Paganini, ended his days in the Jefferson County, New York, almshouse, never having achieved, because of his many idiosyncracies, the acclaim he richly deserved. The famous Norwegian violinist Ole Bull once heard him play and proclaimed, "The man's a genius!"

His name was Nick Goodall, far better known as Nick the Fiddler, and he lived for many years in the Watertown–Elmira area in New York. There still are old-timers who repeat stories about him told by their elders. Most certainly he was a genius, albeit a mad genius, perhaps.

Biographers have found it frustrating to trace Nick's early life. One popular version which may have some truthful elements in it was that he was born in 1849, either in the United States or in England. His father was a first violinist in the orchestra at Ford's Theater in Washington, and he was playing when Lincoln was assassinated by Booth. Young Nick was present at the time and was so unhinged by the happening that he had to be sent to an asylum. Discharged some years later, he became a wandering violinist mostly in New York State.

A variant of this story is that at the age of eight Nick was a child prodigy who had toured Europe until brought to this country by his father. President and Mrs. Lincoln supposedly saw him perform in Washington and were suitably impressed. Or else, to change the story slightly, forget the Ford's Theater connection and say simply that Nick's father was his violin instructor, and he was such a severe taskmaster that his cruelties snapped Nick's mind. Or instead, place father and son in Boston, where the father caused him to practice 12 to 15 hours a day, a regimen that led later to Nick's "softness" of the brain. Now convert the father into a stern instructor in the 1st Marine Corps Band and have Nick simply run away from him and his harsh orders. All of these are theories advanced by various writers of the day.

Whatever Nick the Fiddler's origin was, there is no doubt of his great gift. Nick knew the worth of his hands and continually kept them wrapped in bandages, explaining they were sore. As a result his hands remained as soft and pliable as those of a babe. And when he played, audiences were enraptured. He was often asked to perform at church concerts, but whether he would show up or, if he did, whether he would stick to the promised music was a matter in the hands of the Almighty. At one church affair, after having been admonished to play only sacred tunes, Nick broke into such melodies as "Pop Goes the Weasel" and "The Girl I Left Behind Me." Yet on other occasions, in churches, indeed in taverns, country stores, in hotel lobbies, wherever the impulse struck him, Nick would hold listeners enthralled to the works of Chopin, Liszt, Bach, Brahms, Berlioz, Beethoven, and Paganini.

Once, Ole Bull, the most renowned violinist of the era, was giving a concert in Elmira. Told of Nick the Fiddler, he agreed to hear him play. A performance was arranged in an empty theater, and Nick sat silently on the stage, staring off into space, unmindful of Bull. Bull waited some 15 minutes, but the eccentric fiddler did not begin. As Bull rose to leave, Nick drew his bow. For three hours Nick's violin sang eloquently, and Bull sat unmoving. After the performance, Bull made his famous evaluation of Nick the Fiddler as a genius.

Shortly after this, a theatrical promoter named Nichols decided to launch Nick on a one-man musical tour. Nick agreed and the first performance took place in Troy, New York, before a packed house. For two hours Nick the Fiddler thrilled the audience, and the manager finally attempted to close the brilliantly successful performance. He reckoned without Nick, who had agreed to play, and play he intended to do. On and on the performance went until slowly the audience started to leave in small groups. Some time after midnight the last of the audience had departed, but Nick fiddled on. He would have fiddled even if Troy burned. The night watchman dropped off to sleep, but the strains of Nick's music continued the entire night. Finally with the first rays of the sun, Nick put down his violin and trudged off over the hills for Elmira. His grand tour ended after one long, long night.

Thereafter, no promoter dared present Nick the Fiddler in concert alone, not knowing if he would play or, if he did, if he would ever stop. Nick fiddled to his own drummer. Conductor Milan Lewis did feature the eccentric violinist in concerts in upstate New York, but in some cases the program had to proceed without Nick, who simply refused to play. In Malone, New York, Lewis found Nick shooting pool in the poolroom of a hotel. He actually took a horsewhip in hand to drive the great musician to the concert. Other promoters and conductors fared little better with Nick, who would sometimes sit on stage and take 20 minutes to slowly tune his violin.

Nick, it must be said, really did not like to perform on stage, much preferring to trudge from village to village, playing when the mood hit (most often at the local tavern, where he would be rewarded with unlimited brew). The villagers would swarm to hear him play. If he didn't feel like it, there was no pleading with him, for he never responded to such invitations. However, when he played, the rapture was complete, unparalleled. A silence fell, and only the magic of Nick's violin would be heard.

Nick cared nothing for money or his appearance. He dressed plainly, with a red flannel rag around his neck and thick, leather-laced hiking shoes on, winter and summer. In later years Nick performed less and less, and in the end he was taken in at the almshouse. When he died at the age of 35, he was given a pauper's funeral. It was said, fittingly, that the cost of his burial and grave came to less than the price his violin was sold for.

Kusz, Charles (1849–1884)

MR. HATE

By all known criteria, Charles Kusz was no more than your normal, everyday bigot until he headed west in 1875, at the age of 26. He had hated huge segments of the population previously, but it was only after making a fabulous mining strike in Colorado that he enjoyed the ability to feed his prejudices to the fullest. Taking $150,000 in profits, he left Colorado for New Mexico Territory, heading for the then-thriving mining and cattle town of Monzano, where he went into newspaper publishing.

Personal journalism in 19th-century America was often marked by bigotry, vendettas, and vitriolic sentiments seldom allowed published in the 20th century; even so caustic a publisher as William Loeb of the *Manchester, N.H., Union-Leader,* who typically referred to Henry Kissinger in print as "Kissinger the Kike," would have seemed a scoutmaster compared to Kusz.

Kusz's newspaper was titled *The Gringo and the Greaser,* embracing the nicknames used by the Mexicans and Americans respectively to disparage one another. The entire paper was printed in italics, a style Kusz felt to be both necessary and appropriate; since he wrote the entire contents, he thought every word of his prose was worthy of emphasis.

Kusz never met a Mexican or "greaser" he liked, and he made a point of saying so, applauding every bullet-ridden Latino corpse in each issue of his rag. The same was true of cowboys (he used the words *cowboys* and *rustlers* interchangeably). He reflected the "townie" attitude of the era; cowboys were supposed to come off the trail to be gouged by the businessmen, saloon keepers, and gamblers of the town, then slink off quietly after being stripped of all their pay. Second only to Mexicans, Kusz hated all Roman Catholics, filling his columns with diatribes on Romanism. He also attacked local schoolteachers and the entire educational system of the region, finding it hard, apparently, to accept the idea of free schooling that allowed so much riffraff into the educational process.

Kusz was an embarrassment to the entire community, even to those who agreed with his brand of Americanism. They were never sure when Kusz's stomach would turn over some other group or ideas, his venom spewing forth in hot type.

On the evening of March 26, 1884, Kusz was at home having dinner with a friend—where he found one can only be speculated—when two rifle bullets crashed through the window, killing him. Considering the number of logical suspects, it was hardly surprising that the murder was never solved. It was left for Western historian Denis McLoughlin to offer the most logical solution of the crime. The killer most likely was, he asserted, "a gringo, a greaser, a Roman Catholic, a rustler, or a schoolteacher; elementary."

Garrett, Henrietta Edwardina Schaefer
(1849–1930)

THE LOVE-STRUCK RECLUSE

When 81-year-old Henrietta Edwardina Schaefer Garrett died in her musty Victorian mansion in Philadelphia in 1930, she left a tribute to unrequited love, the real-life equal of that in Dickens' *Great Expectations*. Henrietta had lived for 35 years in the past and had allowed her grand house to turn dilapidated.

Progress had stopped in the house with the death, in 1895, of her husband Walter Garrett, heir to the formidable Garrett snuff fortune. Henrietta kept the mansion as it had been when her beloved Walter was alive. He had not enjoyed electricity or the telephone, and Henrietta was determined to have nothing she could not have shared with him. She threw a temper tantrum, it was said, at the suggestion that a leaky copper tub be replaced by a modern one. Even the servants had to play their roles, wearing the long Victorian dresses and high-button shoes of Gay Nineties' vintage.

When Henrietta married Garrett, 18 years her senior, in 1872, it was the stuff of fairy tales. She was the daughter of immigrants living in a ramshackle house in Freed's Alley in a Philadelphia slum. They met only because Garrett had joined the volunteer fire company in which her brother was also a member. Their marriage shocked the city's social set and many people, including Garrett's two sisters, snubbed the couple. The groom angrily separated himself from all his old social and business ties, devoting himself to pleasing his new bride.

Henrietta often spoke of their union as being idyllic, save for the fact that they remained childless. Perhaps if there had been children, she would have gotten over the loss of her husband after 23 years of marriage.

Grief-stricken, she withdrew from life, rarely leaving the mansion and decreeing that all her beloved Walter's possessions be left undisturbed. Apparently, she even hesitated to spend money now that her husband could no longer enjoy their wealth. For 20 years after Garrett's death, Henrietta seldom was seen outside the mansion, and when her brother, her last close relative, died in 1913, she turned into a total recluse.

The only traffic from the mansion of Ninth Street was that of one of her three servants, her cook, housemaid, or personal maid, off on some money-saving errand. Henrietta would send them blocks just to save a penny on a loaf of bread. Quite naturally, the belief spread among the public, and with her servants as well, that the widow had lost in the stock market most of the $7 million fortune she had inherited. That was untrue. By the time she died in 1930, Henrietta's fortune, through canny investments by a broker named Charles Starr, had grown to $17 million. Starr later claimed Henrietta's estate, producing a letter of hers which he purported to be a will. It left him everything but a meager $62,500 in other bequests. Starr's claim was only one of a staggering total of 3,500 from alleged kinsmen of either Henrietta or Walter Garrett. The finding of a pair of moldy baby shoes among the late widow's possessions produced hundreds of claims from alleged children of the couple.

A rumor spread that Henrietta's personal maid, Carthage Churchville, spiteful that her mistress had left her so little, had hidden the widow's will in her coffin. By that time Carthage herself had died and could not deny the story, so Henrietta's coffin was opened by court order. Inside was Henrietta, clad in Victorian black, but no will.

Several gigantic hoaxes involving forgeries of family Bibles and the like were exposed. Court case piled on court case until all but two claims were disallowed, and even one of those became an international cause célèbre. After legal costs of about $3 million, it was decided that Henrietta had had three first cousins: Johann Schäfer, ex-mayor of Bad Nauheim, Germany; Howard Kretchmar, a Chicago osteopath; and Herman Kretschmar, a St. Louis bachelor who once did five years in prison on a murder charge. All three men died in their nineties but had survived Henrietta. In 1939, the Nazi government made a formal demand for Schäfer's share of the estate, but while the case was pending, World War II broke out. In 1946, the U.S. government laid claim to Schäfer's legacy as a "spoil of war."

In time the United States won its claim of $4 million, and the Kretschmar heirs got the remaining $8 million. The legal case transcripts concerning Henrietta's estate ran over a half million typewritten pages. There is little doubt that the grieving widow of Ninth Street would have cared nothing about it all. As far as she was concerned the world had stopped revolving back in 1895, when her husband died.

Matthews, Robert (fl. early 1800s)

MATTHIAS THE IMPOSTOR

About 1820 a young carpenter named Robert Matthews drifted into New York City from some unknown country hamlet. It soon developed that he considered himself to be the second most important carpenter in history. New Yorkers, then as now, were a fast-moving lot, and they paid him little mind. And so the carpenter moved on to Albany, New York.

There he became known as a bad egg on the job, lecturing his fellow workers and supervisors alike for their evil ways. It got so that his fellows rained down blocks of wood on him whenever he started one of his harangues. Not surprisingly, Matthews got fired from several jobs; he viewed this as a God-given opportunity to pursue his exhortations full time. On street corners he warned the burghers of Albany that they faced cataclysmic disaster, unless they followed his lead. He let his beard grow long and biblical, put on grotesque clothing, and took for himself the name of Matthias.

The prophet, it must be granted, made one convert, an adoring fellow workman who accompanied him carrying a large white banner inscribed: "Rally Round the Standard of Truth." But Albany did not rally.

Matthias shook his fist at Albany, and the vengeful prophet left the city to its certain fate of coming damnation. Matthias moved westward, through forest and on to the prairies, preaching his gospel. Cutting back to the Southeast, he visited Mississippi and Tennessee, and then went on to Georgia, where he preached to the Cherokee Indians. Somehow the Georgia authorities did not appreciate the stirring up of their Indians, and Matthias was hurled into prison.

Only when Matthias promised to leave Georgia and take his message up to the wicked North was he released. So Matthias moved on to Washington, where he was totally ignored. But this was not so when he once more reached New York City. By now he traveled on an old, half-starved horse; he warned the citizenry of the sins of intemperance that would doom New York, as it had already doomed Albany. When was Albany going to sink into the flames? he was asked, and he replied, "Soon. Soon!"

In their own fashion New Yorkers took to Matthias the Impostor, as they dubbed him. He became one of the sights of the city that locals took their out-of-town visitors to see. Matthias obliged with fierce looks and prodigious exhortations, as he paraded through the city with hordes of small boys following him. Sometimes they pelted him with garbage, and Matthias would look skyward occasionally and implore the Father to forgive them, for they knew not what they did. More often, he indicated he would arrange to send them to a very special place in Hell. In fact, Matthias warned that he might just have to go West once more to rally the red men against the white heathens.

Eventually Matthias the Impostor stepped into the mists. We do not know whither he indeed carried his message of vengeance to the Indian; but it is a fact that for the next half century the white man's woes with the Indians were monumental.

Ferguson, Jack; and Wells, Pete
(fl. mid–19th century)

THE GOLD FIELD SPENDTHRIFTS

During the great Gold Rush that started in 1859 in Colorado, it became common for miners who struck it rich to react in bizarre manners to their new stations in life. However, a special niche must be reserved amongst the mindless, devil-may-care prospectors for two illiterate old gold hunters, Jack Ferguson and Pete Wells, who found the richest gold pocket in California Gulch in the early 1860s, which brought in for them a "panful of almost pure gold in a day."

Fortunately the pair was ideally suited to each other. If one was a spendthrift, it only made him the image of the other. Each evening the pair repaired to the saloons of Oro City, and when they returned home in the early hours of the morning it was "without a color in their possession." What nuggets Ferguson could not squander on drink, Wells lost at the gaming tables.

We have the account of a fellow miner to attest to Ferguson and Wells' frivolous attitude toward gold. Ferguson invited the miner to his shack, which consisted of nothing more than a filthy bunk against one wall and a washstand with equally dirty toweling against the other. The miner recounts:

"Ferguson went to the stand and, pushing the cloth aside, revealed a gold washing pan full of nuggets. I would not undertake to say how much yellow stuff there was, but there could not have been less than $10,000. He then produced a bag five or six inches deep, and taking a small spice scoop, filled up the bag. Again I am unable to name the sum, but the bag could not have held less than $800 or $900. . . . Such a bonanza did these two appear to be possessed of, that their gambler friends built a saloon and gambling house on the very brink of their claim so as to make sure of having first access to the wealth these two were taking out and squandering daily."

Needless to say, the gamblers stuck to the eccentric prospectors until at last their find was exhausted. Ferguson and Wells departed the Gulch penniless; they were still, however, the closest of friends, neither berating the other for squandering a hoard that could have kept them in comfort for the rest of their lives.

Logically, this should be the end of their sad tale, one entitling them to honored entry in the folklore of the gold fields, but there is more: Ferguson and Wells struck a new Eldorado, across the high Mosquito Range in South Park. There, in a bleak gorge above the timberline at the source of the South Platte, they hit yellow. Word made its way back to Oro City, and soon the gamblers and saloon keepers packed their gear and took out in pursuit of the pair.

For a time this new mining camp at Montgomery burst into an opulence of riches, and Ferguson and Wells had a new chance to achieve security and wealth. Of course, that didn't happen. They had too many barkeeps and tinhorns to support. When Montgomery's day of fortune passed and withered away, Ferguson and Wells—the Damon and Pythias of the gold fields—faded away into serene obscurity.

Higginbotham, Joe (fl. mid–19th century)

BUCKSKIN JOE

Like another nomadic prospector named Dan Pound (*q.v.*), Joe Higginbotham, called Buckskin Joe because he always wore buckskins, wandered the high mountain country of Colorado in search of gold during the Rush of '59. However, he was at heart not a prospector but a man seeking the freedom of solitude.

The world Buckskin Joe craved was that consisting of a burro, bag of beans, water cans, pick, shovel, gun, and blanket. He loved this new land, and he loved the mountains; he undoubtedly reveled in being the first white man, maybe even ahead of the red man, to explore this particular mountain or to happen onto that small valley or drink from this spring. No one thought Buckskin Joe queer. After all, he was prospecting and that meant "goin' where others ain't."

Imagine Higginbotham's surprise . . . no, horror . . . when he awoke one morning by a huge rock he had used as a windbreak during the night, and he caught the unmistakable glint of gold in some crevices. Just below was a stream and sure enough, there was gold, lots of it, in the water too. This was exactly how many claims were found—by pure blind luck.

Joe got hold of a jug and got himself liquored up and promptly told the first prospector he ran into of his find. Higginbotham knew what he was doing. Soon men would be all over the area mining for gold. In fact, the mining camp was named Buckskin Joe in honor of its discoverer. Not that that meant anything to Higginbotham; he had long vanished, never earning for himself even an ounce of gold.

Happily, there was still unmapped country out there, where the true richness of life could be found. And while men dug and fought and killed back in Buckskin Joe, Buckskin Joe himself was trudging the wilderness. What he was seeking, perhaps even he did not know, but he was content. He could hardly care that back in Buckskin Joe they were calling him a "crazy coot."

Pound, Dan (fl. mid–19th century)

THE IMITATION PROSPECTOR

They were dubbed prospectors or desert rats, but among them were many who were more like hermits, eager to escape civilization. As disguise, these men—called by Irving Stone the "breed of hunter-nomad who pretend to search for gold but do not really want to find it"—went about with their jackasses, picks, shovels, guns, and blanket rolls. They lived in the great outdoors, hunted and survived on game. When they so much as saw smoke curling upward on the horizon, they moved on, viewing it, whether of white or red man's origin, as the unwelcome sign of civilization.

Grizzled Daniel Pound was one of these, having for years prospected, first in the California hills apparently and later, in 1859, in the Pike's Peak area of Colorado. He carried through his hoax of prospecting to the extent of sometimes even building sluice boxes to wash out the dirt from the rocks he mined. It made for a cover story that indicated there was nothing queer about him, that he led his solitary life because of a need for secrecy to protect his potential finds. What Pound was really searching for was solitude.

But even in the mountain paradise where few men trod, sometimes another prospector, one serious about his vocation, found him. One day in South Park, a prospector gazed into Pound's pan and cried; "You've got gold there!"

"The hell you say," Pound answered. It was for him the moment of truth. Pound kicked over his sluice boxes, loaded his pick, shovel, blanket roll, and rifle on his patient burro and disappeared deeper into the mountains. (See Higginbotham, Joe.)

Collins, Lizzie (fl. 1850s–1860s)

THE COLLECTOR

For a time in antebellum New Orleans it was considered great evening sport among the young blades of the city to get one of their number drunk, cut off all the buttons on his trousers, and deposit him on the doorstep of his lady friend. The inebriated youth would then have much to explain. He would have to claim most vehemently and convincingly that he was the victim of a prank and that he had not been carousing with the city's lowest of low women on Gallatin Street.

A man losing his buttons was at the time one of the well-publicized perils of hitting the fleshpots. The more sensational newspapers of the day delighted in reporting the craze; a mania for cutting off buttons was attributed to one of the city's most notorious prostitutes.

Lizzie Collins was one of the more enticing harlots of notorious Gallatin St., famed from the 1840s for some four decades as being without a single house of good repute on its entire two-block length. Lizzie worked the dance houses and other brothels of the area, and she could have done exceptionally well as a dedicated yet honest practitioner of her art. However Lizzie was by nature a thief and revelled in robbing her clients.

In one celebrated court case she was charged with appropriating the purse of a Louisiana farmer who imparted to her the intelligence that he had $110 in gold bound to his leg with a handkerchief. While he viewed Lizzie as a creature of a most delicate nature, he sagely refused to drink with her in her place of employment of the moment—Archie Murphy's renowned dive. However, when Lizzie invited him to come upstairs with her, the farmer accepted promptly.

As they marched into Lizzie's darkened chamber, three other women pounced on him and wrestled him to the floor, whereupon Lizzie poured rotgut whiskey down his throat. She covered his mouth, so that the man could either swallow the vile brew or choke. In due course, Lizzie's victim was drunk and defenseless, and she appropriated his money, then summoned the bouncers from the bar downstairs to have him heaved into the gutter.

The farmer, unlike so many other victims, actually pressed the case against Lizzie but could prove nothing against her; she was released, although the newspapers seized the opportunity to warn their readers to beware of Gallatin Street and especially Lizzie Collins.

Shortly after this affair, Lizzie proceeded to "go bad," as the saying went in vice circles, although in a most unique fashion. She developed the peculiar mania of inviting men to her room and *not* taking their money. Instead, she would exhaust them into sleep and then cut the buttons off their pants and hide them away. In no time at all she had the biggest button collection in New Orleans—but very little money.

When she could no longer pay her rent, Archie Murphy kicked her out. Lizzie found other assignations only to continue her odd behavior of collecting buttons instead of cash, and thus she faced regular evictions. When the Union troops occupied New Orleans in 1862, Lizzie accumulated a very fine collection of military buttons, undoubtedly so monumental that a present-day Civil War collector would drool over such a trove.

However, Lizzie's vice days in New Orleans were clearly numbered and, as Herbert Asbury, noted historian of America's most sinful cities, once observed, "Her reputation in Gallatin Street was very bad. The general opinion was that while a man might be willing to take a chance with his money, his buttons should be sacred."

Lizzie's notoriety became so widespread that it was said that a gentleman feared so much as asking his wife to sew back a single button on his attire that had come loose. Soon of course there was no place in New Orleans for her, and Lizzie Collins eventually deserted the city with a wagonload of her possessions, made up, tradition has it, mainly of buttons.

Parkhurst, Charlie (?–1879)

THE SECRETIVE STAGECOACH DRIVER

He was one of the hardest-driving, six-in-hand stagecoach drivers in the Old West, famed for his skill in negotiating his Concord over the rugged trails of California's Sierra Nevada. Charlie Parkhurst turned up in Gold Rush country around 1850. Little was known about his early days, other than what he told folks in bits and snatches. As a youngster in the 1830s, Charlie, orphaned for as long as he could remember, ran away from a New Hampshire orphanage. He became a stableboy in Worcester, Massachusetts, where he learned the art of driving a team of horses at breakneck speed.

Eventually Charlie pulled up stakes and headed west, finally holding the "ribbons" for the California Stage Company in 1851, carving out a heroic reputation for himself. If a stage was running late, Charlie could take over the run and get it on time again. He'd have himself a dram, light up a cigar, flex his broad shoulders and, slashing away with his whip, take his Concord "a-flyin'."

Charlie was pretty much of a loner in his personal life and, although he would get liquored up and chew tobacco with the other drivers, he tended to sleep alone in the stables away from them. He never went "a-whorin' " at a hog ranch with the rest of the boys either, but the fact that he made a fetish out of shaving every day led to the belief that he had himself a little lady tucked away somewhere on one of his runs.

On the trail Charlie was king of the road. His heroism, bordering sometimes on foolhardiness, became legendary. Once approaching a tottering bridge, he whipped his horses fiercely, determined not to be thrown off schedule. The stagecoach thundered safely over the bridge just moments before it collapsed. Highwaymen gave Charlie's Concord a wide berth after he demonstrated his proficiency with firearms a few times. One gang of road agents made the mistake of trying to hold up his stage, and Charlie gunned down the leader and outran the others, bringing in his passengers and cargo untouched.

In 1870 a gray-haired Charlie Parkhurst retired because of illness. He lived out his remaining years in a small cabin near Watsonville in Santa Cruz County. He died in December 1879, and friends who found the body summoned a doctor to ascertain the cause of death. The doctor did, finding the deceased had been a victim of cancer, but he also made a more startling revelation. Charlie was a woman, indeed at some time in her life had been a mother, whether in her California days or previously was impossible to determine. Nobody quite knew what to do about the stage driver with a strange secret, but it seemed only proper to bury her under the only name by which she had been known.

Bethune, Thomas Greene (1850–1908)

BLIND TOM

The field of music is noted for a number of composers and performers, famed or infamous, who fall under the classification of "mad genius." Certainly Italy's castrati singers, such as Carlo Broschi Farinelli, were almost as well known for their erratic behavior and the severe melancholia they suffered as a result of their castration as for their sweet soprano voices.

Equally exploited in 19th century America was a young black slave named Thomas Greene Bethune. He was blind and had, at best, a low-grade mentality; he was also subject to periodic fits of misbehavior, but he was nonetheless lionized as a genius.

In slaveholding America, plantation owners greedily counted their annual crop of babies born to their slaves. These infants represented future earnings for farmers; and so, when Perry H. Oliver of Muscogee County, Georgia, had a female slave who gave birth to a son in 1850, his initial reaction was one of satisfaction—until he discovered the baby, although generally well-proportioned and hardy, was totally blind.

Disgusted, Oliver put the mother up for auction, and when she was bought by General James Bethune, he threw in—rather cunningly he thought—the blind child for no extra charge. More kindly than most slave owners, Bethune took the baby back to his plantation, named him Thomas Greene Bethune, and gave him the run of the place, allowing him to remain around the mansion.

Bethune soon noticed that Blind Tom seemed to compensate for his sightlessness with a brilliant sense of hearing. The boy was fascinated by all sounds—rainwater dripping into a puddle, various farm implements grinding away.

When the boy was four years old, Bethune bought a piano for his daughters, and whenever the girls played, Blind Tom was drawn as if by a magnet to the big house. One night after the family retired, Bethune awakened to hear music coming from the drawing room. When he investigated, he found the room black yet the music continued. Then Bethune's candle flickered its light on Blind Tom playing away, far, far better than Bethune ever heard his own children perform.

Bethune did not punish Blind Tom but urged him to use the piano whenever he wished, and the boy did so, especially when someone played something new. He immediately played it right back. Realizing Blind Tom had a rare genius, Bethune imported a professional teacher from Columbus to instruct the boy. The musician listened to Blind Tom play and threw up his hands, announcing he could do nothing for him. "That boy," he said, "already knows more about music than I will ever know."

It developed that Blind Tom had merely to hear a musical selection—of any length—just once and he could sit down and repeat it flawlessly. At the age of seven Tom made his concert debut in Columbus to enthusiastic applause. With each passing year Tom added to his repertoire, until he could play 5,000 compositions from memory, including the works of Beethoven, Bach, Chopin, Verdi, Rossini, Donizetti, Meyerbeer, Mendelssohn, Gounod, and many others.

In 1860 skeptics, suspecting some sort of fakery, decided to put Tom to the ultimate test. They offered him two brand-new compositions, 13 and 20 pages in length. Tom listened to them intently and then proceeded to perform both effortlessly. When Tom was 12 a Virginia musician produced an original 14-page fantasia, demanding that Tom play *secundo* to his treble. The young virtuoso did so, then pushed the composer aside and repeated the treble.

Tom was taken on a triumphant tour of Europe, where he demonstrated his brilliant piano ability with a perfect sense of pitch. At one performance three pianos were played at once, with two pianists banging away nonsensically on two of them while a third ran through a series of 20 notes that Tom was to repeat. Completely shutting out the outside influences, Tom did so easily.

It must be said that Blind Tom was sadly exploited for his

talents. He was never exposed to general learning, for fear he would lose his uncanny ability. As a result his total vocabulary never exceeded more than a few hundred words, and his voice was harsh and guttural. He shuffled along with his head thrown far back, as though he were searching for some view of light from above.

Tom was given to fits of rage and only two things could calm him down—General Bethune or the playing of music. After such fits had been calmed, Tom would sit down and play. When finished, he arose and applauded himself wildly, jumping up and down with glee—behavior he often repeated on stage.

When General Bethune died, Blind Tom became incorrigible. Often even music failed to soothe him. He had to be withdrawn from the concert stage and, when he died in Hoboken, New Jersey, in 1908, he was a bitter shell of a genius, still famed but often irrational. To the world of music his ability remains an enigma. To the public he remained known as something between a gifted prodigy and a sad freak.

Sutliff, John (fl. 19th century)

THE LOST MOLE

Back at the start of the 19th century, John Sutliff of Plymouth, Connecticut, was a very successful miller. But for years folks knew he was up to something, though he never let on what. Word got around he was doing some strange digging in a mountain behind his mill. Sometimes farmers, wanting to have their corn ground, had to wait an additional half an hour while an assistant summoned Mr. Sutliff with a clanging bell at the entrance of a shaft opening he had dug in the mountain.

It was many years before Sutliff revealed to anyone what he was doing and why. It seemed he had discovered—how, whether by vision, luck, or some other method, he would not say—that the mountain was loaded with gold, silver, and other precious metals in a liquid state. Once he found these pools he had but to ladle out his liquid treasure and live thereafter in luxury. He had started digging while in his twenties and was still at it in his forties, utilizing all the free time he had for what had become the overriding obsession of his life.

Sutliff did not have the luxury of dynamite to ease his labors, nor was he much on the rules of surveying that would have kept him on a straight course. Whenever he hit a massive underground boulder, he simply burrowed around it, often failing to compensate for his detour. The result was that, after more than two decades of digging, it was not at all certain how far he had penetrated into his treasure mountain.

Then one day a townsman heard a noise under the turnpike leading to the mill. He halted his buggy and then watched in amazement as a wheel started sinking into the ground. The man kept a shovel in his buggy and began digging and came upon . . . Mr. Sutliff, the mountain mole. Unfortunately, Mr. Sutliff had totally detoured and now was digging further and further away from his treasure mountain. Mr. Sutliff's chagrin, needless to say, became Plymouth's favorite tale for years.

Sutliff's disappointment was great but he was made of stern New England stuff. He simply backtracked in his tunnel and dug again in another direction, into the mountain, he hoped.

Alas, after yet another two decades, he still had not found his great treasure. By then the weakness of old age forced him to cease what had become more than 40 years of frantic digging. Retired to his rocker, old Mr. Sutliff maintained his dream. Whenever a lad owed him something for services rendered, Mr. Sutliff would offer to let the youth work off his debt by digging in his tunnel. Alas, even such surrogates had no better luck than Connecticut's human mole and when he died, the liquid hoard of his treasure mountain remained untapped, as it does to this day.

Curran, John (fl. late 19th century)

THE JAIL GROUPIE

The "jail groupie" was a fairly common sideshow at almost every large American jail of the 19th century. These were persons with no official status who were attracted to prison surroundings and found ways to meld into the bleak scenery. Few however matched old John Curran, who became a sort of unofficial guide in the Tombs, the much-storied old prison in New York City.

Nobody seemed to know where he came from, just that all of a sudden in the early 1870s there he was. He reported to the Tombs every morning and started sweeping up. He ran errands for officers and prisoners alike, and was clearly a lost old man for whom the Tombs became a home. For his sundry favors, Old John was allowed to conduct tours of the Tombs, offering awed visitors startling insight into the seamy side of the prison world. Old John never failed to impress; being a compulsive liar helped enormously, of course.

Curran made up tales and legends about the jail and its inmates. Once he informed visitors that a certain distinguished-looking minister in the corridor of Murderers' Row had just been charged with heaving his mother-in-law out a third-story window in an outburst of unchristian behavior. Actually, the padre was a leading, and indeed a most moderate churchman, there to offer spiritual support to a number of the condemned.

Old John did well financially with the revenues from such informative tours, as well as through the sale of what he called "pieces from the gallows on which fifty were hanged." Old John simply gathered up lumber wherever he could find some for this purpose.

Despite his rascality, Old John was especially popular with prisoners awaiting execution, and he earnestly believed he was an angel of mercy who could save them. For this purpose he peddled magical charms of various sorts to ward off the executioner. Sometimes indeed the talismans did work, as a condemned man received a commutation of his sentence; Old John would be ecstatic. Usually, however, they had to keep their date with the hangman, a development that Curran sometimes took as a personal affront. He might disappear for a few days of mourning. When he reappeared, however, he would be sporting a supply of old clothes, which he'd assure gullible customers had been part of the dead man's ward-robe.

From time to time a new prison administration sought to bar Old John from the premises as an unseemly eccentric in an institution of justice. Curran invariably foiled their directives by finding a way to sneak through the forbidding walls of the prison, leading one journalist to observe that the Tombs was easier to break into than out of. There was a considerable body of public opinion that felt Old John should be permitted his duties at the jail, that he was an old man who otherwise would most likely become a public ward if not, in time, a resident at Matteawan, the state institution for the insane. Eventually, each warden bowed to this sentiment.

In 1897 the Old Tombs was ordered torn down to be replaced by a more modern structure on the same site. Old John was frequently seen standing forlorn outside the deserted prison as the razing began. What happened to him is unknown. One story had it that he retired to a remote farm in the far reaches of Maine. Another, more fitting perhaps, had him dying of a broken heart at the loss of his iron-barred home.

Riley, James "Butt" (late 19th century)

FRISCO HARDHEAD

Like San Francisco's Oofty Goofty (*q.v.*), James Riley, better known as Butt Riley, was famed for his peculiar physical prowess. When he lost that, his mental deficiencies, so the observation went, came to the fore. Riley was one of San Francisco's most vicious hoodlums, and indeed the police dubbed him King of the Hoodlums. Unlike other gangsters he eschewed the use of a gun, insisting he had a more potent weapon—his head. He claimed he possessed the thickest skull in Christendom, and he demonstrated this by using it in all sorts of criminal endeavors.

Leading a mob of hoodlums on a looting raid on Chinese opium houses, he batted down the doors, using his head as a pile driver. He also engaged in numerous fights and butting contests (once butting a 160-pound man exactly 10 feet in the air). In time this overuse of Riley's skull caused him to walk around talking to himself, but even in his dim-wittedness, no one accepted the challenge to go head to head with him.

Riley had other physical attributes that added to his fame. He was handsome indeed and was much sought after by the prostitutes of the Barbary Coast in the late 1860s, when he had not even as yet obtained his majority. He boasted that when he granted his favors, he reversed the natural order of things and collected payment from the lady. The great hardhead even went so far as to sell photos of himself to the inmates of the brothels, each Monday marching through the Barbary Coast area with a loaded satchel of his latest poses, which sold for 25 cents "straight" and 50 cents nude. Many a harlot kept framed photos of Butt Riley over her bed, which was, according to legend, extremely disconcerting to a number of clients.

Riley also garnered quite a bit of money by betting 50 cents or a dollar on whether he could splinter doors of various thickness. Finally, he won five dollars for butting a hole in a door made of heavy oak timbers, but the consequence was a very severe headache. He was frightened further when, immediately thereafter, a couple of female admirers complained about his sexual performance as well. Riley gave up butting lumber, restricting himself to human victims.

In 1871 Riley picked the wrong victim at that pastime as well, a young carriage painter named John Jordan. Twice in a saloon brawl he sent Jordan flying, but as Riley charged at him the third time, Jordan pulled out a self-cocking English revolver and shot his tormentor in the chest.

Riley was rushed to a hospital, where doctors predicted he would die of his wound, but he was such a remarkable physical specimen that he recovered. However, he lost his great strength both for fighting and for loving. The worlds of violence and vice lost interest in him. Hoodlums who had previously flocked to his banner for criminal forays now ignored him, sometimes even beating him up for old time's sake.

In 1876 Riley was convicted as a common housebreaker and sent to San Quentin for 15 years, where he was often described as being "stir crazy." After that, the former Frisco hardhead faded into obscurity.

Oofty Goofty (?–1896)

MASOCHIST'S DELIGHT

Of all the queer characters California's Barbary Coast melodeons (music halls) spewed in the late 19th century, none delighted audiences more than a performer named Oofty Goofty. Known to press or public by no other name, he first appeared in a Market Street freak show in San Francisco.

Masquerading as a wild man recently captured in the wilds of Borneo, he was supposedly imported to San Francisco at enormous expense by showmen eager to impart new scientific knowledge to the eagerly and easily awed. An attendant fed the wild, caged man huge chunks of raw meat, which he ripped into ravenously, pausing only long enough to growl, rattle the bars, and scream fearsomely, "Oofty goofty! Oofty goofty!"—hence his name.

Gawking audiences were thrilled and quite possibly sickened by his performances, which drew record crowds for about a week, until problems developed. Oofty Goofty was covered with road tar from head to toe and decorated with large amounts of horsehair, to give him his ferocious appearance. Unfortunately, he was unable to perspire through this costume and became deathly ill. The wild man was rushed to a hospital where doctors tried vainly for several days to remove the coating without at the same time ripping off his skin. Finally they simply poured tar solvent over him and laid him out on the hospital roof, where the sun successfully finished the job.

The incident brought Oofty Goofty considerable fame, and he became a much sought-after performer at leading Barbary Coast beer halls and variety houses. His new act consisted of singing one song—terribly. Then with great ceremony he was thrown into the street, to the wild applause of the audience.

If the act was a success, it meant even more to Oofty Goofty. He was always kicked with considerable force, landing on the concrete sidewalk with a thud. He became aware of the fact that he felt no pain, that he was largely insensitive to pain.

Thereafter, Oofty Goofty was done for the most part with his theatrical career, preferring instead to eke out a dangerous, punishing existence allowing himself to be pummeled by the denizens of the Barbary Coast—for a fee. For the price of a thin dime a gentleman earned the right to kick Oofty Goofty as hard as he could; for a quarter he could work him over with a walking stick. Oofty Goofty's pièce de résistance was his 50-cent offering, which allowed a customer to slam him with a baseball bat. He became a familiar figure, not only on the coast but in other parts of San Francisco; he carried his bat into barber shops, saloons, or just up to groups of men at street corners, doing his spiel: "Hit me with a bat for four bits, Gents? Only four bits to hit me with this bat, Gents."

Oofty Goofty was knocked flat hundreds of times but was able to continue his unique vocation for some 15 years. But one day in the 1890s, he was worked over with a billiard cue by the then heavyweight champion John L. Sullivan. Sullivan's punishment injured Oofty Goofty's back, and he afterward walked with a permanent limp. In addition Oofty Goofty's career was ruined; the slightest blow now caused him to moan in agony.

There was not a happier man in America than Oofty Goofty when James J. Corbett defeated the great John L. shortly thereafter; he looked upon Corbett as his avenging angel. But Oofty Goofty's fall from fame was greater even than Sullivan's. Without his peculiar physical characteristic, Oofty Goofty sank to the level of a nonentity. He died a few years later.

Curran, John "One Lung" (?–c.1900s)

THE COP-HATING BARD

Within the social circles of the late 19th century New York underworld, Johnny "One Lung" Curran occupied a hallowed niche. His claims to fame were three: he was gallant to the ladies; he was the acknowledged bard of the criminals; and, above all, he bore a nearly pathological hatred for policemen. Many are the tales of this notorious brawler beating up men in uniform for no good reason save that they were there.

Despite the tubercular condition that gave him his sobriquet, Curran was a sub-chief of one of the great street gangs of the era, the wild Gophers. This gang ruled Hell's Kitchen, a tough section ranging from Seventh to Eleventh avenues and from Fourteenth to Forty-second streets. Newspapers noted that the police had not the brute power or violence that the Gophers, One Lung Curran in particular, mustered. It was a polite way of saying that the police were afraid of them.

Being afraid of a brute like One Lung was rather understandable. A celebrated case in point was the time a girl friend wailed to him that she was being chilled by the winds blowing off the Hudson River. Ever the gallant, One Lung walked over to a policeman and blackjacked him to the ground. He stripped off the officer's coat and presented it to his lady fair, who took it home and, being an accomplished seamstress, turned it into a military-style lady's jacket. It was such a fashion hit in Gopher society that other gang members went out to club down and denude policemen by the dozen.

When One Lung was not holding his fellow thugs enthralled by his flaky acts, he entertained them with verses of his own composition. Once, for example, when One Lung was in the tuberculosis ward of Bellevue Hospital, a rival gang in Greenwich Village, the Hudson Dusters, laid low a policeman, Dennis Sullivan, who had made quite a name for himself harassing thugs. Sullivan was fallen on by a score of hoodlums who beat him with blackjacks and stomped on his face, inflicting terrible wounds. He was hospitalized for several weeks and was close to death. When news of the assault reached One Lung, he sat up in his bed and penned a poem, even though it meant bestowing honor on another gang. It started:

> Says Dinny, "Here's me only chance
>   To gain meself a name;
> I'll clean up the Hudson Dusters,
>   And reach the hall of fame."
> He lost his stick and cannon,
>   And his shield they took away,
> It was then that he remembered
>   Every dog has got his day.

One Lung's masterpiece went on for a half dozen more verses describing the assault in loving detail. It led to an era of good feeling between the Gophers and the Dusters. The latter had One Lung's poem printed up on parchment-like paper, distributing copies to every saloon and barber shop in their bailiwick. The Dusters also saw to it that a good supply reached the police at Officer Sullivan's home precinct on Charles Street as well as the victim himself in the hospital.

One Lung remained a terror to the police, with his fists and pen, until he died of tuberculosis at the beginning of this century. Indeed, his verse outlived him. For years the aforementioned ditty was sung in the streets by the juvenile toughs of New York's West Side.

Alee, Johnny (1853–1887)

"THE EATIEST FOOL"

It is impossible to come up with the fattest man of all time, the problem being complicated by the circus fat people, for whom preposterous claims are made. Few such fat persons truly weigh more than 500 pounds, although promoters often claim double that, then clad them in loose-fitting garments for the added billowy effect. Thus it may well be that Johnny Alee of mid–19th-century North Carolina was the fattest American. Among his neighbors in the tiny crossroads community of Carbon, North Carolina, he was held to be 1,132 pounds, but that was not a figure medically attested to; therefore Robert Earl Hughes (1926–1958), at 1,069 pounds, is popularly called the fattest American.

However, if Johnny Alee was not the fattest, he was, as folks around Carbon, North Carolina, put it, "the eatiest fool." No psychological quirks nor glandular disorders held sway in the public perception. Alee was just a man who took a powerful interest in gorging.

Born in 1853, Johnny was always on the tubby side but hardly exceptionally so until he was 10. Then he developed his great appetite. He ate ravenously, and by the time he was 15 he could barely support his own weight, and he could no longer leave by the front door of his house. Grown men could barely wrap their arms around his thighs.

Johnny seems to have enjoyed his celebrity although apparently not nearly as much as eating. Friends, neighbors, and the curious were always welcome at the Alee homestead, as long as they brought along a picnic basket or two for Johnny to feast on. Even children gave up their chocolate cakes to watch big Little Johnny devour them in a few quick bites.

In time Johnny could only walk with great difficulty, and the 15-foot trek between his huge chair and the table where he gorged was a major moving project. It became part of the area's folklore that getting from the table to the chair made Johnny expend so much energy that he worked up his appetite all over again.

Quite naturally, Johnny's overweight problem proved the death of him, if not for the traditional reasons advanced by doctors. Alee was 33 years old at the time. He hauled his weight along to a spot in the parlor where he could peek out the door. Suddenly the flooring splintered, and Johnny plunged through to his armpits. He dangled there helplessly, six feet off the ground, since the parlor section was suspended some 10 feet above the ground on log stilts. His neighbors tried to rescue him by rigging up a block and tackle to lift him back to safety.

But before they were ready they noticed that Johnny's heavy breathing had stopped. Doctors later decided the eatiest fool had died of heart failure, from fear of tumbling to the earth, which he had not touched for almost 20 years.

Harden-Hickey, James A. (1854–1898)

KING WITHOUT A COUNTRY

James A. Harden-Hickey can be said to have crowded an incredible number of peccadillos into a relatively short life. Not many men managed to crown themselves king, author a tome dedicated to the joys of suicide, and be so conversant with the thoughts of the greats in the arts and sciences that they suffered no compunctions about putting their own grand ideas in their words.

Born into wealth, New Yorker Harden-Hickey was educated in France, where he was much taken with the court of Napoleon III. He always considered himself cut from the cloth of royalty, and he spent his life proving that exotic idea to his fellow man. He was aided in this by marriage to a bride even richer than himself, Anna

Flagler, heiress to a steel and oil fortune. Her father, tycoon John Flagler, thought his son-in-law to be rather a fop, given as he was to courtly dress; but the older man didn't know the half of it. Harden-Hickey was not one to waste time dreaming about what he would do if he were king; he determined to become one.

This man in search of a kingdom found his lush domain in 1893, on the uninhabited island of Trinidad, some 700 miles off the coast of Brazil. It was not of course the larger British West Indian island of Trinidad off the coast of Venezuela; but at 60 square miles it was enough to be a modest man's empire.

King James I, aboard a full-rigged schooner, claimed Trinidad and established a colony of 40 Americans there. He saw grand opportunities for exploiting the island's natural resources, especially by mining the plentiful stores of bat guano.

King James I did not relish living in his kingly climes all year around, preferring the American scene much of the time. So he opened his country's chancellery on Thirty-second Street where, although the U.S. State Department paid him no mind, he could still receive visitors and those interested in purchasing stamps (with his likeness). If they were lucky, the visitors might also see James I sporting his handmade crown.

Because James I felt it might be a bit pretentious parading around the United States with his kingly title, he also more conservatively dubbed himself Baron James A. Harden-Hickey, certainly more the right thing when one mixes with the masses.

Besides his royal duties, Harden-Hickey turned to the pen, churning out several works presenting his personal philosophy. His most noted work, rather more infamous than famous, was *Euthanasia: The Aesthetics of Suicide*. He stated in the preface: "We must shake off this fond desire of life and learn that it is of little consequence when we suffer; that it is of greater moment to live well than to live long, and that oftentimes it is living well not to live long."

The tome, which can only be described as the ultimate how-to book, offered some 88 poisons and 51 instruments for doing oneself in. Harden-Hickey most preferred "wolfs-bane," but if one did not have access to such a poisonous plant, which grew most prevalently in the Alps, he heartily recommended a trusty pair of scissors. "May this little work contribute to the overthrow of fear," the author rhapsodized. "May it nerve the faltering arm of the poor wretch to whom life is loathsome. . . . The only remedy for a life of misery is death; if you are tired and weary, if you are the victim of disease or misfortune, drop the burden of life, fly away!"

Of course, the reader did not have to take Harden-Hickey's word. His book offered 400 quotations "by the greatest thinkers the world has ever produced." Among them were: "Nature is kind and considerate in giving us the power of dying; there are a thousand ways out of life, though but one way into it"; "The best way never to fear death is always to be thinking about it"; "The wise man lives as long as he ought, not as long as he can."

These quotations are given here without attribution since Harden-Hickey was much too modest in ascribing them to others. He made virtually all of them up himself.

If he was taken to task for his literary forgeries, Harden-Hickey had little time to worry about it. More serious crises faced James I. In 1895 Great Britain, that imperial power, simply seized his island of Trinidad as a coaling station. Suddenly James I found himself a king without a country. He fumed and raged, petitioning the United States to come to his aid, a position the American government found less than compelling.

The following year Britain turned the island over to Brazil, which upset James I all the more. He declared he would launch a war against England for her treachery and, after conclusion of that conflict, he would deal with Brazil's effrontery as well. He recruited a number of mercenaries for his planned attack on England, but it may well have been that these individuals were more impressed with their advance pay than their combat potential against a great power. In any event Harden-Hickey's armed forces started melting away when the pay dried up. Harden-Hickey's wife and father-in-law refused to fund his wild campaign, and he was left alone, wallowing in self-pity and experiencing loss of the desire for life.

In February 1898, Harden-Hickey harkened back to his own book and, in a modest hotel room in El Paso, Texas, he ended his life. He rather mundanely used morphine—not wolfs-bane or scissors.

Gardner, Marshall B. (1854–1937)

"THE GENIUS UNAPPRECIATED"

The idea of a hollow earth is not a new one. Although it was first popularized in America by Captain John Cleves Symmes (*q.v.*) in 1818, Cotton Mather speculated along similar lines a century earlier and, in doing so, drew heavily from one of the more eccentric theories put forward by the great English astronomer Edmund Halley, of comet fame.

In 1913, the mantle was picked up by a man from Aurora, Illinois, Marshall B. Gardner, who was in charge of maintenance of machinery for a corset firm. Nothing enraged him more than the suggestion that his theory was based on doctrines advanced by earlier hollow-earth advocates. In a brilliant example of the old adage about the pot calling the kettle black, Gardner poked fun at Symmes, rejecting his "fantastic notion" that the earth consisted of numerous concentric spheres.

Gardner expounded his theory in a book, *Journey to the Earth's Interior*, which he was forced to print privately. Because he picked up a cult of followers, he was able to expand the book in 1920 to 456 pages. He saw all the earlier hollow earthers as "cranks" who "deny all the facts of science and get up some purely private explanation of the formation of the earth."

Having expressed that thought, Gardner proceeded to boggle the minds of scientists with his own notions, which were likewise based on few established facts and many private fantasies. Ridiculing Symmes' thesis, he insisted that only the outer shell of the earth was definitely known to exist. Inside the hollow earth, he announced, was a sun 600 miles in diameter, which offered perpetual daylight to the interior. There were openings at both the North and South Poles, each 1,400 miles wide, through which outer-shell beings could enter and interior residents could leave. This was where Eskimos came from, he said; furthermore, it explained their legends of a world of never-ending summer. Why had the Eskimos left this paradise? Perhaps they were driven out by great mammoths—like the frozen mammoths found in Siberia.

Gardner then debunked the various expeditions to the North Pole, simply explaining that none of the explorers ever reached it. He attacked the "professional freemasonry" of scientists for the fact that his theories did not get a fair hearing. After all, he pointed out, he was shattering all their neat little explanations of the world. Indeed, Gardner offered his own simple explanation of the aurora borealis. It was produced by interior sunlight streaming out of the northern opening of the earth.

When Gardner published his expanded work in 1920, he predicted the public would soon embrace his views and discard those of establishment scientists. The only reason the public had not gone wild over his 1913 edition, he claimed, was the distraction of the Great War. Gardner was not completely deluded in this. Thousands came to his lectures and listened to his paranoid claims of being "the genius unappreciated." He was philosophical about it; Galileo had also had the same woes, receiving honors only much later.

In 1926 Admiral Richard Byrd made his epic airplane flight over the North Pole. There was no Symmes hole, and no Gardner hole. The corset factory man was shattered. He ceased all his writings and public speaking. But before he died in 1937, he insisted his idea still had some merit.

It must be noted that some followers of Gardner still carry the banner; they hold to his idea of large openings at the poles. They insist the openings simply have not been found. They ask about that warm-weather little pest, the mosquito, that some polar explorers have described. Where else could the little beast have come from, if not Gardner's world?

Tattenbaum, William (1855–1881)

THE SAGA OF RUSSIAN BILL

A long-haired Russian named William Tattenbaum was one of the most colorful figures to hit Tombstone, Arizona, which he did in 1880. He was a flamboyant contrast to the grimy desert rats and saddlebums attracted to that glittering silver mecca amid the sagebrush.

A saddle-sore cowboy coming to Tombstone was always warned by his comrades to be ready for anything—and that was good advice. There wasn't anything like Tombstone for miles around. A town of some 500 buildings in 1880, no less than 100 of them were licensed to dispense alcoholic beverages; 50 more could be called businesses of ill fame. But there was much more, including such magnificent sights as the Bird Cage Theater, Crystal Palace Concert Hall, Schieffelin Concert Hall, and the Elite Theater. Their patrons included the odd, the painted, the dandyish, and the foppish, among others, but few matched Tattenbaum, who quickly achieved a measure of notoriety as the town fool. He was to the awed westerner quite a sight, described by many as "a white Chinaman." He had long hair and would spend hours grooming it, to the delight of old and young alike.

And Russian Bill, as he was called, sure could tell tall ones. Among his crazy chatterings was a claim that he was late of the Czar's Imperial White Hussars, the son of the Countess Telfrin, a wealthy Russian noblewoman. Why had he left? He had faced a court-martial for striking a superior officer. He also told of his many feats of daring, which Tombstonians considered to be down-right lies. They were unimpressed when Russian Bill decked himself out in the finest cowboy raiment and armed himself with the best in shiny six-guns.

Townsfolk much preferred to regard him as an eccentric and the butt of humor. As a character, he was later perpetuated by Hollywood; the likes of comedian Mischa Auer played the Russian-Bill type in movie westerns.

Russian Bill strived for better. He ingratiated himself with Curly Bill Brocius and the rest of the outlaw Clanton Gang, especially the mysterious Johnny Ringo, a strange cowboy who mingled culture with meanness. Ringo was fond of quoting Shakespeare, and one can imagine the face-downs between Ringo quoting the Bard and Russian Bill countering with everything from Plato to Tolstoy. Alas, there was no one else at the outlaw camp at Galeyville to record or probably even comprehend the verbal jousts. Ringo had a killer reputation, which held the other gunmen in line, but Russian Bill enjoyed no such immunity from ridicule. If the outlaws were awed or baffled by his recitations, they were thoroughly amused by his hair grooming. Besides, he was to be tolerated because he could run errands for the gang.

There is little doubt Russian Bill wanted to be taken for a great bandit, but there is no evidence that he was. If anything, the most he ever became was a "horse-holder" during the gang's forays. His pleas for an active role were met by raucous laughter.

To escape such derision Russian Bill struck out in 1881 for New Mexico Territory in an ill-fated horse-stealing enterprise of his own. He quickly fell into the hands of the Law and Order Committee of Shakespeare, New Mexico Territory, where unfortunately his reputation as a softhead was not known. Had they been aware of Russian Bill's eccentricities, he might well have gotten off with just being run out of town. Instead, he and another malefactor named Sandy King were given a speedy trial in the banquet room of the Grant House hostelry. Shakespeare's vigilantes were noted for the swiftness of their justice, and Russian Bill and King were strung up without further ado from a ceiling beam in the very room where the verdict was rendered.

When news of the hanging drifted back to Tombstone, many folks were upset, feeling it was an unkind act toward a feeble-minded character, but what was done was done, most decided. The final word to the Russian Bill saga was not written until 1883, when the Countess Telfrin with the aid of agents traced her erratic son as far as Tombstone, and finally to somewhere in New Mexico.

Tombstonians were rather chagrined to learn that all of Russian Bill's ramblings were true. He had been a lieutenant in the service of the czar. The embarrassment in Shakespeare, needless to say, was even more acute when the townsfolk learned they had hanged "an honest-to-God son of a countess." To save the countess needless grief and protect the town from a troublesome investigation by Washington, it was decided that the wisest course was to report that Tattenbaum had met with an accidental death.

Not long afterwards Shakespeare turned into a ghost town, but as late as the 1950s a small marker indicated Russian Bill's grave.

Gates, Bet-A-Million (John W.) (1855–1911)

THE KING OF THE PLUNGERS

Waiting for a business meeting to start, two men in a New York office watched raindrops slithering down a windowpane, as if their lives depended on it. Then one raindrop plunged downward suddenly, and one of the men roared: "My win! That makes $50,000 you owe me. Let's go again, double or nothing."

A compulsive gambler, Bet-A-Million
Gates made a lucrative science of
besting the Robber Barons at
extravagant bets.

However, the other man had had enough. He was not the compulsive gambler that the winner, Bet-A-Million Gates, was. In fact, he didn't know how he'd been talked into playing in the first place. His opponent, barrel-chested, heavy-jowled John Warne Gates was the King of the Plungers. He got his nickname of Bet-A-Million when, one day at Saratoga Race Track, he tried to place a million dollars on a horse, causing the bookmakers to run for cover.

Gates would bet on anything—cards, dice, roulette, or he'd make up games like betting on raindrops if nothing else was available. He had used the same tactic in business, speculating, trying to anticipate what the other great movers of the day—financiers like the Morgans and the Carnegies—wanted. Then he'd head them off and force them to pay till it hurt to get it.

Almost anyone with money hated Gates. "The man cannot be entrusted with property," J. P. Morgan railed about the Illinois barbed-wire salesman who had pyramided a $30-a-month salary selling wire to Texas cattlemen into a $50-million fortune. "He's a broken-down gambler," Andrew Carnegie raged. Once, after Gates took Morgan in a $15 million deal, the latter in vengeance retaliated by seeing to it that Gates was barred from admission to the Union League and the New York Yacht Club.

Always crude and boisterous, Gates was only tolerated at the Waldorf Hotel because he was its highest-paying guest, keeping a $20,000-a-year suite there for use as a clubhouse. Because he was such a liberal tipper, management discovered they could pay lower salaries to staffers who were eager for a chance to hit it big with Gates.

Gates had started gambling while still a schoolboy, playing poker with railroad hands in idle train cars in his native Turner's Junction, some 30 miles from Chicago. Gates knew how to stack the odds in his favor and, although in later years he might drop as much as a million dollars in a poker session that lasted several days and nights, he always won far more than he lost. Generally that was because he could always afford to come back, having enough money to double his bet after a loss.

Once, in Kansas City, a local sport begged an audience, saying he represented a local syndicate that wanted to gamble with him on any sort of game.

"You know I don't play for small sums," Gates said. "How much have you got to spend?"

The sport produced a roll of $40,000.

Gates flipped a gold piece in the air. "Heads or tails," he said. "You call it."

The local gambler lost, and Gates pocketed his winnings. The loser became a sort of local celebrity who was pointed out as the man who had lost $40,000 to Bet-A-Million Gates in less than 10 seconds.

Once Gates was dining with wealthy playboy John Drake, whose father had founded Drake University and was a governor of Iowa. With their coffee, Gates suggested they each dunk a piece of bread and bet $1,000 a fly on whose bread attracted the most flies. Gates collected a small fortune. Slyly, he had turned the odds in his favor by first slipping six lumps of sugar into his coffee cup.

From the moment Gates awoke in the morning, he was looking for action. On a train en route to the races at Saratoga once, Gates needed a fourth for bridge and told a newspaperman he knew casually: "We play for five a point, but I'll guarantee your losses and you can keep what you win."

When the game ended, the reporter tallied up his points and gleefully told Gates he was due $500 at five cents a point. Gates leaned back and howled with laughter until tears came. He wrote out a check for $50,000. They had been playing for $5 a point.

These and many other bizarre incidents made Bet-A-Million Gates a popular hero. That as much as anything got to Morgan, who was himself labeled a "robber baron." He regarded himself far less an unprincipled speculator than Bet-A-Million.

Finally though, Gates had his run of bad luck. He found himself without cash and down to his business investments, and they were held as collateral, payable on demand to his nemesis Morgan. It is said that Gates literally dropped to his knees, begging Morgan not to destroy him completely. Morgan relented to the extent of letting Gates keep a portion of his former holdings, provided that he got out of Wall Street and out of New York—and stay out forever.

Gates moved to Port Arthur, Texas, where he was only a shadow of his former affluence and influence. He searched around for a new gamble. In 1901 Spindletop, the greatest gusher in petroleum history, had been brought in. Gates formed his own oil company with several backers and hired an army of geologists and drillers. They brought in a long string of dry holes, but then they started to hit winners. In 1902, Standard Oil offered to buy Gates' company, called The Texas Company, for $25 million. Gates just laughed.

By 1911 Gates was personally worth somewhere between $50 million and $100 million. He sent his firm's latest financial statement to Morgan. Later that year Gates died in a Paris hospital while on vacation with his wife. He had already broken his promise to Morgan, having been living in New York in the new and sumptuous Plaza Hotel since it opened in 1908. On his instructions, Gates was buried in a kingly mausoleum not far from Wall Street. Probably to his way of thinking, Bet-A-Million had taken another pot from old J.P.

Brady, James Buchanan "Diamond Jim" (1856–1917)

GREATEST OF THE GOURMANDS

One of the great fashion plates and most valiant, voracious eaters the world has ever seen, Diamond Jim Brady could be said to have eaten his way to success. Born to poor, working-class Irish parents in New York, Brady started out as a baggage handler at a railroad station. He rose to be a champion railroad-equipment salesman when the railroad was king. He did it by holding clients, such as visiting Midwest railroad nabobs, in awe of his diamond-encrusted appearance and compulsive gluttony. A railroad man might head back to Kansas City and, instead of bragging that he had closed a million-dollar deal, he would recall his experience of a lifetime—breaking bread with the famed Diamond Jim.

Making money was not an end in itself for Diamond Jim; it merely allowed him to follow his coarse and flamboyant epicurean ways. Or, as he put it with delightfully insurmountable vulgarity: "Them as has 'em wears 'em." Brady was at the moment discussing the Christmas-treelike glitter that had earned him his nickname of "Diamond Jim." When Brady went to his dresser drawer, he could choose from 30-odd timepieces, many worthy of being museum pieces and ranging up in appraised cost to $17,500 apiece. The combined weight of one of his diamond rings and his number-one scarfpin, each adorned by a single stone, was 58 karats. One of his many watch chains scaled in at 83 emerald karats. A single set of shirt studs, vest studs, and cuff links cost him a piddling $87,315.

He also maintained a wardrobe of 200 custom-made suits and at least 50 glossy hats. All this was part of Brady's selling technique, and as an entertainer of clients he has been labeled the father of the lavish expense account. But of course Brady really displayed his glitter and gilt for the glory of it, and he dined for the sheer joy of ravenous feeding.

He once thus explained his eating style: "Whenever I sit down to a meal, I always make a point to leave just four inches between my stummick [sic] and the edge of the table. And then, when I can feel 'em rubbin' together pretty hard, I know I've had enough." The celebrated New York restauranteur Charles Rector described Diamond Jim as "the best twenty-five customers we had."

Rector's mathematics could not be faulted. Brady's checks for typical feedings would come to monumental numbers. An average day of Brady's gluttony started off with a breakfast of hominy, eggs, muffins, corn bread, flapjacks, chops, fried potatoes, a beefsteak or two—all washed down with a gallon of orange juice, his favorite drink, since he never touched wine or liquor.

By 11:30 A.M. pangs of hunger hit Brady, and there was no way he could survive until lunch an hour later. A pre-lunch snack of two or three dozen clams and oysters kept him going. Then at lunch Brady wolfed down more clams and oysters, a brace of boiled lobsters, some deviled crabs, a joint of beef, and several pieces of pie. Of course this took another gallon of orange juice as a chaser. Teatime meant a platter of seafood washed down with a stream of Brady's second favorite liquid, lemon soda.

Then, happily, came dinner, when Brady could get down to some serious eating. It would start with two or three dozen Lynnhaven oysters, especially selected for Diamond Jim. This was followed by a half dozen crabs and at least two bowls of green turtle soup. Then followed a number of main courses, say six or seven lobsters, two canvasback ducks, two huge portions of terrapin (turtle meat), a large sirloin steak, with assorted vegetables. Jim would then be offered a pastry platter; invariably he simply emptied it. All this would be washed down with another gallon or two of orange juice. Then Brady would cap the meal by nibbling down a two-pound box of chocolates.

Brady always had a bit of a sweet tooth; once in Boston he sampled the wares of a local candy maker and was so impressed that he wolfed down a five-pound box of the stuff, announcing, "Best goddamned candy I ever ate." He wrote out a check for $150,000 so that the little company could expand its facilities and keep him in supply; the money was to be refunded in trade.

There are those who considered Brady to be basically an unhappy fat man who drowned himself in food. He proposed marriage to famed singer-actress Lillian Russell. She spurned him, although she remained his constant dinner companion. But the truth was that Diamond Jim loved his way of life too well to ever change.

He once staged a dinner in honor of one of his racehorses, Gold Heels. The grand feeding of 50 guests ran from 4:00 P.M. until 9:00 A.M. the following morning. The tab for the food and champagne (and a gusher of orange juice for the host) topped $45,000. Brady also presented "party favors" for his guests which, brought in on velvet cushions at midnight, consisted of a diamond-studded stopwatch for each gentleman and an elegant diamond-studded brooch for each lady. The gifts cost about $1,200 each.

Naturally, medical experts kept warning Brady he was killing himself with his enormous meals; indeed many doctors were particularly alarmed by his voluminous intake of citrus juice. Still, it was no small accomplishment that Diamond Jim lasted until 56 before he developed serious stomach trouble. He lived another five years after that. A postmortem on his body revealed that his stomach was six times the normal size. Much of Brady's fortune, including the revenues from the sale of his jewelry, went to the James Brady Urological Clinic, which he had established at Johns Hopkins in Baltimore.

Wittrock, Frederick (1858–1921)

THE GRAND CONFESSOR

"Terrible" Fred Wittrock was a man born too late for his calling. Such publications as the *Police Gazette* led Wittrock, the owner of a small St. Louis store, astray. He read ravenously about the doings of Billy the Kid and Jesse James, and then he brooded on his own dull existence.

Finally in 1886 Wittrock sold his store, bought himself a six-shooter, and purchased several black outfits, trying to decide which would look best, and most threatening, on him. Then he launched the outlaw career of Terrible Fred Wittrock.

Amazingly, he actually went out and pulled a rather impressive robbery, holding up the St. Louis and San Francisco Express just outside St. Louis, netting $10,000 from the Adams Express Company safe. He gained entrance to the express car by using forged credentials that indicated he was the railroad's new night superintendent.

Wittrock was not however sublimely happy at the outcome. He had nice booty but not the satisfaction of achieving fame. After a time the story of the cunning robbery faded from print, and Wittrock was stuck with loot but no headlines. In an effort to rekindle the investigation, Terrible Fred wrote a letter to the *St. Louis Globe Democrat* revealing "the inside story" of the robbery and informing the newspaper that the bandit's tools could be found in a St. Louis baggage room.

Law officers and a reporter went to the baggage room and discovered a six-shooter, mask, blackjack, express company money envelopes, and an old song sheet. Written on the song sheet was Wittrock's address at a local boardinghouse. Wittrock was tracked down within 24 hours. Taken into custody, he begged deputies and the press to refer to him as "Terrible Fred," which he said was what all his outlaw confederates called him.

Wittrock got a long prison term and at least a slight reputation as a criminal. However, Wittrock was not satisfied, and so from behind bars he confessed to a number of other robberies. Some were real and others imaginary capers, and eventually law officials stopped paying attention to his confessions.

When Terrible Fred was released, he tried without success to interest publishers in his "memoirs." Alas, not even the *Police Gazette* took him seriously. Poor Fred lived out his years spinning tales that nobody listened to save for some goggle-eyed school kids. It wasn't much but to Wittrock it was at least a measure of fame.

Senior, Stephen (1859–1924)

THE PERTH AMBOY MISER

Stephen Senior was a well-known character in Perth Amboy, New Jersey. It is not a large town now, and in the early part of the century it was even smaller. People had a way of knowing each other's business. Everyone knew Old Man Senior. He was a poor man who relied on the kindness of others to eke out a precarious existence. He lived in a hovel that he had more or less built himself. He bought his bread at a bakery just at closing time for half price, sometimes even less, and he made the same arrangements at delicatessens, cheaply buying prepared foods and salads that would otherwise spoil over the weekend.

Through the cold Perth Amboy winters, Senior never spent a penny for fuel. He gathered up coal along the railroad tracks and around factories. He obtained wood from boxes discarded behind food and retail stores. The winter of 1924 was a particularly bitter one, and Senior, then 65 years old, was ailing, for many weeks hardly leaving his bed. The porous walls of his crude shack could not prevent the subzero blasts of wind from chilling his abode. Finally faced with a shortage of coal, he summoned a coal dealer, inquiring about his prices. Senior was outraged at the thought of spending the better part of a dollar for a few bushels of fuel, and he drove the dealer from his hovel door with threats and a shower of wooden blocks. He then ventured forth into the snow to retrieve his precious wood with more imprecations and threats at the coal man. Did he think a poor man could afford to spend such a monstrous sum for warmth?

Three days later Old Man Senior was found frozen to death in his bed. His desperate fight to stay alive was evident: he had stuffed the cracks in his walls with rags and newspapers, and when he ran out of his supply of them, he had used other insulation—paper money. Not a few dollars but thousands and thousands. When searchers lifted up the linoleum they found a padding of money to reduce wear and tear on the linoleum.

By the time authorities had concluded their search of the dead man's property, they turned up a fortune of well over a half million dollars in investments and cash. It turned out that Senior owned a considerable amount of real estate and received a large rental income through an agency, used so that the residents of Perth Amboy would know nothing of his wealth.

He had not deigned even to live on his own property, having built his shack on unclaimed real estate. Senior obviously had seen no reason to deprive himself of rental income on his own property or, worse yet, to enrich another landlord for providing him with living space.

What joy Senior must have had contemplating his wealth, and how much greater was that joy because his was a secret kept from mortal man. Was it joy, or what Robert Burton called, "A mere madness, to live like a wretch, and die rich"?

Prince, Frederick Henry (1859–1953)

THE GERM-FREE PRINCES

If one were to have named the most eccentric couple of Boston North Shore society during the first half of the 20th century, it would have had to have been Frederick Henry and Abigail Norman Prince. Prince was often described as the wealthiest man in New England, with a fortune estimated at $250 million garnered in railroading and in outright ownership of the Chicago stockyards. He had a reputation as an outstanding horseman and one of the most outspoken American capitalists—in that order. The ranking of these attributes was based on the observation that while he might on occasion be sans checkbook, he was almost never without his riding crop, even at formal or social affairs. His interest in matters equine was further held up to public view in 1929 when, in a moment of pique, he bashed a groom, a polo professional, over the head with a polo mallet—all for the inexcusable offense of riding him off the field in the heat of a practice match. The groom's offense was almost the equivalent of the unwashed storming the Bastille.

The ensuing trial for $50,000 damages was covered by the Boston newspapers with almost the zeal shown in another Massachusetts court case, the trial of anarchists Sacco and Vanzetti. Indeed, besides drawing the standard newsmen contingent, the Prince affair also attracted the society department reporters. It was perhaps in keeping with Prince's behavior that a jury award of $20,000 to the groom was appealed by the defense for four years, finally being settled out of court for, it was reputed, the original sum of $50,000.

During his tribulations, Prince could count on unlimited support of his doting wife, Abigail. She shared all of Prince's interests and biases, including of course an interest in horsemanship, polo, foxhounding, and the like—activities in which the couple indulged at various homes in Boston, Newport, Aiken, (S.C.), and Europe. From the time he married Abigail in 1884, Frederick doted on her, determined to protect her from the germ-ridden outside world.

Early on, he forebade his wife to handle money, paper or coin, lest through the filthy lucre Black Death, chronic septicemia, or even more dreaded diseases like V.D. be conveyed upon her. Of course, since they lived in a world where money was a necessity,

Prince supplied his wife with a personal bursar, an Irishman named Thomas, who handled all financial transactions. Thomas seemed much like a member of the horse-loving family, never being seen in any other dress than riding breeches, canvas leggings, and hard Derby hat. There were those journalists who advised their readers that he slept in his gear, to be ready at a moment's notice to fulfill his mistress' slightest whim.

However, the Princes understood full well that germs did not restrict themselves to the currency of the realm, and that other risks of infection abounded. Mrs. Prince was not permitted to sleep in the same bedroom on successive nights lest germ intelligence learn of her whereabouts. She slept in a specially built large cradle which was wheeled to a different room each day, thus outwitting the germs. The cradle was disinfected each day, and the new room's walls were draped with sheets which were also scrupulously sprayed with antiseptics.

Indeed, it must be noted that Abigail lived well into her eighties under the regimen, dying in 1949. Prince lived to the ripe old age of 93, a testimonial indeed to the virtues of disinfectants and large sums of money—especially if such filthy lucre could be kept at arm's length, at least.

Billings, Cornelius K. G. (1861–1931)

HORSEBACK BILLINGS

As with Charlie Gates (*q.v.*), speed was C. K. G. Billings' grand obsession, especially fast horses and fast boats. Fortunately Billings had the wherewithal to cater to his whims, having been born into millions. He was also a leading capitalist, real-eastate investor, and chairman of the board of Union Carbide. However, such activities hardly held his interest or his time. He was obsessed with fine horses and, above all, fast living. He sought to gain access to high society with fast and free spending.

He owned a sleek 240-foot yacht, the *Venadis*, the operating cost of which ran to a quarter of a million dollars a year. It was a fast, sleek craft that, by night, could be taken for a Cunarder. It was credited with having one of the fastest times between New York and Palm Beach, where it was a standout during the society season, even if Billings himself was not; the owner was considered too grotesque and ostentatious in his tastes.

It could not be said that Billings did not try hard. The *Venadis* had to anchor three miles out at sea in Florida, and Billings' arranged for its houseguests to be hauled back and forth between ship and shore in a fleet of brass-bound, mahogany-finished small boats shuttling off every half hour. Spankingly dressed stewards served drinks aboard all the ferries; Billings' own dinghy, a shallop close to the size of the average small yacht, carried a Hawaiian steel-guitar quartet who performed while the master sipped rum served in hollowed coconut shells.

Undoubtedly Billings was at times frustrated by his lack of acceptance by high society—certainly he spent money freely enough to merit some consideration—and one may assume that his order for the *Venadis* to speed back north was born of such rejection. On one of the yacht's speed forays, it rammed with the steamer *Bunker Hill*; there was a resultant loss of two lives. Undaunted but presumably a bit contrite, Billings swapped the *Venadis* for Morton Plant's somewhat smaller but still speedy *Kanawha*.

If Billings loved speed on water, he was most ecstatic about it

"Gaudy" and "grotesque" were two of the more restrained adjectives used by society writers to describe C.K.G. Billings's wacky horseback dinner indoors at Louis Sherry's famous restaurant.

on the turf. A dedicated sportsman, he bred many top horses, trotters, saddle horses, and racers, even buying into some race-tracks. Raised in Chicago, where his father became president of the Peoples Gas Light and Coke Company, Billings entered the company in 1879. He succeeded to his father's post in 1887, moving on to other business posts later, devoting however only that time to business that did not interfere with his true love: horses.

Early in the 1900s, he moved to New York and purchased Fort Tryon as a site for his stable. Upon opening his stable, he catered an outdoor dinner at which all the guests rode horseback in evening clothes. Billings considered the event such a success that he decided to repeat it in a more gaudy and grotesque manner in 1903. He staged a zany horseback dinner indoors, at Louis Sherry's famous restaurant. The guests, all men, sat in the saddle astride horses that had been conveyed up to the ballroom by elevator. They dined, at an estimated $250 a plate, on pheasant from feed bags, guzzling champagne from large rubber casks.

The overall cost of the feast was placed at $50,000, which included the planting of sod on the ballroom floor. Society writers were unimpressed by the bizarre affair, noting it was uncomfortable for all and that the steed's soiling of the banquet room floor diminished the elegance of the event.

Billings was only bewildered by such carping, wondering once again what he could do to impress certain people.

Ketchum, "Black Jack" Tom (1862?–1901)

THE SECOND STUPIDEST OUTLAW

It has somehow become a Hollywood legend that the Old West was peopled by outlaws who were intelligent or even brilliant characters. In actuality, that sterling breed could probably be counted on the fingers of one hand. Billy the Kid, for instance, could more rightly be classified as a murderous juvenile psychopath.

However, when one is searching for the flakiest in the West, it is hard to go beyond "Black Jack" Tom Ketchum. It would be kind

Hanged in 1901, outlaw Black Jack Ketchum is rightly remembered for his "numb skull."
(National Archives)

to describe Black Jack as merely a stupid outlaw. After a fashion, he himself concurred with that sentiment. Whenever a caper of his went wrong, he would methodically beat himself on the head with the butt of a six-shooter, snarling, "You will, will you (slam)? Now take that (pop) . . . and that (bang)!"

Such therapy never did seem to work. It hadn't, some years earlier, when Ketchum, then working as a cowboy, returned to Clayton, New Mexico, from a cattle drive and was handed a note from a pretty young thing named Cora, who had promised to wait for him. The letter was the "Dear John" sort, indicating she had run off with a cowpuncher named Slim, who weeks earlier had even watched Ketchum kiss his lady fair good-bye. Cora's final lines really affected Ketchum. "No more than you got out of sight than we went to Stanton and got married."

Colonel Jack Potter recorded the sad tale in *Sheriff and Police*, telling how Ketchum went down to the bank of the Perico River to lash himself with his twisted saddle rope, "while cursing all womankind."

It was this bitter experience that drove Black Jack and his

brother Sam to Wyoming's notorious Hole-in-the-Wall country, to take up fulltime outlaw life. According to some western experts, Ketchum became one of the leaders of the Hole-in-the-Wall gang. This was not precisely accurate for, while some of the denizens of the area could more logically be called members of the Hole-in-the-Head gang, most were too smart to follow Ketchum. One of the superior intellects of the bunch, Butch Cassidy, was thoroughly bewildered that anyone would follow such a self-skull-smasher.

Many of Black Jack's planned crimes turned into disasters, and if each member of his gang got $10 for his share, it could be considered a superior outing. Needless to say, Black Jack's gun and skull both took regular beatings.

Late in 1898 Black Jack led his men on a train robbery, that of the Twin Flyer, near Twin Mountains, New Mexico. It was to prove a memorable heist even though the total loot came to less than $500. Black Jack hadn't experienced such a bonanza in some time and resolved to pull another train job. He could think of nothing better to do, however, than to stage a replay, hitting the same train at exactly the same spot. As a matter of fact, he hit the Twin Flyer a total of four times, which was, as Butch Cassidy could have informed him and probably did, asking for trouble.

The last caper occurred on July 11, 1899, and the law was waiting. Most of the gang was captured, including Ketchum, who was wounded in the shoulder. In due course Ketchum was convicted and hanged. His execution was considered such an important event in 1901 that even the *New York Times* dispatched a correspondent to cover the event, which turned out to be rather grisly.

After the black cap was adjusted over his head, Ketchum yelled out, "Let 'er go." When the trap was sprung, the weights proved to be poorly adjusted and the terrific jerk ripped Ketchum's head from his shoulders. It was left to some western wit to note that poor Black Jack could never get anything right. (See also: Ketchum, Sam.)

Bivens, Joseph, Jr. (c.1862–1912)

"COXEY" BIVENS THE CAVEMAN

This country, especially in the 18th and 19th centuries, had more than its share of cave dwellers; among them, Joseph "Coxey" Bivens, Jr., deserves special mention as well as the gratitude of archeologists. A by-product of Biven's life-style was the uncovering of many relics of the Iroquois and Algonquian Indians.

To the residents of New York's Delaware Valley Bivens was an "odd coot"; at the same time he was a most engaging "river rat," with his unfailing ability to guide fishermen to spots where the "really big ones" were biting.

As a boy he loved his Delaware River and was constantly exploring it. When his father died in a railroad accident, followed shortly to the grave by his grieving mother, young Bivens left the family home for refuge on his river. He fished for food, gathering such bait on the shores as dobson fly larvae and lamprey eels, both of which were great for catching bass; he then sold the bait to sportsmen, who were grateful not only for it but for Bivens' guidance in finding the best fishing spots. As a result, they often stood him for drinks at a nearby tavern.

It was for Joseph Bivens a complete existence. He found a cave, where he lived in relative comfort, apparently laboring industriously in it, leveling the floor with paved stones. Sixty feet long, ten feet high, it made spacious living quarters.

If Bivens withdrew in many respects from society, he maintained a certain social consciousness. He was much upset by the great Panic of 1893, which threw three million persons out of work, and he was much taken by Jacob Sechler Coxey, better known as "General" Coxey, famed for leading his "army" of unemployed to Washington in 1894, demanding jobs through a public works program. Bivens liked very much the idea that workers involved in these construction jobs would be paid $1.50 a day, and he talked enthusiastically of joining the "army." He promptly gave up the idea, however, when he learned that he would be required to walk the whole way to Washington. By that time, he had been so identified with the Coxey cause that he was thereafter nicknamed "Coxey" Bivens; to this day his river refuge is known as Coxey's Cave.

Coxey remained there for another 18 years, until his death in

1912. Since caves in the area were overrun with snakes, it was a popular belief that Coxey had a cure for snakebite. More likely he simply developed an immunity after being bitten several times. He often carried rattlesnakes in his pocket and displayed them to passersby who requested the sight. Coxey realized other people were rather different than himself, "queer" by his standards.

When he died in September 1912, the *Narrowsburg Democrat* reported:

> The death of Joseph Bivens, of Narrowsburg, although occurring two weeks ago, is still being heralded in the county papers because of the peculiar life which he led. "Coxie" [sic] as he was called, was a man of good education but fell by the wayside like many another good man. He eked out a meagre existence working around the village and . . . had lived in a cave across the river from Narrowsburg. It was hardly a cave but simply an over-hanging rock with a few boards as a shelter. Last winter relatives induced him to live with them during the cold spell. He remained two weeks and then went back to his cave.
>
> The cause of his death was a fall he had from a tree which he was repairing with an iron band to keep it from splitting. He lived a number of days after the fall and seemed all right, when he suddenly passed away.
>
> Joseph Bivens, although down and out, was a man well respected by everybody in his home town. Well-educated and of good character, always willing and anxious to do a good turn for a friend, he will be remembered by all with a feeling of deep regret for his loss.

Coxey, as it developed, left his mark on Delaware Valley archeology. He "discovered" his cave, which was in fact more substantial than the above account makes out, but he was by no means the first resident there. In the 1920s, a Pennsylvania archeologist, Dr. Max Schrabisch, found a number of Indian artifacts in Coxey's cave, unearthed by Bivens. This led to general excavations at the site and, under the flat stones that Bivens had laid, hundreds of Indian relics were discovered. The arrowheads, potsherds, net sinkers, and Indian pipes unearthed made the cave one of the most prized archeological finds in the area.

As late as the 1950s, an impoverished family attempted to take up residence in Coxey's Cave, but the local welfare department soon rescued them instead. Coxey Bivens' ways were no longer to be tolerated.

Ketchum, Sam (1864–1899)

THE STUPIDEST OUTLAW

It would be grossly unfair, in a work that credits Black Jack Tom Ketchum (*q.v.*) with being one of the great eccentrics of western outlawry, to omit mention of his brother Sam, amazingly known as Black Jack's even less smart brother. While Black Jack Ketchum was in prison awaiting trial and execution, the leadership of the Hole-in-the-Wall gang passed by default to Sam Ketchum. Brother Black Jack had been caught after four times robbing the same train at the same spot in New Mexico. It turned out that planning robberies was not Sam's strong suit either, if he indeed had any. Undaunted, Sam came up with what he regarded as a surefire plan: he and the boys would hold up the same train at the same time for the *fifth* time.

Sam was mortally wounded in the attempt.

Creffield, Edmund Franz (1868–1906)

JOSHUA II

He was most definitely a prophet not to trifle with. When Edmund Franz Creffield came to Oregon, he declared he was on a mighty mission, searching for the Second Messiah. Quite incidental to that, he found time to shake up the city of San Francisco with a mighty earthquake. Certainly Joshua Elijah or Joshua II—the identity he appropriated for himself—believed in his mighty mission and his power to cause upheavals and so did a number of followers, virtually all of them women. The earthquake happened in 1906, but it was a long time coming. For a time Joshua Elijah was not only the sole prophet but also the sole communicant of his Church of the Bride of Christ.

Creffield had been born in Germany and come to America in

his teens. There he joined the Salvation Army, and by 1902 he was a commander of the group when he turned up in Corvallis, a rural village in western Oregon. Perhaps it was the climate but, for whatever reason, he transformed himself into Joshua Elijah Creffield with the avowed mission of fathering the Risen Christ. He expected to carry out this divine duty in Corvallis.

Feeling a need for charisma, he grew himself a beard that covered much of his face and let his hair flow down well over his shoulders. It may be that poor Corvallis was plagued by America's original hippie, but the townsmen had more to worry about than Joshua's appearance. The ladies, from matron to teenage girl, were just wild over Joshua. It turned out he was leading the women of the town in regular secret meetings in their various homes while their husbands were off at labor and the children at school or play. All this was of course to help Joshua find his new bride. There was a good deal of sermonizing from the Scriptures and the like, but invariably Joshua would shout, "Vile clothes, be gone!" and soon his devoted females were writhing naked on the floor. Teenage girls cut classes to take part in the meetings, and wives left dough unkneaded and meals unprepared. They were too busy all afternoon obeying Joshua's call to "Roll, ye sinners, roll!" There followed almost inevitably a closer inspection of his flock by Joshua in search of potential Mothers of Christ.

Such goings-on could not be long kept secret in a place like Corvallis, especially after four girls, ages 14 to 16, had to be shipped to the Oregon Boys and Girls Aid Society and a married woman committed to the state asylum at Salem. The townsmen figured out that mad Joshua was the source of all their woes, and a deputation called on him to get out of town. Creffield dismissed them with a wave of the hand, threatening to invoke God's vengeance. Apparently the men were impressed; at least they departed.

Joshua's meetings then turned wilder, and he took to leading 20 or so of his female followers to some river-bottom land south of town, where they could romp around in scenery more conducive to nudity and rolling away their sins. Alas, one day a photographer in the grass took some Brownie shots of exactly what was transpiring at these outdoor religious orgies, and soon well-fingered prints were circulated not only in Corvallis but in surrounding towns as well.

Suddenly Joshua noticed that quite a few of his followers weren't coming around much anymore. Distressed husbands and angry fathers shipped a number of women off to stay with relatives elsewhere. Joshua countered this by announcing he'd found himself a wife, Maude Hurt, daughter of a leading family. Slowly, the meetings got back into a regular swing.

Finally male sentiment reached the tar-and-feathering stage, and in January 1904 Joshua was duly dispatched from town, thoroughly pitched and feather-decorated.

There was however no keeping a good messiah down, and Joshua soon sneaked back and was uncovered in flagrante delicto with the wife of a prominent citizen. Joshua escaped a buckshotting, but the husband took out a warrant charging adultery, and Joshua's reluctant father-in-law, Victor Hurt, offered a $150 reward for his capture. Maude got a divorce.

Joshua remained at large three months until he was caught, bone skinny and dirty, hiding all the time right under the crawl space of the Hurt house. Several women had fed him scraps they smuggled out of their kitchens. He was put on trial on the adultery charge, convicted by a jury of men, and shipped off to the state prison for two years.

Joshua was released in December 1905 and moved to Seattle, where Maude Hurt soon rejoined him, and they remarried. They moved in with Mrs. Creffield's brother and his wife, Mr. and Mrs. Frank Hurt of Seattle. Joshua named Frank Hurt as the Gabriel of his movement and ordered him to establish a commune for the faithful at Waldport, on the Oregon coast.

Joshua also announced he had at last picked his Bride of Christ, 17-year-old Esther Mitchell, one of the prettiest and most obedient rollers back in Corvallis. He advised the men of Corvallis not to interfere or else he just might bring down the fury of his wrath on Seattle, Portland, Corvallis, and San Francisco. In fact, he said he'd be doing that soon anyway and advised all those wishing to be saved from the destruction to come to his Garden of Eden at Waldport.

Then Joshua himself headed back to Oregon. On April 18, 1906 the telegraph wires hummed with news of San Francisco smoldering in smoking ruins. Joshua was gleeful. "Didn't I tell you I would call down God's curse? This is only the beginning."

Quite naturally the converts started pouring into Waldport, led by Esther Mitchell. Other Corvallis women were restrained only because their menfolk locked them in their cellars. Some men grabbed their shotguns and headed for a showdown with Joshua. However, when they got to Waldport they discovered Joshua had fled, with his religious bride Esther, undoubtedly having been fortuitously forewarned from on high.

Early in May, young George Mitchell, Esther's brother, heard that Joshua had turned up in Seattle once again, and he headed there, a .38 tucked under his arm. George found Joshua standing on a street corner, stepped up behind him, pressed the revolver to his neck and pulled the trigger. The guru collapsed in a pool of blood, dead. Despite the protests from Esther and the Hurts that Joshua would soon arise, he was planted, very much dead, in Lake View Cemetery.

George Mitchell was brought to trial for killing Creffield, but the juicy tale of Joshua's sexual escapades guaranteed he would be found not guilty for killing his sister's lover. Applause ringing in his ears after the verdict came in, George headed for Union Station to catch a train back to Oregon. As hundreds of tourists watched, Esther Mitchell appeared at the train station and walked up behind her brother and shot him through the head.

She eventually was committed to an asylum while Maude Hurt took poison while awaiting her own trial. She had bought the gun Esther used.

In June all that remained at the Garden of Eden commune, five women and a baby, were found almost naked and near to starvation. They had been living on nothing but mussels. Somehow they hadn't heard that Joshua had gone to his reward. They were still waiting his return and were sure that he had already carried out his destruction of much of the outside world. They had to be forcibly shipped back to Corvallis.

That town for long thereafter remained on the alert for any invasion of outsiders. In 1936 the good burghers of the town even refused to allow Socialist presidential candidate Norman Thomas to speak there. They had had quite enough of prophets of any kind.

How, James Eads (1868–1930)

THE MILLIONAIRE HOBO

Few heirs who turned down a fortune were at the same time more ridiculed by many and applauded by some than James Eads How, who became known as the "Millionaire Hobo." How was the grandson of James Eads, the famed bridge builder, and when his mother, Eliza Ann Eads How, died she left him a quarter of a million dollars. Eads refused to touch the money, insisting that he believed it was wrong to live on money that one had not earned oneself.

Instead he took to the open road, becoming famed, or notorious some would say, as a tramp in threadbare clothing. He trekked almost exclusively by foot, although he "rode the rods" along with other hoboes; he made his way around the country working at whatever he could get.

In some places he was welcomed as a hero; but in others he was castigated for being a fool, and some folks denied him work, saying he was taking jobs from those in true need. He was arrested on a number of occasions for vagrancy, and sometimes escorted to a town's limits and told to leave.

At times How was found in dire physical shape for lack of food; this was not always caused by privation because of want of money. How also had the eccentric idea that any bodily ailment could be cured by total abstinence from food, and it was virtually impossible to shake him of this conviction. Whenever he was committed to a hospital for treatment for his condition, How refused to pay any bills, insisting he had no money of his own.

In 1930, How picked his way to Cincinnati, where an old family friend and attorney, Nicholas Klein, lived. He got as far as Union Depot in Cincinnati. There he fainted. Travelers' Aid called Klein to tell him a strange, unkempt man had passed out from hunger and was asking for him.

The puzzled Klein hurried to the station, only to find How sitting on a bench, stooped, his head bowed. His face was haggard and seamed, his laborer's clothes shabby and torn. "I scarcely recognized him," Klein said later.

Klein immediately rushed How to his home, fed him, and called a doctor. The doctor found How dying on the edge of starvation. After he was somewhat revived by food and sleep, he was able to talk and said he doubted he would live. He told Klein that was why he had come, to confer with him about making a will. How had managed to survive in a rich America, but now in a nation several months deep into the Great Depression, he had been unable to find work or food.

To his ex-wife he left only "whatever she may be entitled by law" (which proved to be negligible) and $5 each to a brother and stepson. He repeated this was not to demonstrate any disaffection toward them but because of his firm belief that no one should seek to live on inherited wealth, on money he or she had not worked for. The rest of his estate, he said, was to be set up in trust for "benefit and behoof of the workers of the World, especially for the education of the disemployed."

Ironically, because How had always rejected his inheritance, it had been kept in cash; thus it had escaped the great debacle of the stock market and had grown to over one million dollars. The Depression might well have killed How, but it had not damaged the fortune How had so detested.

Green, Ned (1868–1936)

THE PROFLIGATE SPENDTHRIFT

As the son of Hetty Green (*q.v.*), (America's greatest female miser), Ned Green never shared his mother's fondness for penny-pinching. During her lifetime, he managed to keep his spendthrift ways relatively under control. However, on inheriting half of his mother's $100 million in 1916, Ned, a six-foot-four-inch, 300-pounder with a wooden leg, gave to the term *cash flow* a new and torrential meaning. Until his death two decades later, he managed, in boom years or bust, to spend money at the phenomenal rate of $3 million a year.

Ned as a child knew the misfortune of lacking money, even though his mother, Hetty, was astoundingly rich. She hauled him to school in a cart and, in lieu of heavy clothing, stuffed his clothes with newspapers to keep out the biting wind. Because his mother was too stingy to pay for medical attention for him when he was

Profligate son of a miserly mother, Ned Green squandered $3 million a year in life and still left behind an estate so vast to result in a reduction of the Massachusetts tax rates. (Library of Congress)

involved in a childhood sledding accident, his knee became infected and eventually his leg had to be amputated.

Ned never seemed to exhibit any bitterness toward his mother because of her parsimonious treatment of him. During her final hours he tenderly eased her passing by bringing in trained nurses to minister to her. However, he insisted they attend her in street clothes rather than their uniforms. Nurses cost as much as one dollar an hour, and the loving son realized the thought of squandering such a sum would send Hetty into immediate death throes.

Hetty did allow her son some profligate activities while she was alive. Some said it was because of guilt feelings over Ned's loss of a leg. Thus, when Momma sent him to Texas to see what he could do on his own, running one of her railroads, Colonel Green—as he was known to the Texans who handed out such titles in direct proportion to one's bankroll—was soon soaring over the irons in a private Pullman car named Mabel (after a Chicago prostitute he was exceedingly fond of). Hetty had made Ned promise—at the pain of being disinherited—that he would not marry, and Ned agreed, contenting himself with a long string of mistresses, most recruited from the finest call houses of the era, including Chicago's fabulous Everleigh Club.

When Hetty died, Ned came into his own, launching on his great never-ending spending spree. Ned's business interests were far flung, and he was required to sit on numerous boards of Hetty's financial empire. Business affairs bored him, however, and he generally was silent during directors' meetings, speaking only to make motions to adjourn.

Ned Green had more serious matters of concern, ranging from stamp collecting (he had the world's largest collection), teenage girls (not the world's largest accumulation, perhaps, but a substantial one consisting of a few dozen, many of whom he promised to put through college; alas, most flunked out), racing automobiles, $1 million yachts, and diamond-studded chamber pots.

Jewelry was one of his greatest passions. Ned collected diamond-encrusted chastity belts as well as chamber pots. He often traveled with a diamond broker who acted as sort of a court jeweler so that he could make purchases, properly appraised, as the mood struck him. Quite commonly Ned would make his buys in a jewelry store, while his limousine was double-parked outside.

Within a month of Hetty's death, Ned married Mabel and ensconced her in a mansion in New Bedford, Massachusetts, her presence irritating the high-society neighbors almost as much as the blimp he kept moored to the property.

One of Ned's crowning ambitions was to own the world's largest private yacht and, unable to build because of the Great War, he sought to purchase vessels belonging to J. P. Morgan or Vincent Astor. Neither was willing to sell. In frustration Ned had to settle for a Great Lakes passenger boat named *United States*, which was available for $1 million. Although it had 5 decks and a displacement of 2,054 tons, Green was unhappy with its length of a mere 225 feet, less than either the Morgan or Astor models.

To amend this sorry defect, Ned had the vessel sawed in two and 40 additional feet added to the length at midship. The *United States* was equipped with the best of everything, its main cabin sporting an open fieldstone fireplace and its nine master suites, all lavishly furnished by John Wanamaker, having their own baths. The craft required a staff captain, a navigating captain, and a crew of 71. It took 660 tons of coal a year just to keep the fire lines and shower baths activated. Ned had his wish, the largest and costliest private yacht in existence, but the distinction didn't last long. Under circumstances never fully fathomed, the *United States* sank one day in 16 feet of water, while at its moorings. Ned trimmed his sails after that, acquiring a smaller vessel called *Day Dream,* which had sleeping accommodations for merely 70.

Ned was never fully accepted by high society. Some of his dinner parties consisted of his favorite food as a main course—oversized hot dogs—and his wine cellar was sniffed at by connoisseurs as, in the words of one, "simply dreadful." Still, Ned had no time for slights. He was the darling of the winter season in Florida, speeding into Miami, on the way handing out $20 gold pieces to every cop he saw (a practice that earned him special dispensations on traffic regulations).

He furnished a Mississippi showboat and threw lavish parties attended by hundreds of people he didn't know. Ned in the meantime busied himself with his various collections. It is to be lamented that death cut him off in 1936, when he had just started his newest passion, collecting whale penises, leading off with a most impressive 14-footer.

Oddly, despite Ned's mad expenditure of $3 million a year on yachts, girls, diamonds, hot dogs, and other sundries, his estate was still estimated at over $50 million and inheritance taxes to Massachusetts worked out to be well over $5 million—equal to all other inheritance taxes collected by the state from all other estates that year. This windfall allowed Massachusetts to pare its tax rates by 30 percent in 1939. It was a form of altruism that Hetty Green would never have abided, but her wastrel son was still squandering money in his grave.

Mallon, Mary (1868–1938)

"TYPHOID MARY"

In a sense Mary Mallon, who became known worldwide as "Typhoid Mary," was a genuinely pathetic eccentric. For almost two decades she was coinsidered the most dangerous woman in America, hounded by her fellow man, although she was guilty of no intentional wrong. Like the leper of old, she was branded unclean. She was simply a walking epidemic, her body swarming with typhoid germs, although she never showed any of the symptoms herself. From 1897 to 1915 she worked as a cook, from the New York area to Maine, and infected 57 people with typhoid, of whom at least three died. It was believed that her toll of infected and dead was probably greater, but that the illness was not always correctly diagnosed.

Her first known spreading of typhoid fever occurred in 1897, when the buxom blonde Irishwoman turned up as a cook for a well-to-do family in Mamaroneck, New York. Within a week and a half of her employment, every member of the household—the entire family and the servants—came down with typhoid. All save Mary Mallon, who disappeared before doctors could examine her.

For the next decade Mary moved from job to job as a cook in private homes or restaurants in New York and New England, and everywhere Mary went someone came down with typhoid and away she went. In 1906 she turned up in Oyster Bay, New York, working for another well-to-do family. One evening shortly after her employ, Mary Mallon made a lavish dinner for a number of guests; shortly thereafter several of them turned up in the hospital, sick with fever soon diagnosed as typhoid.

By that time, Mary Mallon had disappeared again, but she had been identified; within a year she was run down by public health officials in New York City. When Dr. George Soper, the city's sanitary engineer, explained to her that she was the first known typhoid carrier in the country and that he wished to have her submit to medical tests, she flew into a rage and sent him fleeing from her attack with a rolling pin and carving knife. Finally, five burly policemen came around and subdued her.

The case then became public knowledge, and she was dubbed Typhoid Mary by the press. She was hauled off to hospital isolation and subjected to a year of tests. It was found that she was indeed a carrier. The typhoid germs had most probably settled in her gall-bladder; removal of the organ might well eliminate her problem. Not being of a particularly scientific bent and feeling no pain from her gallbladder, Mary refused the operation.

In the meantime a public debate developed on the morality of keeping her incarcerated; she obviously had committed no crime. Hurriedly a number of states passed Typhoid Mary laws, which would prevent her from ever cooking within their jurisdictions. Finally in 1910, after a number of indecisive court battles, Mary won her freedom on condition that she refrain from working as a cook or engage in the handling of foods, and that she report to the city Health Department every three months.

Immediately on release Typhoid Mary disappeared, and for five years, frequently changing her name, she managed to elude health authorities. She went right back to working in kitchens, in-cluding stints at a Broadway restaurant, a sanitorium, and a Long Island hotel. On these occasions, she got away just before the au-thorities closed in. In 1915 there was an awesome outbreak of ty-phoid at the Sloane Hospital for Women. Twenty-five nurses and attendants were stricken, and two died. Mary was discovered to have been in the kitchen "spreading germs among mothers and babies and doctors and nurses like a destroying angel." She had fled but was soon recognized as a cook in a Long Island home, and she was taken into custody for the last time.

Typhoid Mary was sent to a hospital on North Brothers Island, which she was to leave only in death. For years she did nothing but brood and read books, but later on she was happy to be kept busy as a lab technician keeping records. Typhoid Mary died November 11, 1938, at the age of 70, after 23 years of confinement.

Jenkins, Florence Foster (1868–1944)

FIRST LADY OF THE SLIDING SCALE

One of the most fabulous concerts in the hallowed history of Carnegie Hall was staged October 25, 1944, a bright moment in the grim days of war. Performing was the noted coloratura soprano Florence Foster Jenkins, and so great was the demand for tickets that they were scalped at the then-outrageous price of $20 apiece. More than 2,000 lovers of music had to be turned away. It had been so at many of Madame Jenkins' public performances of the previous more than 30 years. Police often had to be called out to herd off gate-crashers at such events.

The remarkable aspect of it all was the fact that Madame Jenkins had a voice that was not even poor but downright preposterous. As one observer put it, "She clucked and squawked, trumpeted

Florence Foster Jenkins, the noted if controversial coloratura soprano, at the unveiling of a bust of herself. Of her singing, a *Newsweek* critic once noted, she "sounds as if she was afflicted with low, nagging backache." (Wide World)

and quavered." Critics could say that she could not carry a tune, that she was "the first lady of the sliding scale," that she lacked a sense of rhythm, and that her voice in reaching for high notes simply vanished from the hearing of the living, taking the audience to the upper registers and then over a precipice into sudden silence. As *Newsweek* commented, "In high notes, Mrs. Jenkins sounds as if she was afflicted with low, nagging backache."

Different audiences reacted in various ways to her performances. Some roared with laughter until tears rolled down their cheeks, while others sat in utter silence, according her unique voice an attention befitting the world's greatest singers.

Some may find it surprising then that many distinguished musicians and singers—including the great Enrico Caruso—held for her genuine affection and respect. Hers was the gentlest of all madnesses, one that was completely harmless, although tinged with something between ghastliness and magnificence. Her determination to sing was simply unquenchable. People may have inevitably laughed at her singing but, as one critic conceded, "the applause was real."

Born into a staid Wilkes Barre, Pennsylvania, banking family, young Florence Foster took music lessons and at the age of eight had a piano recital in Philadelphia. At 17, she asked to go abroad to seek a professional career in music. Father Foster, holding to the Victorian line that women belonged at home serving tea, refused. In anger, Florence eloped with a young doctor, Frank Thornton Jenkins. It was not a successful marriage, and they divorced in 1902.

Cut off from all aid by her father, she earned a bare existence as a teacher and pianist. In 1909 Father Foster died. He had not carried his anger to the grave, however, leaving Florence a large inheritance. Free of money worries for the rest of her life, Madame Jenkins in her forties launched a career in her first love, singing.

By 1912 Madame Jenkins staged her maiden concert, footing the entire costs herself, performing for society club women. She soon was performing regularly in Newport, Washington, Boston, and Saratoga Springs. The club women who rallied loyally to her were no doubt more tone-deaf than discriminating. However, it was all for a good cause. Madame Jenkins' recitals usually made considerable amounts of money, and the proceeds were given to needy young artists. Madame Jenkins also contributed much of her income to such causes. As a close friend said, "She only thought of making other people happy."

Her recitals soon attracted the attention of critics, and their first reactions were always moments of great note. In time some critics took to composing marvelously ambiguous reviews that added mirth to what were otherwise profoundly distressing experiences for them.

Madame Jenkins was in her element. She recorded her voice; such an original recording is today a collector's item. She was unrivaled in her live performances, all of which were staged with appropriate lavishness, bordering on the ridiculous. In one number, amidst a cascade of flowers and greenery, Madame Jenkins offered one of her favorites, "Angel of Inspiration," properly bewinged in an angel's outfit. For "Clavelitos," she wore a large red flower in her hair, a bright Spanish shawl, and fluttered an enormous fan. At the proper cadences, she also heaved handfuls of rosebuds upon the audience, sometimes getting so carried away by the spirit of it all that she tossed out the wicker basket as well. It was a sensational showstopper, and the ecstatic audience often applauded wildly for an encore. She would order an assistant to hurry into the audience to harvest the blossoms so the routine could be repeated.

At times, of course, the raucous laughter grew so intense that Madame Jenkins could not overlook it. She simply rationalized it as the work of boorish hoodlums acting on orders from singers afflicted with "professional jealousy," employing a sort of reverse claque system.

In 1943, at the age of 75, she was involved in a taxi collision and, for a time, entertained the thought of filing a lawsuit. However, she found the trauma had given her the ability to sustain "a higher F than ever before." Delighted, she sent the driver a box of expensive cigars instead and scheduled another performance.

In 1944, Madame Jenkins, urged on by her fans, made her grand performance at Carnegie Hall. At her age, she realized her career was nearing its end; such a recital would be the appropriate crowning achievement.

She offered all her grandest selections, although in "Clavelitos" she refrained from hurling the basket. Some reviewers felt it incumbent to mention such facts as "her singing was hopelessly lacking in semblance of pitch" or that "she was undaunted by . . . the composer's intent." However, on the whole, the reviews were extremely gentle and not without feeling. One noted "a certain poignancy to her delivery" and another wrote, "Her attitude was at all times that of a singer who performed her task to the best of her ability." Robert Bager of the *New York World-Telegram* perhaps summed it up best: "She was exceedingly happy in her work. It is a pity so few artists are. And her happiness was communicated as if by magic to her listeners who were stimulated to the point of audible cheering, even joyous laughter and ecstasy by the inimitable singing."

What really impressed most critics and virtually all of her audience was Madame Jenkins' ability to soften the ridicule and disarm derision. That she did so with remarkable, even touching, self-deception only enhanced her rapport with her listeners.

One month after her triumphant Carnegie Hall performance, Florence Foster Jenkins died, but in her three-decade career, she had long ago written her own epitaph. "Some may say I couldn't sing, but no one can say that I didn't sing." If the self-deception was not all encompassing, there was no doubt she was correct in her belief that her courageous singing brought extreme pleasure to her audiences.

MacFadden, Bernarr (1868–1955)

BODY LOVE MACFADDEN

Magazine publisher and health faddist, Bernarr MacFadden is proof of the axiom that yesterday's eccentric can be tomorrow's prophet. There is no doubt that MacFadden was a "nutball," as a former protégé, Walter Winchell, described him. Yet by the time he died, *Time* magazine, which never held him in too high esteem, did have to note that MacFadden was "the modern pioneer of such things as the low-heel shoe, the bed board, enriched flour, sunbathing, brief swimsuits and many of the foods known today to be richest in vitamins."

He more than anyone made people muscle- and exercise-conscious; he did more to curtail the sales of worthless patent medicines; and he above all changed the reading habits of the country. MacFadden was the inventor of confession and fact-detective magazines, as well as newspaper lonely-hearts and gossip columns. It was MacFadden who introduced to the world the new technique of peephole writing; he, after all, originated the column written by a young Walter Winchell, who had come up with a crackling kind of slanguage, which he was so proud of that he always read his col-

On his 84th birthday, Bernarr MacFadden, sporting a parachute halter and red long-johns, danced a jig on the west bank of the Seine after making a jump from a two-engined plane to prove his health theories. (Wide World)

umns aloud. MacFadden developed another top columnist, Ed Sullivan. His right-hand man was Fulton Oursler, who wrote of MacFadden in tones he later reserved for God in his bestselling *The Greatest Story Ever Told.*

At one point in the late 1920s, MacFadden owned 10 extremely profitable magazines, including *True Story, Physical Culture,* and *Model Airplane.* He was also the creator and publisher of the *New York Evening Graphic,* easily the worst newspaper in America, as well as nine other newspapers. He was by then worth an estimated $30 million.

Although he remained hale well into his 87th year—he attributed that mostly to the fact that he never saw a doctor (he called them quacks)—it was doubtful for a time that he would survive his childhood. He was born in 1868, of a consumptive mother and a father who was the town drunk. Ailing and believed to have tuberculosis, he ran away from home at 12. He soon saved up enough money to buy a pair of dumbbells and took up body-building. In 1898, MacFadden launched *Physical Culture,* his first and always favorite magazine. It proved to be an immediate success.

The press delighted in calling him "Body Love MacFadden." At his magazine offices, he sat at a desk in the middle of the floor while his editors labored on balcony levels above him. At any instant, MacFadden might pounce on top of his desk and lead his editors in required exercises; from his vantage point he could spot any slackers.

The *Graphic's* office always looked like the most unlikely place for a newspaper. It was also the mecca for the physical-culture nuts who followed MacFadden. Once, the staff arrived for duty, only to find characters hanging by their hair from pipes all over the place. It was a competition to see who was the man with "the strongest hair in the world."

The *Graphic* allowed MacFadden's wacky mind to run unrestrained. William Randolph Hearst, no amateur at the art of fakery himself, was outraged with the way MacFadden doctored photographs to illustrate ridiculous stories. Otherwise blasé New Yorkers pounced on certain issues of the *Graphic* when word went out that it was outrageously sexy that day. Newsboys promptly hiked the price of the two-cent paper to a nickel or even a dime.

Some typical MacFadden stories are best reflected by their headlines, such as:

- "I STABBED MY WIFE FORTY TIMES BECAUSE SHE KEPT LEAVING THE CAP OFF THE TOOTHPASTE"
- "I KILLED HIM, WHAT'LL I DO?" [The paper was deluged with suggestions from readers, almost all unprintable.]
- "I VIOLATED THE MORAL CODE OF STAMFORD"
- "I AM THE MOTHER OF MY SISTER'S SON"
- BEAT TWO NAKED GIRLS IN REFORM SCHOOL
- RICH RED DROPS FREE LOVE

The classic tale, still told in journalism schools, concerned a patient who escaped from a booby hatch and promptly raped a girl. The way the headline came up at the *Graphic*, it read: "NUT BOLTS AND SCREWS." MacFadden agonized for a half an hour but finally decided it wouldn't do. However, since he felt the copy editor who came up with that gem was really trying, he gave him a five-dollar raise on the spot.

MacFadden's competitors were incensed by his ethics and called his rag the *Porno-Graphic;* in truth it remained so bizarre that, although it sold well, it could not make money because advertisers avoided it. Not so with MacFadden's magazines. It was agreed that MacFadden instinctively grasped the lowest common denominator of public taste. Still, in eight years of publication, he lost $8 million on the newspaper.

In his magazines, he was accepted as one of the great arbiters on health matters. Many readers followed his advice, taking 20-mile hikes, eschewing breakfasts, steaks, and alcohol, and instead gobbling down nuts, raw carrots, and beet juice.

MacFadden's wife divorced him in 1930. Under his direction, she had provided him with four girls, conceived by following MacFadden's rules of sex determination. Then Body Love decided he'd like four boys. His wife provided three, then finally rebelled at his "no-doctors" rule. That finished *that* marriage.

There's no doubt that in later years MacFadden's fortune dwindled, drained by his physical-culture schemes and his penny restaurants, which he started on the basis that the cheapest foods were the best. MacFadden's overhead proved too high. In the 1940s he sold all his magazines.

MacFadden remained in the public eye however. When he was 80 he married a woman half his age and took her off to the wild rugged life. He celebrated almost every birthday after 80 by parachuting from an airplane at low altitude into some river. He did it in New York's Hudson River, and at 84 he took Paris by storm, dropping into the Seine. Amid cries of "Bravo, MacFadden!" he danced a jig and announced he'd continue his jumps every year "until I am 120 and then I'll try to live until I am 150.

He didn't make it though. In October 1955 he died of a cerebral thrombosis. But he was healthy till the day he died, and no doctor had ever laid hands on him in his adulthood, except for examinations he needed to get his pilot license.

MacFadden may have died just in the nick of time. He'd just about finished running through his $30 million. He was down to his last $50,000 or so in cash.

Connelly, James Leo "One-Eyed" (1869–1953)

WORLD CHAMPION GATE-CRASHER

A hobby that became a half-century obsession made a one-eyed former boxer named James Leo Connelly the acknowledged world champion gate-crasher. He lost an eye in a boxing accident at the age of eighteen, and thereafter he decided "to take me other eye and see the world." One-Eyed Connelly's world was mostly sporting events, later on, political conventions, and he boasted he saw every heavyweight championship fight since 1897, except for three that did not strike his fancy—all without paying, since he figured the sporting world "owed" him for the loss of his eye.

He crossed the United States 102 times on gate-crashing missions, also making forays into Australia and Europe. He pulled off his amusing, amazing tricks by posing as an ice man, carpenter, deliveryman, vendor, or whatever other role or dodge he found effective.

One-Eyed launched his oddball career in 1897, when he announced to New York friends that he intended to go to Carson City, Nevada, to witness the big championship bout between Bob Fitzsimmons and Gentleman Jim Corbett. When his friends laughed at the idea, since he was as usual dead broke, he made a number of bets that he could get to Nevada and furthermore get into the "big go" for free. Connelly made it to Carson City by riding the freights, then he approached promoter Dan Stuart with an awesome tale. He said he had been in a local saloon and overheard a couple of mean mugs plotting to bump off fight referee George Siler if the fight didn't go the way they were betting. "They're planning to plug him from ringside with a six-gun."

Promoter Stuart was terribly shaken and wanted to know if One-Eyed could identify the toughs. "Not by name," One-Eyed said, with a straight face, "but if I saw them again, I'd recognize them." Naturally the fight promoter went for the bait and gave him a choice seat with the idea that One-Eyed would point out the villains as soon as he spotted them. One-Eyed never did, but he thoroughly enjoyed the fight in which Fitzsimmons dethroned Corbett in 14 rounds.

After the fight, promoter Stuart was furious, realizing he had been conned by "a cocky Irishman," and his howl reached all the way back to Manhattan so that One-Eyed's cronies paid their wagers without protest. One-Eyed Connelly's reputation was made and, although promoters vowed to keep the great moocher out of their arenas, he continually outwitted them, just as he promised newspaper reporters he would.

In 1899 he crashed the match between Fitzsimmons and Jim Jeffries in Coney Island by parading through the gate with a case full of stage money. He gave a gateman a quick flash and announced, "Change for the box office."

Connelly never permitted his "business career" to interfere with his gate-crashing duties, mainly because he had no career, holding on to various jobs only long enough to gain a stake and to allow him to spend his summers as a park-bench sleeper. Occasionally, he did stints as an elevator operator, circus roustabout, waiter, newsboy, or steeplejack, all endeavors he instantly abandoned when there was an event he had to attend. The last named occupation stood him in good stead in Milwaukee once when, because the promoter had vowed to keep him out at all costs, he simply sneaked in during the night preceding the fight. He climbed to a girder well above ringside, lashed himself there, and went to sleep. When he was spotted during the ring contest, the fans gave him an enormous ovation. The promoter, by public demand, was forced to buy One-Eyed a steak dinner.

In 1908 Connelly stowed away aboard a ship to Australia for the title match between Tommy Burns and Jack Johnson in Sydney. He got caught and had to work for his passage, but this did not violate his gate-crashing rules. Once landed, he easily got into the fight by posing as a deliveryman lugging a huge carton marked "Boxing Gloves."

Shortly after World War I, he trekked to England for the bout between Joe Beckett and Georges Carpentier. He crashed it easily but then disaster struck. One-Eyed made it to ringside and, just as the fight started, he actually shook hands with the Prince of Wales, who was so amused by his exploit that he handed him a gold sovereign. Unfortunately, while Connelly was involved with royalty, his back turned to the ring, Carpentier scored a quick kayo; One-Eyed had crossed the ocean only to miss seeing the fight.

At the contest between Jack Dempsey and Carpentier in 1921 in Jersey City, Connelly was tossed out of 13 of 15 entrances, but he made it through the fourteenth. He recalled, "I borrowed a pail of coffee and a basket of sandwiches from the telegraph crew, and the gateman thought I was a vendor." With similar magic he crashed the Dempsey-Tom Gibbons battle in Shelby, Montana, in 1923, by pretending to be an iceman lugging an 80-pound block of ice through the door for the coolers.

As his fame grew, some promoters became reconciled to Connelly's inevitable presence. The legendary Tex Rickard once offered him a pass to a fight. One-Eyed rejected the offer as contrary to the rules of gate-crashing. Then, at the night of the fight, he slipped in and ensconced himself in Rickard's private box.

In the 1920s, One-Eyed's interest in public affairs perked up, and he took to crashing political conventions. At one Democratic nominating session, he easily got past security guards by carrying a door he had appropriated from a nearby cafe. In 1928, at the Democratic convention in Houston, Texas, Connelly was recognized by a cop who handcuffed him to a bench outside the convention hall. That was just raw meat to One-Eyed, who simply picked up the bench and paraded through the gate, explaining, "They want this on the speaker's platform."

Connelly's interests were not limited to boxing and politics. During the 1930s, he could be counted on each year to crash the Kentucky Derby, the big Indianapolis auto races, and the World Series. When, however, it was once suggested that he crash the Army–Navy football games, he was offended. "That wouldn't be patriotic," he sniffed.

In 1945, Connelly, by then in his mid-seventies, announced his retirement from the gate-crashing racket, describing it as a younger man's game. Over the next eight years of his life, he supported himself as a greeter at a saloon owned by friends, an elevator operator, and an usher at political and sporting events.

In Chicago's Wrigley Field, during the World Series between the Cubs and the Detroit Tigers, he stopped a suspicious character heading for a choice box seat.

"Who are you?" he demanded.

"P. K. Wrigley, Jr.," the man answered, producing identification showing him to be the owner of the Chicago team.

"That," the dubious Connelly declared, "is for the birds." He gave the man the bum's rush.

One-Eyed Connelly was fired for that one, proving to him that the angels were not on the side of the anti-gate crashers after all.

Lawson, Alfred William (1869–1954)

THE GREATEST

Alfred William Lawson, Supreme Head and First Knowlegian of the University of Lawsonomy, at Des Moines, Iowa, often estimated he was born ten or twenty thousand years ahead of his time, that much more advanced was he over the so-called thinkers of the 20th century.

His biographer, one Cy Q. Faunce, declares:

> To try to write a sketch of the life and works of Alfred W. Lawson in a few pages is like trying to restrict space itself. It cannot be done. . . . Who is there among us mortals today who can understand Lawson when he goes below a certain level? There seems to be no limit to the depths of his mental activities . . . countless human minds will be strengthened and kept busy for thousands of years developing the limitless branches that emanate from the trunk and roots of the greatest tree of wisdom ever nurtured by the human race.

Born some 20,000 years ahead of his time, self-proclaimed visionary Alfred W. Lawson, founder of the University of Lawsonomy, appeared before the U.S. Senate Small Business Committee. Lawson was little surprised that the logic of his "Suction and Pressure" theory eluded the congressmen. (Wide World)

Faunce was right about one thing—few mortals would understand Lawson, although the suspicion, based on writing styles, would not die that Faunce was really Lawson himself. There were a few thousand praises Lawson felt inhibited saying in the first person. Thus it was left for Faunce to announce, "The birth of Lawson was the most momentous occurrence since the birth of mankind."

Altogether, Lawson churned out more than 50 books and pamphlets in which he developed what he called the new science of Lawsonomy, perhaps best defined in his 1923 work, *Manlife*. The publishers of this tome declared: "In comparison to Lawson's Law of Penetrability and Zig-Zag-and-Swirl movement, Newton's law of gravitation is but a primer lesson, and the lessons of Copernicus and Galileo are but infinitesimal grains of knowledge." Lawson of course was the publisher of *Manlife*.

Lawson saw the cosmos as being without either energy or empty space; to him it merely was composed of substances of varying densities. Substances of heavy density simply moved toward those of lesser density through the actions of the two "great discoveries" of Lawson—Suction and Pressure. The underlying principle behind it all he called Penetrability. "This law was too far reaching for the superannuated professors of physics," Lawson wrote, ". . . but little by little the rising generations of advancing scholars have begun to grasp its tremendous value."

One thing these scholars would have to master, Lawson said, was the theory of Zig-Zag-and-Swirl; this he defined as "movement in which any formation moves in a multiple direction according to the movements of many increasingly greater formations, each depending upon the great formation for direction and upon varying changes caused by counteracting influences of Suction and Pressure of different proportions."

Actually some scientists grasped what Lawson was saying about Zig-Zag-and-Swirl, and Suction and Pressure, but they hadn't the vaguest idea of any significance to be applied to them. Lawson was annoyed, promising to devise a "Supreme Mathematics" for computing his complicated theses.

He never did, being almost totally obsessed with Suction and Pressure which, he said, governed all that happened in the universe. When a radio played, he said, one's ear sucked it up, hence sound. The eye sucked up light; the lungs oxygen; the mouth food. Excretion was a most important element in Lawsonomy, presenting pressure in its most efficient form. What was sex of course but the attraction of Suction (female) for Pressure (male)?

The most important suction apparatus of all, as far as humans were concerned, Lawson said, was the earth itself. He pictured the earth as a great sucking machine that absorbed, through a "mouth" at the North Pole, substances sent by the sun and gases from meteors. The earth was filled with arteries inside itself, which carried life-giving matter to all its parts, while "veins" flushed waste substances away. Eventually these wastes reached the South Pole— earth's anus. The wastes were then expelled by pressure. Some additional excretion was done away with through "volcanic pores" on the earth's surface.

Born in London in 1869, Lawson grew up in Detroit. Besides becoming the greatest scientist of the ages, he was also a professional baseball player for 19 years (never rising above the minor leagues), novelist, nutritionist, economist, and airplane enthusiast. His baseball career almost destroyed his life, he later said. He began to chase after money and, worse still, he became addicted to tobacco, liquor, and meat, three terrible vices according to Lawson. He paid the price: his teeth decayed and his health failed. When he was 28 he gave up all these vices with a superhuman effort. From then until his eighties, he was to assert he was in perfect health.

Lawson abandoned baseball in 1907, but he had not as yet gotten fully into Lawsonomy. He instead moved into aviation, where he had considerable impact. In 1908 he started the first popular aeronautical magazine, *Fly,* the premier issue of which showed on the cover a young woman soaring through the clouds on the back of a giant eagle. Lawson coined the word "aircraft." In 1919 he invented and built the world's first passenger airliner. There was considerable speculation that the thing would never fly, but Lawson himself piloted it round trip between Milwaukee and Washington. The following year he enjoyed considerable success with a 26-passenger version, the first with sleeping berths. Then one of his planes crashed, and his company did the same shortly after.

This sorry development left Lawson with all the time in the world to come up with Lawsonomy, and he devoted the rest of his life to his science—with brief sojourns into nutritionism and economics. He advised everyone to follow his example of gobbling down a dish of fresh-mown grass with every meal. During the Depression he attracted huge crowds with his crackpot Direct Credits Society, which proposed the use of "valueless money"—not redeemable for anything—as well as the cancellation of all interests on debts. Only such drastic action, he insisted, could cure the economic ills of the world, caused by the "pig-like maniacs known as financiers."

But all that fell to the wayside, compared with Suction and

Pressure and spreading the word about Lawsonomy. In 1943 Lawson formed the Des Moines University of Lawsonomy on the campus of the long-defunct University of Des Moines. The course of study ran 10 years and no other texts were used but the works of the master himself. Teachers were called Knowlegians, senior professors were labeled Generals, and Lawson was known reverently as Supreme Head and First Knowlegian.

Lawson insisted the school was nonprofit, but in 1952 he was hauled before the Senate's Small Business Committee. The members asked him to explain the huge profits he had made, which were based on the school buying and selling war-surplus machine tools "for educational purposes." It soon became clear to Lawson that he towered intellectually over all the senators, and that they could never hope to understand him. Somehow he got them talking about Lawsonomy, mechanics, and deep theories. Nothing much came of the Senate expose, but two years later Lawson sold off the university property to a land developer. By that time the school had 361 students, all studying at home. Lawson felt surrounded by treacherous enemies, but in the end, he said, he knew his ideas would triumph. Lawsonomy would spread, generation by generation, until a new species would be created—a super race who could communicate by telepathy (another form of Suction and Pressure) and would have great longevity. Lawson died that same year.

Voliva, Wilbur Glenn (1870–1942)

KING OF THE FLAT EARTHERS

The religious zealot and the pseudoscientist have one thing in common: they are extremely narrow-minded and opinionated. However, when one combines the traits of both the religious zealot *and* the pseudoscientist in one individual, the result inevitably moves to the point of insufferability.

A strong case can be made that Wilbur Glenn Voliva was the most insufferable crank in 20th-century America, a man with nothing short of a paranoid belief in his own greatness. He regarded those he disagreed with, or, more precisely, who disagreed with him, as "poor, ignorant conceited fools," and he boasted, "I can whip to smithereens any man in the world in a mental battle. I have never met any professor or student who knew a millionth as much on any subject as I do."

Voliva's claims to fame, one can see, were obviously manifold. He gained notoriety for running Zion City, a peculiar fundamentalist community in Illinois and certainly the foremost theocracy in America. He was outspoken on matters of science, knowing the secrets of how to live 120 years and being the leading "flat earther" of the early 20th century.

One might fault his scientific knowledge, but there was no doubt that Voliva understood how to become a millionaire out of religion. Ordained a minister in 1889, he had come to Zion City around the turn of the century to join the Christian Apostolic Church founded by another odd individual, the Reverend John Alexander Dowie (*q.v.*), a Scottish-born faith healer. Dowie, an arch-fundamentalist, set himself up as general overseer of his religious community; he personally owned everything, every house, factory, and church building in Zion City. Dowie saw in Voliva all the traits he admired in himself, and he made Voliva his chief aide.

Flat Earth theorist and zealot Wilbut Glenn Voliva challenged the world to prove the earth wasn't flat, but none took up the charge. Those who "accept the absurdities of modern geography," he said, "are straining at gnats and swallowing camels." (Library of Congress)

By 1905 the ambitious Voliva had forcibly removed an ailing Dowie from power, and for the next 30 years he ran Zion City with an iron hand. Most of its citizens, members of the sect, worked for Zion Industries, which sold the rest of "Godless" America everything from fine lace to fig bars.

Under Voliva, Zion City had stricter blue laws than any city in America. Tourists learned to avoid the area, since they faced instant arrest for such irreligious activities as smoking cigarettes or whistling on Sunday. Voliva did not exactly make it against the law for women to wear high heels, but he did want them shipped off to insane asylums. Among the banned in Voliva's fiefdom were tan shoes (a particular affront to his sensibilities), pork products, oysters, and doctors.

A baldish, paunchy, grim-faced man, Voliva seldom laughed about anything. "We are fundamentalists," he once said. "We are the only *true* fundamentalists." And Voliva, following Dowie doctrine, demanded complete literalness in acceptance of the Bible.

This of course led him to his firm belief that the earth was flat. Good-bye Columbus, Magellan, and all the others with their addled brains who did not understand the earth was really just a pancake—circular, it was true, but not spherical. The center of this pancake was the North Pole; the outer circumference was a solid wall of ice, which other people mistakenly called the South Pole. It was a good thing that that ice wall was there, Voliva explained, because otherwise all the oceans on the earth would spill over, and nitwitted explorers would sail right off and plunge into Hades. Poor Magellan just didn't understand he was simply sailing in a circle along the edges of the pancake, Voliva said, not unsympathetically.

It seemed odd to Voliva how much 20th-century man had regressed from the wisdom of the ancients who knew the stars really were much smaller than the earth and rotated around it. Voliva also knew better than to believe what the fool scientists said about the sun. As he and every one of his 10,000-member sect knew:

> The idea of a sun millions of miles in diameter and 91,000,000 miles away is silly. The sun is only 32 miles across and not more than 3,000 miles from the earth. It stands to reason it must be so. God made the sun to light the earth, and therefore must have placed it close to the task it was designed to do. What would you think of a man who built a house in Zion and put the lamp to light it in Kenosha, Wisconsin?

Voliva had yet to find an astronomer who knew the first thing about the sky, stars, and earth. They simply did not understand Voliva's scriptural and scientific tenets. In *Leaves of Healing*, the sect's periodical, Voliva wrote:

Can anyone who has considered this matter seriously, honestly say that he believes the earth is traveling at such an impossible speed? If the earth is going so fast, which way is it going? It should be easier to travel with it than against it. The wind always should blow in the opposite direction to the way the earth is traveling. But where is the man who believes that it does? Where is the man who believes that he can jump into the air, remaining off the earth one second, and come down to earth 193.7 miles from where he jumped up?

Each year Voliva took out an ad in Chicago and Milwaukee newspapers offering $5,000 to anyone who could prove to him that the world was not flat. Needless to say, no one ever did. Despite his scientific ignorance, or perhaps because of it, Voliva remained an absolute power in Zion City. But by 1935 other churches began to get in, and he started losing some of his influence. Perhaps this was because he had proved to be rather off the mark in his predictions of the end of the world. He variously set the date of doom in 1923, 1927, 1930, and 1935, with nothing at all happening. Even his death in 1942 must have come as a bit of a shock to him. His special diet of buttermilk and Brazil nuts meant that he would live to be 120, he told his followers, many of whom munched along with him.

Today Zion City still sports some who remember and honor Voliva, but many of the women now wear high heels, lipstick, and short skirts. Some even smoke. Yet it may still be regarded as a bastion of the forces of Middle America. To Voliva, however, it would undoubtedly seem a modern Sodom or Gomorrah.

Stuyvesant, Augustus Van Horne (1870–1953)

THE LAST STUYVESANT

There is something about several million dollars that seems to bring out the exuberant in most people, but there is the occasional rich recluse who shuts the world out from his or her life. Usually the reason for such behavior is deep-seated: a fear of society, a contempt for one's fellow man, a broken or grieving heart. In the case of A. Van Horne Stuyvesant, the last direct descendent of wooden-leg Peter Stuyvesant, the autocratic, strong-willed Dutch governor of New Amsterdam, it was said to be simply a matter of shyness. He was, at least after his late forties, almost totally withdrawn from life. Whenever he met anyone, especially women, he was painfully ill at ease, unable to look the person in the eye.

He cut quite a picture in his sober, faintly pin-striped suit, high white collar, bow tie, black oxfords, and sweeping white mustache as he strolled, almost always alone, near his mansion at Fifth Avenue and East Seventy-ninth Street in New York. The only other place he was ever seen during the last few decades of his life was the old Stuyvesant family church, St. Mark's-in-the-Bouwerie, at Second Avenue and East Tenth Street. He would emerge from a handsome Rolls-Royce town car every second or third Sunday and visit the family vault. Eventually he would be the eighty-fifth and last interment there. He would pause to read the old inscription:

> In this vault lies buried
> Petrus Stuyvesant
> Late Captain General and Governor
>   in Chief of Amsterdam
> In Nieuw Netherland now called New York
> and the Dutch West Indies.
> Died A.D. 1673
> Age 80 years.

Here all the Stuyvesants were buried, including most recently his two sisters, Katie in 1924 and Annie in 1938. After paying silent homage, Van Horne strolled about the church graveyard for a few hours, studying the various markers. Then he returned to be ushered into the Rolls by a chauffeur dressed in plum-colored livery.

Either shyness or contempt spurred millionaire recluse A. Van Horne Stuyvesant to keep society only with his family. He survived his sister Anne (pictured with him) and ventured from his Fifth Avenue mansion only to visit the family vault. (Wide World)

Driven back uptown, he would be seen on a regular basis the rest of the time only by his servants. Possibly his only other social contact, besides sitting silently at services in either St. Mark's or St. James churches, was in 1941 when Parks Commissioner Robert Moses induced him to emerge into public long enough to unveil a statue of Peter Stuyvesant in Stuyvesant Square Park. Van Horne had no occupation, but he dabbled in real estate anonymously through brokers and lawyers, building up his fortune.

Both Van Horne's sisters were more outgoing than their brother, but they lived with him throughout their lives, never marrying or even bringing in friends out of respect for his privacy. Both left their shares of the Stuyvesant fortune to him. All three had agreed that, with his passing, all their money would go to

St. Luke's Hospital for the establishment of a Van Horne Stuyvesant Memorial Hospital for the poor living on former Stuyvesant
farmland.

The mystery of Van Horne's withdrawal from social contact
quite possibly is as tantalizing as that of the newspaper mogul's
dying word, "Rosebud," in the film classic *Citizen Kane*. Was Van
Horne's retirement and shyness simply an attempt to recapture a
lost innocence, something a new world and a changing New York
City would not permit? His withdrawal began with a "new" menace
to society after the war—the rise of the dreaded Bolshies and the
attendant Red scares. Shortly before the millionaire's death, a butler may well have inadvertently revealed to a journalist the secret to
his master's reclusive existence. "All Mr. Stuyvesant does," he revealed, "is sit in front of a picture of Franklin D. Roosevelt and
cuss."

By that time, "That Man in the White House" had been dead
some seven years. Still Van Horne had not forgiven FDR. He remained the symbol of the forces, one psychiatrist suggested, that
were trying to strip the last of the Stuyvesants of his only means of
protection in a hostile world—his fortune.

Poillon, Charlotte (1870–?) and Katherine (1872–?)

STRONG-ARMED PINUPS

Today perhaps the Poillon sisters, Charlotte and Katherine, would
not be considered sex symbols by anyone except fans of lady wres-
tlers. They were large, imposing, hard-bellied women scaling in at
210 and 200 pounds respectively, and indeed Charlotte had once
gone a bizarre four rounds with heavyweight champion Gentleman
Jim Corbett. But around the turn of the century there was something to the Poillon charm.

It was an era not completely taken with the wispy beauty of the
Floradora and Gibson Girls, and the pages of such arbiters of female pulchritude as the *Police Gazette* offered pinups of girls, including the Poillon sisters themselves, who might now be regarded

as cow-eyed, heavy of jowl, and thick of limb; but at the time they represented beauty at once stimulating, daring, exciting, and spicy. The Poillon sisters were all that and, some would say, rather punchy besides.

The yellow press, from Pulitzer and Hearst to Richard Fox's *Police Gazette*, reveled in reporting the romantic and often bizarre capers of the maidens Poillon. Both had escaped stormy marriages, probably to the delight of their spouses, to become the titantic sweethearts of Broadway—and they were quite prepared to beat the hell out of a gent who thought otherwise.

Their idea of being star-eyed romantics was to befriend rich, elderly men and talk them into engagements. When they turned to crude behavior and the men subsequently tried to break off with them, they sued for breach of promise. In 1903 they sued wealthy William G. Brokaw for $250,000, and they got $17,500 when they promised not to drag him through the courts. This was a rather hefty settlement in a time when a dollar was worth many times what it is today.

The sisters haunted the better hotels and restaurants stalking lovers and victims. Their behavior was enough to provoke protests from other tenderhearted guests. In 1907, when a hotel manager reprimanded them for flirting with married guests in company of their wives, the sisters hurled him down a flight of stairs. They did the same to another hotel manager, who they felt had overcharged them. This put them in the prisoners' dock and in the newspapers.

There were many such incidents. In 1909 they were evicted from New York's Hotel Willard for another breach of etiquette. It took three bellhops and three other men to wrestle Charlotte out to the street—but not before she decked all three bellhops. Charlotte on another occasion was similarly evicted from Charley Rector's, a posh Broadway restaurant, in 1912. She sued for $25,000 but lost. Rector's rather frightened maitre d' testified that the lumbering lass had entered the establishment dressed as a man and had not been interfered with until she slammed two waiters to the floor as she bulled her way to a table reserved for other diners. When Charlotte left the court, she added her booming voice to the feminist cries by observing, "It's a d----- man's world!" The censorship belongs to the press of the day.

As late as the 1920s, when the sisters were in their hefty fifties, they continued to make love-nest headlines. In some cases the men claimed they had been too frightened to reject the sisters' attentions. In 1923 an elderly businessman, for a time smitten with both sisters, charged them with fraud after they trimmed him of several thousand dollars. The Poillons refused to enter a plea. They sat in court cutting up paper dolls and making anti–Semitic remarks about their Jewish lawyer. When the judge banged his gavel, Charlotte responded by battering the defense table with her fist. Remarkably, the sisters' lawyer still won the case.

By the late 1920s, with both sisters in their late fifties, the sisters dropped out of the romantic news. There were reports that they had each married and settled down, or that they had jointly trotted off to a mental institution. In any event they vanished from view except for a brief return to the limelight by Charlotte in 1929.

A New York City department store had set up a promotion exhibit on the street with a prizefighter working out with a punching bag. Suddenly Charlotte exploded out of the crowd, proclaiming the boxer to be "a bum" and shoving him aside. She took over lambasting the punching bag and was hired to replace the male pugilist. Charlotte kept punching for about three weeks, and then she disappeared again.

A romantic era had ended.

Smith, William (c.1870–?)

THE FUTURE MAYOR OF CHICAGO

A young black dandy, thief, and gambler, William Smith provided Chicago politics with one of its lighter moments. In the 1890s, he fully expected to become the city's first black mayor and chief pimp at one and the same time. Hattie Briggs, one of the most notorious, hard-driving, and sometimes softheaded black madams of the Little Cheyenne vice area, became infatuated with Smith and showered him with money. She set him up in a fancy saloon and announced she had great plans for her "loving man."

Smith promenaded around Little Cheyenne in lavender pants, white vest, yellow shirts, bright blue coat, patent-leather shoes with white spats, all topped off with a silk hat. His shirtfront gleamed with diamond studs, his fingers with diamond rings, and he carried a gold toothpick behind his ear—all gifts from Madam Briggs.

Smith also carried four different colored pencils in his vest pocket and kept a liveried messenger boy in ready attendance to deliver his important epistles. Sometimes he scribbled a note to Hattie demanding a thousand or so for pocket money, which resulted in immediate compliance.

Smith's problems arose because he also authored a number of letters to the mayor and the chief of police, some of which actually got to City Hall, where they caused a mixture of bafflement, wonder, and outrage. Smith would note that the payment of protection money required a more immediate response to the desires and needs of the saloon keepers and brothel owners of the city.

Hattie Briggs was not unamused by her precious pet's actions and urged him on, catering to his every whim. Hattie announced to her cohorts of Little Cheyenne that she was making so much money, she was going to buy up all the saloons and brothels in Chicago, and have Smith elected mayor. This prophecy caused Smith to dance wildly about in anticipation. He announced that his first official act would be to abolish the police force, replacing it with bouncers from all the leading brothels.

Such announcements by Smith made him a delight in most vice circles, but to the police he was considered an affront. They resented his grandiose claims of political influence and saw nothing remotely entertaining about efforts to separate them from their graft. As a result in April 1892, the annoyed police descended on Smith's lavish dive and tore it apart, damaging Smith as well in the process.

For his troubles Smith was fined a hundred dollars for disturbing the peace, and in time his saloon license was revoked. Thereafter they arrested Smith three or four times a day, and when Hattie Briggs protested, they gave her the same treatment, no longer concerned with the years of protection money coming from her.

Soon she and Smith were being picked up 10 or even 20 times in a 24-hour period. Eventually the harassment became so unbearable that Hattie packed up her girls, her bedding, and other furnishings, and relocated across the state line.

William Smith came along but, despite Hattie's consolations, pouted about having lost the mayoralty after her lavish promises. Not even several new wardrobes pacified him; according to one version circulating in Chicago vice circles, William absconded with two of Hattie's most prized "boarders," who promised to "do right" by him ever after. Hattie Briggs was said to have been heartbroken about her lost lover who was never heard of again.

Wilks, Sylvia Green (1871–1951)

HETTY GREEN'S DAUGHTER

It is to the eternal credit, or at least distinction, of Hetty Green (*q.v.*) that unlike so many other eccentrics she begat two others. Her children, Ned and Sylvia, went on to their own dubious fame of being in the same strange league with their mother.

Son Ned turned out to be the complete spendthrift, running through his share of Mama Green's fortune at the rate of $3 million a year. A wag once said Ned simply didn't like money. Sylvia Green Wilks did like money. In fact she adored it, and indeed she held on to most of what she got and became one of the world's richest women, being worth more than the Queen of England or the combined wealth of two of America's most famed heiresses, Doris Duke and Barbara Hutton. On a comparative basis, she was worth more in ready cash than even the Aga Khan. She had so much cash that she kept $31 million in a non-interest-bearing checking account in New York's Chase National, a fact that kept the bank's executives in a state of constant anxiety for fear that one day she would march in and demand instant payment.

As much as Sylvia liked money, she didn't like people. She may not have been a total recluse—indeed she could show up for spirited court battles when a fortune was involved—but she could disappear from sight for months or years at a time, totally uncaring about the society of her fellow beings.

Part of Sylvia's behavior—shy, untrusting, ungraceful—was traceable to the teachings of Mama Hetty, who lectured her on the evils of fortune hunters, the contesting of wills, and the worthlessness of lawyers. For fear of fortune hunters, Hetty made her son promise never to marry while she was alive. But she withdrew that stipulation as it concerned Sylvia when the daughter was 38, enabling her to marry 63-year-old Matthew Astor Wilks in 1909. Wilks was, after all, the great-grandson of John Jacob Astor and a millionaire in his own right. Of course Wilks did have to sign a prenuptial agreement giving up any claim to Sylvia's money. The reverse was not true. When Wilkes died in 1926, Sylvia picked up a considerable additional fortune from his estate, including the $5,000 Hetty had willed her son-in-law in order to reward his good grace in signing the original marriage contract.

What few friends Sylvia had agreed she had become almost as

penny-pinching as her mother. Having been constantly bombarded with lectures on the joys of frugality for years in a dismal Hoboken flat where she waited on miserly Hetty, sewing, cooking, and doing the dishes, this is not surprising.

Sylvia did hire a vast number of servants, clearly a reaction to her years of manual serfdom, but otherwise she kept a tight rein on expenditures. An enquiring New York reporter once estimated her fortune thusly: $30 to $45 million in New York City mortgages; $40 to $60 million in nontaxable municipal bonds and industrial securities; $10 million in farming and oil tracts; and $10 million in real estate.

Neighbors in Massachusetts around the various Green–Wilks mansions had plenty of tales to tell about Sylvia's bizarre behavior. Sometimes, despite her reclusive character, she felt impelled to visit neighbors, but she walked about in such slovenly dress that on several occasions the woman of the house thought she was a beggar or peddler and did not open the door. At other times she would call on a neighbor for a cup of coffee, wearing a ravishing fur coat over a common housedress.

Sylvia was capable of breaking with her mother's firm rule against charity. She once donated the site of her father's old home in Bellows Falls, Vermont, to the community for a park as a memorial. She had the mansion bulldozed, which upset many in Bellows Falls since it had been a local landmark, having been built in 1804. One citizen asked Sylvia why she had not given the home to the town to be used as a community house. She responded sourly, "Why don't you give yours?" It was a long time after that before Bellows Falls was found deserving of any further charity from Sylvia.

If Sylvia's good deeds toward humans were limited, she set a different value on animal life. She kept a number of collies and doted over them, much as Hetty Green did for a pet terrier. Sylvia's main affection however was for birds. If a tree on any of her estates had to be chopped down or was struck by lightning, Sylvia had a birdhouse erected on the stump so that any birds living there would not be dispossessed. She had a chart picturing various species of birds hanging in her living room and could readily identify any bird flying over the estate.

Probably the most vivid picture New Englanders had of Sylvia was the black-clad recluse showing up in New Bedford with four armored cars some time after her brother died in 1936. As the four-car convoy sped through New Bedford, the town's entire police force joined in escort. At South Dartmouth more police joined the convoy as it continued on to Round Hill, where Ned Green had lived. It took four hours to load up the cars at the mansion, with a platoon of gun-drawn guards discouraging the curious from coming near. Then the convoy sped off.

Sylvia had picked up her inheritance of Ned's $20 million gem collection. She had little interest in diamonds and virtually all of the collection was sold off, including Ned's prized diamond-studded chastity belts. What Sylvia did with her brother's famed library of erotica was not determined. One theory was that she personally burned it.

If Sylvia could shake off the influence of her late brother, she could not as readily dismiss the ghost of the long-gone Hetty Green. Hetty might well have kicked up in her grave at the thought of her daughter spending $11,000 a year for a penthouse apartment on New York's Fifth Avenue, but she would have been partially pacified by the fact that Sylvia hauled with her much of Hetty's old and dilapidated furniture. In 1940 Sylvia traded in her penthouse for two lower-floor apartments—one on the third floor where she lived and one on the fourth for the old Green furniture.

Sylvia also occupied the same office space at 111 Broadway that Hetty had used for years, and she dabbled there in various types of financial paper. She had an office manager who kept her out of direct contact with bond salesmen and with charity solicitors of all sort. Hetty had never given a dime to charity, and Sylvia in her later years pretty much maintained that policy. When Sylvia died on February 5, 1951, she had no really close relatives. Her estate after taxes came to more than $90 million. It went to 63 charities. Her mother might not have even guessed there were so many.

Schmidt, William Henry "Burro" (1871–1954)

THE HUMAN MOLE

Stricken with tuberculosis at the age of 24, William Henry Schmidt went west in 1895, to improve his health and, he hoped, to strike gold. He was successful in both goals. Although he remained frail of body, the clear air of California's El Paso Mountains did wonders for his breathing. And after a decade of prospecting he found a vein in Copper Mountain, near Randsburg.

The trouble was, Schmidt decided, there was no sense in working the claim until he could tunnel through to the far side of the mountain, where he could pick up a road to the smelter. With the aid of two burros, Jack and Jenny, he started his gigantic undertaking of cutting through a half mile of solid granite in 1906, using only hand tools and dynamite when he could afford to buy some. "Burro" Schmidt, as he became known, labored around the clock, seven days a week, sleeping only whenever fatigue overtook him.

His project passed from necessity to obsession; in time, progress came to the mountains after all, and road and rail links connected the two sides of the mountain, making Burro's efforts needless. But Burro wasn't about to quit; his fight was with "that damn rock," and he intended to win it. Foot after foot, year after year, Schmidt burrowed onward, bringing out 2,600 cubic yards of rock. Well-wishers, many of whom admittedly thought him crazy, showed up from time to time with gifts of food and supplies. College pranksters once stole all his tools, but a Good Samaritan bought replacements. In 1938, 32 years after he had started digging, he hit daylight: he had tunneled through 1,872 feet of rock.

The press, the curious, and even the professional geologists came to marvel at Schmidt's grand obsession. The one-track-minded prospector had beaten his mountain, and he was lionized by Robert "Believe It or Not" Ripley. The fame came in handy, considering the fact that his vein turned out to be of limited value. However, encouraged by a business promoter, Schmidt turned his tunnel into a tourist attraction and lived quite well on the revenues until his death in 1954. Nobody thought him crazy anymore, a little eccentric maybe, but not crazy.

Fort, Charles (1874–1932)

THE ENIGMA

It has never been easy to chronicle the career of Charles Fort, and to this date there is no adequate biography of him, only the weak efforts of profilers who generally present him as an enigma. Was he a hopeless crank, a tantalizer of the human mind? Or was he a practical joker carrying off what writer Ben Hecht called a "Gargantuan jest," never believing one iota of his own wildly insane "hypotheses"?

He wrote four books that espoused his theories of "Fortean Science." Theodore Dreiser, a lifelong friend who considered Fort a true genius, found them "full of marvelous data of the most mysterious and provoking character, all of which has been deliberately ignored by the scientists." Fort in fact presented the kinds of theories loonies embrace. No doubt he would have reveled in the modern U.F.O. craze had he lived.

Fort, a large, retiring, bearlike man with thick glasses and a walrus mustache, spent the last 26 years of his life in the British Museum and in public libraries, collecting notes and clippings that filled cubbyholes and shoeboxes in his apartment in the Bronx. These told stories of happenings that science often could not explain, such as black rains; ice falling from the sky; the appearance of Chinese seals in Ireland; eerie lights in the heavens; lost planets; frogs, crabs, and blood falling from the sky; unexplained disappearances; people bursting spontaneously into flames; all poltergeist tales.

After ridiculing the explanations of organized science, he came up with his own. Fort had no doubt that there was a universe parallel to the one we see, and he suggested that the earth may well only rotate once a year. Was this so amazing, he wondered, since it was obvious to all that God "drools comets and gibbers earthquakes." The stars, he suggested, were not actually bodies in space but mere apertures in a gelatinous shell that surrounded earth, and that what we saw was light shining through those holes. He warned aviators to mind their flying, else they ran the dire risk of becoming "stuck like currants" in it.

Above us was a sort of super sargasso sea, in which had been collected rubbish blown from earth and other planets over the eons.

He argued that also in the sky were fields of ice as big as those floating in the Arctic Ocean, and thus we have winter. Then too there were huge fields of water and vast expanses of land covered with caterpillars drifting above us. How else explain the many instances of caterpillars raining down on earth, which his research had discovered?

Fort would have nothing to do with such conventional explanations of the well-authenticated instances of red rains as that they were the result of reddish-colored dust becoming mixed with water. Why not one of the following:

> Rivers of blood that vein albuminous seas, or an egg-like composition in the incubation of which the earth is a local center of development—that there are super-arteries of blood in Genesis-trine; that sunsets are consciousness of them: that they flush the skies with northern lights sometimes. . . .
>
> Or that our whole solar system is a living thing: that showers of blood upon this earth are its internal hemorrhages—
>
> Or vast living things in the sky, as there are vast living things in the oceans—
>
> Or some one especial thing: an especial time: an especial place. A thing the size of the Brooklyn Bridge. It's alive in outer space—something the size of Central Park kills it—
>
> It drips.

Fort was amused that science had no explanation for reports of persons standing in clear view in the middle of the road one moment and vanishing forever from human view the next. He noted that Ambrose Bierce disappeared in Mexico at the very same time that Ambrose Small did in Canada. Was it not logical that someone up there was collecting Ambroses?

When Dorothy Arnold, a celebrated society heiress, disappeared in 1910 in New York City, the police staged an intensive hunt but never found a trace of her. How could they, Fort asked; they had never checked up on the significant fact that a white swan appeared on a pond in Central Park at approximately the spot she would have reached had she gone in that direction. It was elementary.

Fort grew up in Albany, New York, in an unhappy family in which his mother died when he was four. He was often mistreated by his father, and he left home in his teens. A poor student, he nonetheless made an interesting writer. At 17 he was selling features to a New York syndicate and the *Brooklyn World*. Later he had a job on a Queens newspaper until it folded. Then he traveled around the world on the cheap, almost ending up on a chain gang in the American South and contracting malaria in Africa. When he returned to the United States he married Anna Filing, an Englishwoman.

They lived in abject poverty at first, constantly parading in and out of pawnshops, even breaking up chairs to use for firewood. Fort worked at odd jobs and finally started selling stories to newspapers and magazines. Dreiser published some in his *Smith's Magazine,* and he became Fort's lifelong admirer.

In 1905, Fort began collecting his notes on strange happenings. Shortly thereafter he inherited a small fortune that left him free to pursue his chosen task full time. He and his wife shuttled between New York and London so that Fort could continue his research at the British Museum. The first book on his research, *The Book of the Damned,* appeared in 1919. Dreiser had taken the manuscript to his own publisher, Horace Liveright, and announced it would have to be brought out or he (Dreiser) would take his own writings elsewhere.

Over the next 13 years, three more Fort books appeared—*New Lands, Lo!,* and *Wild Talents.* All were jammed with showers of periwinkles and frogs, bleeding statues and paintings, poison fogs, showers of beeflike substances, as well as with deluges of stone wedges and even cannonballs. In a foreward to *New Lands,* Booth Tarkington was thrilled by the author's power to describe "cyclonic activity and dimensions."

It must not be inferred that the public snapped up Fort's work. The books sold in underwhelming numbers. However, many literary figures embraced Fort's works, including—besides Tarkington and Dreiser—novelist Tiffany Thayer (Fort's closest friend and, except for Dreiser, perhaps his only one), Ben Hecht, Jon Cowper Powys, Edgar Lee Masters, Burton Rascoe, and Alexander Woollcott. In 1931 these writers and other interested parties formed the Fortean Society: to expound Fort's theories to confound and bait the scientific world. Fort himself refused to join, since he was a believer in absolutely nothing, not even his own absolute truths.

He just spent his every moment collecting more facts. Even after he died in 1932, Fort continued to spark vociferous debate over what he stood for. Thayer, who in 1937 started publishing the *Fortean Society Magazine,* which later became *Doubt,* insisted "Charles Fort was in no sense a crank. He believed not one hair's breadth of any of his amazing 'hypotheses'—as any sensible adult must see from the text itself. He put his theses forward jocularly—as Jehovah must have made the platypus and, perhaps, man. . . ."

One must wonder then, as Martin Gardner did in *Fads & Fallacies in the Name of Science,* a classic study of pseudoscientism, how Fort could spend a quarter century "on such 'minor tasks'—as he once described it—of going through twenty-five years of the *London Daily Mail?* The answer is that more meaning than meets the eye lurks behind Fort's madness."

Gardner saw Fort as a Hegelian. He was apparently much impressed by Fort's observation that "I think we're all bugs and mice and are only different expressions of an all-inclusive cheese." Clearly though, Gardner was not comfortable dealing with Fort, starting off a chapter on him with a certain resignation: "Sooner or later in this book, we shall have to come to terms with Charles Fort."

Others have tried to as well. Ben Hecht, reviewing Fort's first book, declared, "Charles Fort made a terrible onslaught upon the accumulated lunacy of fifty centuries. . . . He has delighted me beyond all men who have written books in this world. . . . He has shot the scientific basis of modern wisdom full of large, ugly holes."

Hecht of course meant little of that. Woollcott held Fort "to have been one of the most magnificent mentalities of modern time." Was Woollcott being any more straightforward than H. L. Mencken, who wrote the United Press following Fort's death, "Your story describing the funeral of Charles Fort lists me as one of his customers. This was a libel of a virulence sufficient to shock humanity. As a matter of fact, I looked upon Fort as a quack of the most obvious sort and often said so in print. As a Christian I forgive the man who wrote the story and the news editor who passed it. But both will suffer in hell."

Despite such disputes Forteans still thrive today. *The Fortean Times,* published in London, is filled with such stirring items as "The Nonstop Toilet of Leek Street," which details the sad fate of Delores Goodyear and family. They have been flushed out of the home in Leek St., Leeds, England. Ever since the family moved into their council maisonette three years ago, the toilet has driven them clean round the bend by repeated flushing itself and flood their home. The family have been rehoused while workmen attempt to solve the riddle. Sentient malice is hinted at in hushed tones: 'For no reason at all it would start flushing, and not know when to stop. It has ruined carpets, lifted tiles, and made the house very damp. It's been a nightmare.' All the obvious causes seem to have been explored, and so the plumbers will resort to their more drastic arts. . . . If thy throne offends thee, pluck it out."

Forteans are amused at these foolish plumbers for failing to see "a connection with poltergeistery." And still the enigma of Fort and Forteanism remains.

Gillette, George Francis (1875–?)

THE EINSTEIN CHASER

Probably the gravest professional insult pseudoscientist George Francis Gillette ever suffered, at least from his viewpoint, was the supreme slight of being held inferior to Albert Einstein. All Einstein had was the theory of relativity while Gillette had his "spiral universe." The short shrift his theories got from the scientific world made Gillette livid with rage, and his adult life was spent on an "Einstein Must Go" campaign.

"Einstein a scientist?" Gillette wrote in one of his privately printed books. "It were difficult to imagine anyone more contrary and opposite to what a scientist should be. . . . As a rational physicist, Einstein is a fair violinist." And as for that bit of nonsense called relativity, that was "voodoo nonsense," "utterly mad," "cross-eyed physic," "the nadir of pure drivel," and a "moronic brain child of mental colic," to Gillette.

The personal history of Gillette is rather hazy beyond the bare fact that he attended the University of Michigan and held engineering positions with several firms. More importantly he wrote four books. In them, Gillette informed his readers that Newton was his kind of scientist, although he modestly had to observe that his spiral universe theory was an improvement on Newton; in fact it "out-Newton's Newton."

Since nobody else has ever quite grasped the full meaning and import of the spiral universe—although the Forteans (q.v. Charles Fort) sort of embraced it—it probably can best be done justice in Gillette's own words.

The "unimote" is the indivisible unit in the theory, and the universe is a "supraunimote"; the cosmos is the "maximote." There is also the "ultimote," which Gillette informs us is the "Nth sub-universe plane."

He explains, "Each ultimote is *simultaneously* an integral part of zillions of otherplane units and only thus is its *infinite* allplane velocity and energy subdivided into zillions of *finite* planar quotas of velocity and energy."

Gillette's universe would be a dull place without what he calls "lumps, jumps, and bumps."

"All motions ever strive to go straight—until they bump. Nothing else ever happens at all. That's all there is, he writes: "In all the cosmos there is naught but straight-flying bumping, caroming and again straight flying. Phenomena are but lumps, jumps, and bumps. A mass unit's career is but lumping, jumping, bumping, rejumping, rebumping, and finally unlumping."

All these findings led Gillette to his "backscrewing theory of gravity." Again only the master himself can do the theory justice. Some of his observations are:

"Gravitation is the kicked back nut of the screwing bolt of radiation."

"Gravitation and backscrewing are synonymous. All mass units are solar systems . . . of interscrewed subunits."

"Gravitation is naught but that reaction in the form of sub-planar solar systems screwing through higher plane masses."

Faced with such obvious facts, Gillette was incensed that scientists ignored him. He became most agitated that he had to print his theories at his own expense. But he added, "The truth seeker is never a fanatic. He has no fantasies to be fanatic about. So he is serene, and humane, civilized." So, in a civilized manner, he said of the scientific world: "Pooh! . . . It will soon attain oblivion by its own efforts."

Probably Gillette's *Rational, Non-Mystical Cosmos* can be called the standard work on his theories, but at 384 pages, it can get to be rather tough going. Most neophyte anti-Einsteinians are best directed to his *Orthodox Oxen* (1929). Some library copies are graced with hand-colored pictures done by the author, but they are considered such classics that most have been ripped off.

Writing in 1929, Gillette predicted that "the relativity theory will be considered a joke" by 1940. "Einstein," he added, "is already dead and buried, alongside Andersen, Grimm, and the Mad Hatter."

Something went wrong. By 1940, Einstein was still thriving, and the world lost sight of George Francis Gillette.

Juettner, Emerich (1875–?)

MR. 880

He was America's most successful counterfeiter, eluding the law longer than any other "maker of the queer" in history. If that connotes a criminal proficiency, the accolade is unearned. For he was not only the most successful but probably the worst counterfeiter ever to match wits with the U.S. Secret Service.

His name was Emerich Juettner, and he lived under the Americanized name of Edward Mueller on West Ninety-Sixth Street in New York City; until his sixties he had never committed a crime of any sort. He was a short, 120-pound, blue-eyed recluse known to his West Side neighbors as a collector of reclaimable junk. It was during the Great Depression, and as he strolled the streets with a pushcart, poking through garbage cans, he was looked upon, with his shock of white hair, skimpy mustache, and toothless grin, as no more than a slightly odd exponent of free enterprise.

Some of the junk he sold to dealers. Those that had once been toys or dolls, he put outside his apartment door, to be appropriated by neighbors with children. It was a laudable effort, considering the fact that Mueller–Juettner literally did not often have enough to feed himself and his dog. Whatever he was, he was not considered to be a scourge upon the city.

In 1938 a counterfeit bill turned up at a cigar store on Broadway near 102nd Street. The odd thing about it was that it was of the $1 variety, a bill which at that time was never counterfeited. A new Secret Service file was started for the miscreant, numbered case 880. It was a case that was to perplex seasoned veterans of the agency. The bill was of incredibly poor workmanship—the numbers were extremely fuzzy, and the portrait of George Washington was ludicrously inept. In addition, the paper was nothing more than ordinary bond, purchasable in any five-and-ten or stationery store.

In the ensuing weeks more of the bogus bills turned up, mostly in Manhattan, especially on the upper West Side, but some were found as far away as New Jersey. Those that could be traced were discovered to have been passed to small merchants, subway clerks, newspaper vendors, bartenders, and the like—all persons who handled hundreds of bills a day and, if they were ever concerned about counterfeits, would certainly only have paid close attention to fives and up.

By the end of 1939, the Secret Service had accumulated some 600 counterfeit $1 bills, some even more clumsy now than the first ones. Apparently the counterfeiter had tried to improve his work and ended up this time rather charmingly misspelling "Washington" as "Wahihngton." What was most exasperating to government investigators was the fact that the victims went right on blithely accepting these patent phonies.

During World War II the stream of bogus ones kept flowing, despite a Treasury Department publicity campaign in New York. More than likely, many persons finding themselves in possession of such incompetent counterfeits decided to keep them as mementos rather than reporting them to the government and seeing them appropriated. By 1947 the government had in its possession more than 5,000 less-than-minor masterpieces by Mr. 880, as agents took to calling their unknown nemesis.

In January 1948 the Secret Service finally got their man, although it was in rather bizarre fashion. A few weeks before the previous Christmas, the two-room flat of old Mueller–Juettner had caught fire. His dog had awakened him to the peril, and the old man saved himself although his old dog died.

Firemen responding to the alarm extinguished the blaze, heaving much of the old man's junk into an alley, where it was covered over by a fast-developing snowstorm. The heartbroken old man went off to spend Christmas with a daughter in Queens.

On January 13 two youths started poking through the fire-damaged junk in the alley, which was being partially uncovered by warming weather. They were highly encouraged when they came across two $1 bills. They dug on energetically until they discovered a set of printing plates. The youngsters took their find to the West 100th Street station house, where detectives immediately identified the bills as counterfeit. The Secret Service was summoned, and soon they found some parts of a small handpress as well as negatives for $10 and $20 bills. These negatives had never been used but the agents were more gleeful about their find of the $1 plates. They had Mr. 880, and Mueller–Juettner was apprehended a few days later when he returned to his flat.

Juettner was identified as a native of Austria, where he had learned the rudiments of engraving. After coming to America as a teenager he worked at many jobs, including that of a gilder of picture frames. He also worked as a janitor to provide for his wife and two children. When his wife died, he moved to upper Manhattan and pretended to his grown daughter and son that he was well able to provide for himself. Actually, he had not been able to even scrape by as a purveyor of junk, and so he took to his part-time career as an inept counterfeiter.

He knocked out a few ones on his handpress in his kitchen whenever he needed food for himself and his dog, or help paying his $25-a-month rent. Outside of that, he passed no bad bills, not wishing to cause anyone more financial harm than that. He made it a point never to stick a victim more than once for this same concern. As a Secret Service agent explained, Mr. 880 had been difficult to catch because he suffered from a "complete lack of greed."

The New Yorker magazine profiled Juettner in an engaging story by St. Clair McKelway, and Hollywood made a movie, with Edmund Gwenn playing the title role of the eccentric Mr. 880.

Meanwhile the real Mr. 880 eventually wound up in court, facing his first offense as a master criminal. Eventually, he was sentenced to nine months in prison, but the judge was clearly more awed than angered by his activities. When Emerich Juettner completed his term, he faded into the obscurity to which his criminal talents so clearly entitled him.

Gates, Charles G. (1876–1913)

GREAT PLUNGER II

Unlike some children of eccentrics, Charlie Gates was, to use with justification the tired phrase, a chip off the old block. He was in many ways a carbon copy of his father, Bet-A-Million Gates (q.v.). He plunged heavily into the stock market, took crazy chances at the gaming tables, and he spent and tipped lavishly—his tips, the New York Times reported, ran to $1 million a year. It may also be said he inherited still less admirable characteristics of his father, namely drinking, taking up elbow-bending in heroic volume while still in his teens.

One trait he didn't pick up from his father however was business acumen. He probably lost double what he ever managed to win in the market and at gambling. But the Gates fortune was so great, it hardly mattered. So disinterested did he become in business that firms on whose boards of directors he served had to retain detectives to find him when his presence was legally required. The detectives may be accused of overcharging for their services, since all they usually had to do to find him was check out the nearest drinking resort.

Charlie Gates lived only for gambling, drinking, and traveling at great speeds in his private train, which roared around the country at his instant whim. A friend once asked him why he spent so many thousands of dollars just to get his train to New York City from 2,000 miles away in 20 minutes less time than it would have taken him at normal speeds. "Speed is life," Charlie responded.

In 1911, he had his train cover the 3,000 miles from Yuma, Arizona, to New York City in 74 hours and 19 minutes, including stops; this pace was unheard-of for the era, working out to better than 40 miles per hour. It might be said to be due to an affair of the heart; at least it was an effort to dissuade his wife from filing for divorce.

In failing health in 1913, having crowded a wealth of charming if debilitating experiences in to his 37 years, Gates went to Cody, Wyoming, in the hopes of reviving his weakened body. He spent five weeks hunting bear and the like, and seemed to be improving. On the last day of his stay Gates started dishing out money. He spent $7,000 for fur coats for friends, and he tipped his chauffeur $1,000. He peeled off $10,000 in cash for his hunting guide. "Hell," Gates said. "I can't live forever and I can't take it with me."

That night he welcomed Buffalo Bill Cody to a rendezvous in his private Pullman car dubbed *Bright Eyes*. One single evening of boozing with that well-alcoholed old reprobate simply killed off Charlie. He died aboard *Bright Eyes* the following morning, as his valet was fixing him a restorative.

"I didn't know he was a tenderfoot," Buffalo Bill is said to have declared upon being informed of the younger man's demise. "I never should have ordered those last six bottles."

Gates had spent at least $70,000 on his brief sojourn in Cody, and the citizens there were mighty upset to lose a live one, especially since he had announced he was aiming to come back. They insisted he must have been poisoned, but the official verdict on the cause of death was apoplexy.

Muenter, Erich (1880–1915)

DR. MUENTER AND "MR. HYDE"

A man who poisoned his wife, sabotaged a ship at sea, exploded a bomb in the U.S. Capitol, and, for good measure, shot J. P. Morgan might begin to suspect that people considered him a menace to society. Not Erich Muenter, Ph.D., a fugitive Harvard instructor who did or was suspected of doing all of the above and more. But he saw himself as the savior of society.

The man the press labeled the "Mad Mr. Muenter" and "Dr. Muenter and Mr. Hyde" did not have the look of madness about him. As an instructor at Harvard he was described by a student in his 1905 German class as looking "like a ghost caught out in daylight"; hardly the description of a man given to violence.

After his wife's sudden death, toxicologists made a belated discovery that her stomach was full of arsenic. By that time Dr. Muenter had had the rest of the body cremated, and he had also done a most thorough job of disappearing himself.

Much to the embarrassment of Harvard, a wanted-for-questioning-regarding-murder bulletin went out for the school's errant instructor, who bizarrely did not vanish quietly. From New Orleans he mailed 100 copies of a printed brochure to the president of Harvard and a number of the faculty. Entitled "A Protest," it excoriated both society in general for its treatment of persons under suspicion and the press in particular for its handling of crime news.

> In the eyes of all who read the atrocious account in the daily papers, I am a brutal murderer, a thing to be despised and shuddered at, an outcast, an enemy of humanity, a wild beast that must be hunted, killed or caged for the safety of the community.
>
> Whether I am guilty or not of all or any of the charges brought against me, what must be my attitude? Why, revenge! The lesson you teach me I shall execute and it will go hard with you. You fiends of hell, if I do not strain every nerve to get revenge, let me never again respect myself.
>
> I can never prove my innocence to you. My only witness is dead. Hence if I could annihilate all of . . . Cambridge at one blow, that would be the thing to do. You will annihilate me; I must anticipate you.

Clearly, the weird doctor had gone round the bend. Police fine-combing New Orleans could find no trace of him.

Actually all Muenter had done was shave off his Vandyke beard and mustache, and move on to Fort Worth, Texas. Being then only in his mid-twenties, he enrolled at the Polytechnic College as Frank Holt, a clean-shaven, earnest-looking freshman. The halls of ivy proved a perfect hideout. Surprising everyone but himself, the brilliant young Holt breezed through four years of college work in 16 months. In 1909 he was made a professor of elementary and advanced German at the school. By 1915 he was back East, teaching at Cornell, accompanied by a Texas bride and two young children. Dr. Holt was doing just fine.

It took World War I to resurrect Erich Muenter. In letters to newspaper editors, he railed against the war, especially against the munitions makers, and he noted that if J. P. Morgan was barred from shipping arms to the Allies—Morgan's firm was acting as munitions purchasing agents in the United States for both England and France—the war would end quickly. The French, he added, would quickly collapse, being a people of notoriously loose morals. "The heads of universities," he noted, "are afraid to expose their young students—particularly the co-eds—to a real Frenchman."

He could not understand why newspaper readers did not rise up and demand support for his position. Infuriated, he determined to set off bombs in important places in the country to forcefully demonstrate the horrors of war.

He sent his wife and children on a trip to Texas and rented a cottage on Long Island, where he fashioned a king-sized bomb. On July 2, 1915, Muenter went by train to Washington and wandered through the corridors of the Capitol building, his grisly package under his arm. Finding the reception room outside the office of the vice president, in the Senate wing of the building, unguarded, he planted his bomb there and slipped away. When it went off, it took no lives but shattered much of the vice president's office. It was powerful enough to blow a watchman off his chair at the other end of the building. The man suffered several broken ribs.

By this time Muenter was back in New York, where a bomb had gone off in Police Headquarters. By this time a letter he had sent to a Washington newspaper was published; in it the anonymous writer said he had planted the bomb as a protest against munitions shipments.

Muenter did not wait to gauge the impact of his bombings on the public. Carrying another bomb, he traveled to Glen Cove, Long Island, where Morgan, Muenter's villain of villains, maintained his estate. On the trip Muenter decided that setting off a bomb there was not enough. He was determined to kidnap Morgan's baby and thus force the financier to "stop the war."

Forcing his way into the house, two guns pressed against the Morgan butler, Muenter demanded the child. What he got instead was Morgan himself barreling down the main stairwell straight at him like an enraged bull. Muenter shot Morgan twice in the chest, but the financier was not to be stopped and slammed into him. In the meantime the butler picked up a piece of coal from a fireplace and knocked the intruder out.

The story made the newspaper headlines the next day, having far more impact than Muenter's bombs. "Holt" was identified as Muenter. Behind bars, Muenter said he was sorry that he was forced to shoot Morgan, whose wounds proved to be slight. But he warned grandiosely that he had also planted bombs on munitions ships. News came that a fire on the *S.S. Minnehaha* had broken out after a bomb blast. But learning that the blaze had been contained, Muenter turned melancholy, feeling all his efforts had gone for nothing.

On the afternoon of July 6, a detective interviewed him and asked, "Do you think you are crazy?"

"I don't know," Muenter replied. "Sometimes I do, sometimes I don't. I've been trying for six months to convince myself of one or two things—either that I'm crazy or that I'm not. I haven't been able to settle that question yet."

Later that night, in an unguarded moment, he dove from the walkway of the third-floor cell, landing headfirst on the concrete floor of the cell block 24 feet below.

Benga, Ota (1881–1916)

THE ZOO MAN

Probably no better example of an eccentric made by society, not born as one, was Ota Benga, a young pygmy brought to America from the Belgian Congo in 1904. Found by the noted African explorer Samuel Verner, he was exhibited at the 1904 St. Louis Exposition, and afterwards he was presented by Verner to the Bronx Zoo director, William Hornaday. Hornaday apparently saw no difference between a wild beast and the little black man; for the first time in any American zoo, a human being was displayed in a cage. Benga was given cage-mates in his captivity—a parrot and an orangutan named Dohong.

The situation produced moral outrage. The black community quite naturally was upset and campaigned for freeing Benga from his captivity. A number of white clergymen also expressed strong disapproval, but not because the pygmy was a human being caged like an animal. What these men of the cloth feared, in fact, was that the Benga exhibition might be used to prove the Darwinian theory of evolution.

Hornaday insisted he was merely offering an intriguing exhibit for the people's edification. He dismissed the objections of a group of black clergymen that the pygmy's captivity was an affront to all black people, insisting that Benga was happy and that he was absolutely free. This statement could not be confirmed by the man in the cage because he could not speak English.

However, Hornaday finally bowed to the threat of legal action and allowed the pygmy out of his cage. This hardly dulled the pygmy's appeal as an attraction to tourists. Dapperly dressed in a white suit, Benga strutted around the zoo with huge crowds trailing him. At night he still returned to the monkey house to sleep. In time Benga's bizarre fate began to affect his behavior. Seeking to elude the mobs dogging his every step, he fashioned a bow and arrows to discourage them. Finally he wounded a visitor slightly.

It was then only a matter of time until Benga left the zoo for good. He came under the sympathetic care of a succession of institutions and individuals, but he never fully shed his "freak quality" attraction to the public. With the passing years the little black man, so long torn from his habitat, grew more hostile in behavior, forlorn, bitter, and, to some, "irrational." Tormented by his fate, and without funds to return to his native land, Benga committed suicide in 1916, using a gun.

Collyer, Homer (1881–1947) and Langley (1885–1947)

THE SHY MEN OF HARLEM

They became New York's most celebrated hermits, the brothers Collyer, living in their three-story mansion on upper Fifth Avenue in a once fashionable part of Harlem. Homer Collyer and his brother, Langley, four years his junior, were the sons of a wealthy Manhattan gynecologist and a cultured mother who read them the classics in Greek. They were trained to be gentlemen-scholars. Homer became an admiralty lawyer, and Langley was both an engineer and a talented concert pianist.

In 1909 their parents separated, an event that had shattering effects on both their lives. They began drawing into their shells, continuing to live in the house with their mother. By the time she died, 20 years later, they had almost totally shut themselves off from the throbbing city outside. Harlem was changing, and more and more black people were moving into the neighborhood. The mansion at No. 2078, now boarded up, was pointed out as the abode of two reclusive millionaires living with their fortune hidden in the house. The misers had stopped paying their water and electric bills, and so they had lost those services. It mattered not; they were content to cook with a small kerosene stove, to haul water from a park fountain four blocks away.

In 1933 Homer went blind, but the brothers did not consult a doctor. Langley told the few acquaintances he occasionally saw that he would cure his brother's blindness himself. He had him eat 100 oranges a week, keeping his eyes closed to rest them. By 1940 Homer was paralyzed as well. Now only Langley was ever seen on the streets, doing all the chores, keeping Homer and himself supplied with food. He foraged in garbage cans, begged food from kindly butchers, and sometimes walked all the way to Brooklyn to buy a loaf of stale bread for just a few pennies. And always he collected bales of newspapers, so that Homer could catch up on his reading when he regained his sight.

From time to time, news photographers caught Langley trying to avoid being seen by climbing over the mansion's grille-iron fence. The Collyer home was also of intense interest to burglars, but to no avail. Several tried to get in, but Langley had barricaded all the

The body of 61-year-old Langley Collyer was found after police removed 120 tons of trash from the family's Harlem mansion. He had been crushed to death by one of his anti-burglar booby traps. (Wide World)

entrances and windows with huge piles of debris, which defied passage. There were numerous passageways through the debris, but most ended in dead ends and were filled with booby traps. Only Langley knew which ones to take. Soon the criminals gave up. Not even a million dollars—the reward they fully expected to find— was worth the risks.

By and large the police also ignored the Collyers. But they could not do so in March 1947, when an unknown caller reported a dead man at the mansion. It took the police a considerable length of time to investigate the tip. Chopping through the locked front door, they found their way blocked by a mountain of cartons, scrap iron, broken furniture, and newspapers. When they finally got inside, they discovered Homer dead on the second floor. He was clothed only in a tattered bathrobe, with his long white hair reaching below his shoulders. His hand only inches away from a dried-up apple, he had starved to death.

The search for Langley proved fruitless at first. Bit by bit, searchers cleared the house, which was jammed almost solid with masses of junk honeycombed by twisting tunnels. Police found 14 grand pianos, hundreds of ancient toys, cartons of molding clothing, thousands of books, bicycles, sewing machines, dressmaker dummies, piles of coal, obscene photographs, scrap iron, barbed wire, tree limbs, machinery, the chassis of a Model–T Ford, and the jawbone of a horse.

At last they found Langley Collyer, much of his body chewed by rats. He had been crushed to death by one of his anti-burglar booby traps as he was bringing food to Homer. In all, the "loot" inside the house weighed more than 120 tons. No millions were discovered. In fact, the total Collyer fortune came to only about $100,000. Scores of relatives soon enough registered their claims to it.

Coneys, Theodore (1882–1948)

SPIDERMAN OF MONCRIEFF PLACE

Recluses abound in this volume, but none was more eccentric than Theodore Coneys. Not unlike many other recluses, he locked himself up in a house, keeping away from the prying eyes of society. However, the house where Coneys hid away was not his; furthermore it was at the same time still occupied by its real owners. Still later, he continued to occupy it after it had become a "ghost house" in Denver, Colorado.

The case of the Spiderman of Moncrieff Place first came to public attention late one evening in October 1941, when a couple living on that street became worried about an elderly neighbor, Philip Peters. Upon breaking into the house, they found him bludgeoned to death.

It would be a long time before the murder was solved; the

genesis of the case traced back about a month earlier, when a 59-year-old tramp named Theodore Coneys approached the Peters house to beg for food. He had known Peters decades earlier but doubted that he would remember him.

Just as Coneys neared the house, Peters rushed out and got into a car to visit his wife who was in the hospital. To Coneys this was a fortuitous development. Instead of relying on the charity of a former acquaintance, he was provided with the chance to steal what he needed. Coneys got into the house without difficulty and, as he searched for money and food, he discovered a trapdoor, only about two and one-half times the size of a cigar-box lid. It opened to a narrow attic cubbyhole. It was obvious that Peters had never used the space, not easy to reach, but Coneys was a thin man and could squeeze through the opening.

Instantly, Coneys changed his plans. He was a tired man; years on the road had worn him out and, whenever he was picked up by the police, he faced the threat of being sent to a mental institution as an incompetent. This made the cubbyhole all the more attractive. He could lead a joyful solitary existence up there with no more worries about finding shelter from the cold and wet. Coneys scoured the house and came up with some food, a pile of rags, and an old crystal radio, and he settled into his new home. The rags made as comfortable a bed as he had had in years.

At first Coneys perhaps thought of his refuge as just a resting station for the winter. But soon he decided to remain as a permanent, uninvited boarder. He listened to Peters shuffling down below and watched when he left the house, whereupon he would descend from his attic home to snack, shave (with Peters' razor), or even take a bath.

On October 17, thinking that Peters had left the house, Coneys was having a full sit-down meal in the kitchen. Actually the old man was just taking a nap. Suddenly the sleepy Peters walked into the kitchen. He gaped at Coneys, whom he did not recognize. Then he started to scream, and Coneys, panicking, grabbed an iron stove shaker and attacked the home owner. Peters fell dead in a pool of blood.

For a moment Coneys considered flight, but he had nowhere to go. He climbed back into his hiding place and remained there with a store of food until, and long after, the body of the victim was found. The police searched the house, but hardly expected a murderous intruder to still be there. They even noticed the trapdoor but concluded a man could not possibly slip through it.

A few weeks later, the widowed Mrs. Peters returned from the hospital with much trepidation. It soon seemed for good reason; several times at night both she and her housekeeper heard strange noises. Once the housekeeper screamed hysterically when she saw a shadowy figure in the hallway. But when she and Mrs. Peters investigated, they found nothing. The housekeeper decided the shadow had been Mr. Peters' ghost and finally convinced her mistress to move out of the house.

Even while the house lay vacant, Coneys remained. He was well-stocked with food and obtained enough to drink from the snow-filled gutters outside his tiny window. The reputation of the old Peters' place as a ghost house grew, particularly when passersby from time to time saw eerie lights at the top of the house. The police checked out such reports but Coneys heard them coming and managed to put out the light in time. The police concluded that neighborhood children were trying to frighten neighbors with mysterious lights from an abandoned house.

Nevertheless the police made routine checks on the house and, in late July 1942, two detectives heard a door shut on the second floor. They charged up the stairs just in time to see Coneys' feet disappearing through the trapdoor. The odd Spiderman of Moncrieff Place, as the newspapers dubbed him, was captured. He was tried for the murder of Peters and, despite a claim of insanity by the defense, was convicted and sentenced to life imprisonment.

Brinkley, "Dr." John R. (1885–1942)

GOAT GLAND BRINKLEY

It has been said that few areas of quackery have had a longer or more insane history than that of sexual rejuvenation, and in the case of "Goat Gland" Brinkley it would be difficult to find a more earnest, if crackpot, believer; or one, for that matter, who had a greater impact.

"Dr." John R. Brinkley gained his title through a Midwest diploma mill. When that institution was discredited, he managed, with the outlay of a considerable sum of money under the table for certain officials, to obtain another medical degree from Italy's University of Pavia. Armed with such an imposing background, Brinkley—a man of earnest mien, neatly trimmed goatee, and spectacles—seemed very much the scientist as he promised to restore men of any age to full sexual vigor.

For the trifling sum of $750 Brinkley would give a man the transplanted glands or testicles of a billy goat ($1,500 for a very young goat). The patient was then supposed to enjoy a complete sexual renaissance. Goat Gland Brinkley, as he came to be called, operating out of the Brinkley Gland Clinic in Milford, Kansas, even allowed patients to pick out the billies of their choice from a backyard pen, thus assuring themselves that they were getting active goats.

Evidently Brinkley qualified for performing this revolutionary scientific advance thanks to his slaughterhouse work for Swift & Co., the meat-packing firm, and a two-month stint in the army (four weeks of which was spent under psychiatric observation). With that background he stepped right into business. Indeed, some of Brinkley's patients showed improvement, reflecting the well-known ben-

Rejuvenator of prowess, Goat Gland Brinkley couldn't resuscitate his business and so, with attorney Anthony Davis (left), voluntarily declared bankruptcy. (Wide World)

efits of the hard sell in the days before sex clinics and surrogates. Brinkley's advertising was right to the point. "Here, here," his offer went. "Just let me get your goat and you'll be Mr. Ram-What-Am with every lamb." And while Goat Gland Brinkley had millions of Americans chuckling in the 1920s, he also had tons of supporters.

The Maharaja Thakou of Morvi hustled all the way from India for the transplant. E. Haldeman-Julius, the publisher of the Little Blue Books, was fooled by Brinkley; for several years he ran the goat-gland man's advertisements free, as well as doing puff pieces about him in a periodical devoted chiefly to debunking American life. Later on, Haldeman-Julius publicly apologized for his errors, but Brinkley was already well on his way. He soon was a millionaire thanks to the public reception of his claims.

To this day, there is not the flimsiest evidence that the glands of any animal can make a man strut about like a rooster, but this did not prevent Brinkley from imparting 5,000 pairs of goat glands—perhaps much more than that—to men from almost every state of the Union. By the time Brinkley was forced to roll up his medical license, he had earned a title from the American Medical Association as a "giant in quackery" and "the greatest charlatan in medical history."

Of course, being opposed by the medical profession fired Brinkley up all the more, since he truly believed his goat-gland theories. He regarded himself as the greatest mind of the century, considering Einstein by comparison to be nothing more than a "foreign upstart." Brinkley had a cure for just about everything, and he was busily working on a form of goat wizardry that would return mental patients to normal existence, with IQs to match their newfound sexual prowess.

Because the forces of government started to wage war on him, Brinkley, sporting his own radio station, moved into politics, three times running for governor of Kansas, and darn near winning each time. In 1930, the Democratic and Republican candidates polled 217,000 and 216,000 to Brinkley's 183,000, but all the goat man's votes had to be write-ins, since he could not get on the ballot. Brinkley claimed he was robbed of the election since some 56,000 ballots were thrown out.

In the next election, famed Kansas editor William Allen White was so frightened of Brinkley that he organized a "Save Kansas" campaign to beat him. In the voting, Alf Landon polled 278,000 to Woodring's 272,000 and Brinkley's 244,000. Brinkley even got thousands of write-ins in adjacent counties of Oklahoma, where he wasn't on the ballot.

It is said that the electoral defeats as well as the loss of his radio license really sent Brinkley over the edge, and he proclaimed, "to hell with Kansas," closed up his Milford gland clinic, and removed to Mexico—just across the Rio Grande, where he set up a new station as well as a clinic. There he pretended to perform prostate operations and peddled a medicine cure-all that contained nothing but blue dye and a touch of hydrochloric acid. Although it was not known at the time, Brinkley moved politically far to the right; he contributed to William Dudley Pelley's Silver Shirts, a native fascist movement.

In 1937 Brinkley opened a new hospital in Little Rock, Arkansas, where he continued his medical quackery, flitting between that city and Mexico. He also continued to entertain his own political ambitions and, in 1941, filed for Texas' Democratic nomination for U.S. senator. Back in Kansas, William Allen White grumbled, "He is irresistible to the moron mind, and Texas has plenty of such."

As it turned out, White's lathering up was needless. By then Goat Gland Brinkley had lost his hold over even the unwashed. Few people cared about him any more. In May 1942 he died of a heart attack at the age of 56. In Milford, a touching inscription appears on the Brinkley Memorial Church, reading: "Erected to God and His Son Jesus in appreciation of the many blessings conferred upon me, by J. R. Brinkley."

Kelly, Alvin "Shipwreck" (1885?–1952)

"THE LUCKIEST FOOL ALIVE"

More than 30 years ago, a group of journalists and historians were asked to name the one person who best typified, for its mindless nonsense, the so-called Roaring Twenties. Alvin "Shipwreck" Kelly scored at the top of the list, far ahead of the goldfish swallowers. In 1952, just a couple of years after this dubious honor, Shipwreck Kelly dropped dead between two parked cars. He had been home on relief, living in a seedy flat on New York's 51st Street between Eighth and Ninth avenues. Locked under his arm when he was found was a worn scrapbook full of yellowed newspaper clippings

Shipwreck Kelly ignored superstition on Friday, October 13, 1939 by standing on his head eating donuts on a plank extended from a Manhattan skyscraper. (Wide World)

about his exploits as the 20th century's most redoubtable flagpole sitter. He carried the scrapbook around to show to anyone he could pester into viewing it.

Alvin Kelly had always strived for recognition, flitting from one career to another with that goal in mind. He was at various times a merchant seaman, rigger, structural iron worker, human fly, high diver, boxer, pilot, aerial athlete, soldier of fortune, sign painter, stunt man, and window washer (at which task he often challenged co-workers to eschew safety belts as he often did).

Kelly told all who would listen, in bars, parks, on street corners, that as a sailor he had survived 32 shipwrecks. On occasion that figure changed to 62. Kelly suffered a lifelong difficulty telling the same story twice. Chances are slim that Kelly survived even one such disaster. In fact his nickname of Shipwreck had an entirely different origin: as a prizefighter known as Sailor Kelly, he spent so much time stretched out on his back on the canvas that boxing fans often chanted, "The sailor's been shipwrecked again!"

Kelly finally found his calling of flagpole sitter in 1924, when he was about 39 although he advertised himself as 32. He liked to say Jack Dempsey was the inspiration for what was to become his life's obsession. He said he was in a hotel in New Jersey on the eve of the Dempsey–Carpentier fight in 1921; when he defended Dempsey against some slurs, a group of drunks tossed him out the window. He managed to grab hold of a flagpole and the inspiration hit him. But on other occasions he told a different story: he was in Florida in 1922 when the heavyweight champion chased him up a palmetto tree. It occurred to Kelly that he had a knack for shinning up to high places and staying there without discomfort. Dempsey, when asked about this version, did allow it was conceivable that he had met Shipwreck some time, somewhere; but he insisted he had never chased him or anyone else up a tree.

Actually Kelly took to flagpole sitting in a logical place—Hollywood. He had performed a steeplejack stunt in a 1924 epic, and a press agent asked him if he could do 10 hours on a flagpole. Shipwreck said, absolutely; and in no time at all he was stationed high above a Los Angeles movie house, shilling some lesser epic of derring-do. He stayed aloft for 13 days and 13 hours. From there on, at one exhibition after another, he came down to cheers of crowds who had gathered to watch. They cheered him for what he did, and they never really asked *why* he did it.

Shipwreck's props included an eight-inch disk that fitted on the top of the pole, to provide him with a platform. He often fashioned a makeshift chair to sit on. He was able to sleep during his performances by locking his thumbs in bowling-ball-style holes in the flagpole shaft. If he swayed while dozing, the twinge of pain in his thumbs caused him to right himself without waking up. He trained himself to catnap five minutes every hour and found he could last almost indefinitely in that fashion. Some who came to marvel at Shipwreck seemed most intrigued about how he disposed of waste matter; after the performance, they studied the special hose run up beside the flagpole.

Love came to Shipwreck because of his exploits in Dallas, Texas, when he did a New Year's act atop a hotel. Inside the hotel, an unimpressed Texan stepped into an elevator and asked the female operator, "Is that damn fool still up there?"

The operator, a young woman named Frances Vivian Steele, slapped the man's face, snapping, "He's not a fool."

While management threatened to fire the girl, news of her defense of his honor was passed to Shipwreck. Naturally he wanted to meet her, a situation that required she be raised to his side by rope and tackle. The result was an aerial handshake, and a trip some time after to the altar.

By 1928 Shipwreck was making $100 a day by his flagpole perching, and in 1929 he did a cumulative total of 145 days up high. By that time he had a son—Little Shipwreck of course—but trouble was developing in the marital bed. "What's the use of having a husband unless he comes home nights?" Vivian wailed bitterly. Finally realizing that flagpole sitting was a compulsion that her husband would never abandon, she packed up and left with Little Shipwreck.

Meanwhile, in the summer of 1930, Shipwreck set a new world's record for flagpole sitting, at the Steel Pier in Atlantic City, staying aloft for 1,177 hours, or more than 49 days. However, Shipwreck's day was rapidly passing. Later that year Shipwreck suffered through a terrible ordeal atop New York's Paramount Hotel. His 13-day, 13-hour, 13-minute stint took place in zero-degree weather with an almost steady downfall of snow, sleet, and freezing rain. At street level shills collected a pitiful $13. America, now mired in the Great Depression, with many people not even having goldfish to eat, had little time for such tomfoolery as flagpole sitting.

Shipwreck kept trying, sure his obsessive act would catch on again. In 1935 he tried an exhibition in the Bronx, but was forced down when police threatened to cut the pole. He enjoyed a brief resurrection in 1939, when he was hired to promote National Doughnut Week by standing on his head on a plank extending out from the 56-story Chanin Building—then still the tallest skyscraper in midtown New York—and eating 13 hand-fed doughnuts. He was 54 at the time.

He managed to scrape by the next few years with stints above saloons, to lure in thirsty clients; by 1942 Shipwreck had been reduced to painting flagpoles at Palisades Amusement Park in New Jersey. One day he slipped, fell five feet—and was hurt.

There were no more stunts for Shipwreck Kelly. He was on home relief, with nothing to show for his eccentric career but a yellowed collection of newsclips that he could hardly get anyone to look at. But Shipwreck did, to the day he died.

Leedskalnin, Edward (1887–1951)

THE COMPULSIVE BUILDER OF CORAL CASTLE

Slaves of unrequited love, as noted elsewhere in these pages, have often become hermits. Yet others, like James Lick, have turned into money-making machines, to prove to themselves and others that they were worthier than they had been treated. A Latvian immigrant, Edward Leedskalnin, was cut from a different mold. He built a castle of gigantic blocks of coral—a masterpiece of construction which to this day baffles engineers as much as the techniques used by the Egyptians in building the pyramids—to shelter his shattered romantic dreams.

In 1912, when Leedskalnin was 25, he became engaged to a 16-year-old peasant girl in his small native village outside Riga. On the eve of the wedding, his bride-to-be broke off the affair, telling him she was in love with someone else.

Shattered but with the flame of love still burning within him, Leedskalnin left Latvia. He decided that if he could accomplish something that would seize the world's attention, he would win back the love of the girl he was always to refer to as "My Sweet Sixteen."

Coming to America, Leedskalnin tried his luck in New York, California, Texas, and finally Florida, where he settled in the little hamlet of Florida City. He had by this time decided on his great enterprise; he would build a monument to his love that would be one of the wonders of the modern world.

He began his work on a great "coral castle" and, when Florida City became too crowded, he moved everything to Homestead, Florida, where singlehandedly he quarried and set in place coral rock segments weighing up to 70,000 pounds each. He carved out an obelisk 27 feet high, three feet higher than the great central trilithon erected by the mysterious builders at Stonehenge, England. Everything Leedskalnin built both in his two-storied castle and in the park—tables, chairs, rockers, bathtubs, a "twisted heart" sculpture—were made of coral rock, without any benefit of cement.

How he lifted the great rocks into place—including that of an eight-foot-high, three-foot-thick wall to keep out the curious—remains a mystery to this day. From time to time he would show visiting engineers his self-made machinery for hoisting huge weights—a simple enough conglomeration of chains, pulleys, and levers—but none of these experts saw how the devices could lift such tremendous weights. The mysterious Leedskalnin never allowed anyone to see him at work and when townsfolks saw him scouring junkyards for scrap parts and chains and wheels from railroad hand cars, they knew better than to ask him what use he intended to make of them. His workshop was at all times littered with wedges, jacks, rollers, slings, sledgehammers, cables, and chisels.

Leedskalnin was vain enough to invite neighbors in to view a new creation now and then. He was particularly proud of his "repentance corner," where he said his children would be punished after the arrival of Sweet Sixteen. It was built along the lines of a colonial pillory, and, the Latvian assured his visitors, "The kids might forget a whipping, but they'll never forget this." At times he admitted the mere presence of the repentance corner might be enough to assure good behavior of children.

Leedskalnin was a frugal man of simple tastes, and thus he lived quite well in his coral castle. Still, a castle is a big place to clean; the Latvian constructed everything so that such labors would be done with the greatest possible ease. His bed could be pulled to the ceiling after he arose so that making it was unnecessary. The legless table was attached to the wall, making sweeping under it a breeze.

The rear entrance to his park was through a nine-ton door, perfectly balanced on pivots so that even a small child could open it with ease. Leedskalnin constructed a telescope weighing 30 tons and towering 25 feet to study the North Star. He mystified horticulturists with a solid rock table in which a flowering centerpiece grew without difficulty.

As the Latvian's castle and park grew, it quite naturally attracted visitors. Leedskalnin did not encourage such visitors, but he permitted them to enter without paying fees although he did accept donations. His proudest boast to them was that in all his years of labor, he had never ruined a single stone, an amazing accomplishment considering the way coral can crumble. He amused people with a rock turnstile which weighed three tons, so perfectly balanced that visitors could push their way through using only their pinkies for leverage.

Leedskalnin never revealed the secrets of his construction methods and spurned all such pleas that he do so. As he grew older, he became more crotchety, considering himself a failure in spite of his incredible works. As the years passed, he came to realize his efforts were in vain. Despite the many letters he wrote back to

Latvia, Sweet Sixteen never came. And when Russia swallowed up Latvia, it became apparent to him that she never would.

He died in 1951 at the age of 64, but his monument remains, his castle and park becoming one of Florida's most unusual and popular tourist attractions. And professional engineers still wonder about how Leedskalnin did it, just as they have puzzled about the Egyptians and their pyramids.

Anonymous (fl. 1890s–1900s)

THE FRENCH MAID

Within the social order of the red-light district of pre-earthquake San Francisco, there were many unusual characters; but none fired the imaginations of local practitioners, press, and public as much as the "French Maid" at Madame Marcelle's Parisian Mansion, one of the more infamous Barbary Coast brothels on Commercial Street.

For years there was much speculation as to the identity of the French Maid, an understandable preoccupation since "she" was actually a middle-aged man who appeared each morning armed with a bundle of women's clothing. He donned the attire, then swept and dusted the house from parlor to attic, never so much as saying a word to the inmates. His task completed, he put back on his regular clothes and left, depositing a silver dollar on the parlor table.

The French Maid made his appointed rounds for several years around the turn of the century, but his identity remained a secret. The ladies of Madame Marcelle's establishment felt he was probably an important politician; a number of journalists theorized that he was a leading banker or businessman; and the *National Police Gazette* speculated that he was a man of the cloth. These conjectures may have merely reflected hostility toward the establishment or, in the case of the *Police Gazette,* toward the clergy. Nevertheless, to many, the expenditure of the not inconsiderable sum of $7 a week— enough in that era for a man to support his family—indicated a man of means.

Only Madame Marcelle knew for sure and could have told. However, she adhered till the end to her belief that a business-woman in her profession who forsook discretion would not long enjoy prosperity.

Diederich, Hugo (fl. 1890s–1920)

THE MAD BARBER

Not many towns of less than 350 inhabitants in turn-of-the-century America could boast of, or need, two barbers, but the Missouri river town of Rocheport qualified for that honor. One was the town's regular barber who handled all the local inhabitants. The other was Hugo Diederich, a German with a deep, thick accent that towns-men loved to imitate. Hugo of Rocheport was much celebrated but never patronized by the locals.

Nobody knew, or at least in later years could remember, exactly where he'd come from or indeed where he went when he finally packed up his razors shortly after World War I; but tales of his barbering by then had become legendary.

It was said that Hugo of Rocheport never got any repeat cus-tomers, that a man would have to be insane to ever sit under his razor a second time, risking again an abrupt demise after learning the perils of that barber chair. That was an exaggeration. Hugo did have repeats, but admittedly they were not Rocheporters. The trou-ble with old Hugo, everyone agreed, was that he was a mad barber, one who could not contain a desire to be the fastest practitioner of the scissors-and-razor set.

Rocheport was at the time a not unimportant rail link, and travelers often found themselves with layovers in the town. There was time to seek out a fast shave, and there was Hugo's shop right by the tracks. Hugo had to make hay when a train was due, and he sought to take care of as many patrons as possible in the limited time. He had to be fast. Fast? Hugo was a shaving fool!

Hugo was extremely popular with railroad engineers because they could jump off a non-stopping train as it was roaring through the station (so the tale went), charge into Hugo's parlor, get lathered up and shaved, and still rush out in time to catch the caboose when it came along.

Once a man rushed into Hugo's shop less than five minutes before a train would make a 30-second stop. Could Hugo shave him in so little time?

"Sure!" cried Hugo.

"But I don't like any pulling or scratching," the man admonished.

"Mister," Hugo replied with pained chagrin, "if I give you one scratch, you get another shave free before the train comes."

Hugo was famed among other barbers in surrounding communities and indeed other counties and states, and it was said many tonsorial experts journeyed to Rocheport to see the master in action. Master he most certainly was, and it was legend among younger barbers that Hugo at either the Chicago or St. Louis World Fair received a medal as the best straight-edge man in the world.

Hugo was truly amazing, with a work-load capacity that awed other barbers. When the railroad crews were in town, he often shaved for 24 hours without a break, staying on his feet for continuous "minute shaves." Hugo liked to brag that his prowess was due to his speed razors, some 1,000 straight-edged blades he had ready for use. He would size up a man's beard instantly for the most likely steel.

Time and again locals would advise him he could build his practice enormously if he cut down on his mad stress on high-speed shaving. The locals liked a barber who had time for a few words, who could discuss the latest news with a measure of leisure. Would Hugo try to do that? "*Ja, ja!*" Hugo responded with hasty assurance, too fast to inspire confidence.

One day when the town's other barber was swamped with customers, one of the permanents screwed up his courage and entered Hugo's shop. No train was due for some four hours which meant Hugo would be idle for that long.

Hugo was mighty pleased to see a local and made an elaborate routine of preparing the lather and toweling the man. It was a monumental effort on Hugo's part. Then he picked up the razor and with a single stroke shaved the whiskers off the entire right side of the man's face. The customer bolted from the chair as Hugo turned to wipe the razor clean.

"What's the matter?" compulsive Hugo cried. "I will shave you quick. I will shave you."

"I know you will," the man said, fear mirrored in his eyes, "but if your razor slipped, my head would fall off!"

He threw off the towels and, half his face still lathered, he raced down the street to have the job completed by the other barber.

Sadly, Hugo must have finally known his days in Rocheport were numbered. With a change in train schedules after World War I Hugo's business fell off disastrously and he left town, the locals not knowing to where and, indeed, caring little.

Adamski, George (1890–1965)

THE FIRST ENCOUNTERER

In the strange world of UFO believers, George Adamski occupies a special niche. Indeed, there are those who consider all exponents of flying saucers to be "nuts," but that still leaves George Adamski, who is considered even within the field as pretty much of an embarrassment.

An amateur astronomer and former head of a mystical cult called the Royal Order of Tibet, Adamski ran a hamburger stand at the foot of Palomar Mountain in California during the 1940s and early 1950s. Then on November 20, 1952, Adamski said he "made personal contact with a man from another world."

Adamski's newfound friend, whom he met in the California desert, was from Venus, about five feet six inches tall, had gray eyes, long hair, a brown jump suit, and oxblood shoes. Later, Adamski said, he made a rash of friends from other planets as well, from Mars and Saturn; those from the latter planet were very much better looking and smarter than most earthlings, he reported in such books as *Behind the Flying Saucer Mystery, Flying Saucers Have Landed,* and *Inside the Space Ships.*

This last contribution was rather important, because his otherworld buddies invited him to take a spin in space. Adamski had a jolly time, especially when having refreshments with an "incredibly lovely" blonde name Kaina and an equally charming brunette named Ilmuth. As much as Adamski enjoyed his out-of-this-world adventures, so much did the spacemen like their adventures on earth, according to Adamski's reports. He met one space traveler at a favorite restaurant, where the alien especially liked the hamburgers and the apple pie. They just didn't know how to make those specialties back on Venus.

In fact, according to Adamski, Planet Earth was becoming overloaded with extraterrestrials going about posing as humans. Their main mission, he said, was to study man's nuclear activities, which very much worried the folks of other planets in the solar system. They were not fond of any big bangs, they told Adamski.

There are those who said that the more whoppers Adamski told, the more he himself accepted the tales. He was a totally committed believer, it was said. And, in fact, no one was ever able to get Adamski to retract the slightest point in any of his claims, right up to the day he died, in a Maryland sanitarium in 1965.

UFO nut George Adamski reported that the space aliens he met were wild about hamburgers and apple pie. (Wide World)

Weyman, Stanley Clifford (1891–1960)

IMPOSTOR FOR FUN

Born Stanley Weinberg in Brooklyn in 1891, Stanley Clifford Weyman was a man of many identities and impostures, and was forever a puzzlement to the police. A fabulous fraud, he was at times a diplomat, a doctor, a journalist, and a draft-dodge adviser. However, he seldom did it for money but rather simply for the art of fooling people, often hilariously doing so. When he did it for profit, it was simply a demonstration of the eternal truth that even fakers must eat. It in no way corrupted his art.

Once late in his career a reporter asked Weyman why he did the things he did. "One man's life is a boring thing," he explained. "I live many lives. I'm never bored."

Weyman wanted to study to be a doctor but his poor Brooklyn parents could not afford such expenses, and instead Weyman, a name he adopted early in life, was forced to look forward to an existence of clerking in stores and counting houses. It was no life for him and Weyman decided he was entitled to more than being a drudge, so he quit his job in a Brooklyn counting house and crossed over into Manhattan. Decked out in a purple uniform, he declared himself to be U.S. Consul Delegate to Morocco.

He frequented plush hotels and restaurants, running up impressive tabs as this mythical diplomat. Once, fresh out of checks, he appropriated an expensive camera and hocked it. This errant behavior led to his unmasking and Weyman, not yet 21 (a heavy beard had made him appear older), was shipped off to the Elmira Reformatory.

Here Weyman reformed, in a manner of speaking. He resolved never again to sink to petty thievery. When he got out on parole the following year, Weyman reported to his parole officer and announced he had a job. He neglected to mention what it was. He then decked himself out as a military attache from Serbia. He also moonlighted as a lieutenant in the U.S. Navy.

It paid off for a time, but finally he was caught and imprisoned again. Paroled a second time, Weyman swore to authorities he would do it no more. But in 1915 he got himself another uniform and became a lieutenant commander in the Rumanian Navy as well as Rumanian Consul General in New York. Aware of the high duties of his position, Weyman decided he should inspect a battleship. He appeared at the U.S. Navy Department office in New York and said he had been ordered by his queen to offer his respects. The navy accepted an invitation to pay an official visit to Rumania's Black Sea ports and, in return, Weyman was asked to inspect the USS *Wyoming*.

Although a mere 24 years old, Weyman in his sky-blue uniform had a severe mein that made him appear much older. He was very stern inspecting the sailors standing at attention, and he even reprimanded a few of them. Later, the important foreigner mellowed, and he invited the officers of the ship to dine with him at the Astor Hotel.

For the occasion Weyman reserved a private dining room with instructions that the bill be sent to the Rumanian Consulate in Washington. Had the *New York Times* not printed a brief, supplied by the hotel publicity department, about Consul General Weyman hosting a banquet for the officers of a navy ship, his imposture might have worked to perfection. Unfortunately, a sharp-eyed police officer spotted the squib and wondered if that could possibly be the same old Weyman. A couple of detectives checked out the banquet and Weyman was once more in custody. Rather piqued, Weyman said, "You could have waited until after dessert."

When the United States entered World War I, Weyman did the patriotic thing. He commissioned himself as a lieutenant in the Army Air Corps under the name of Royal St. Cyr. He was arrested at the Forty-seventh Regiment Armory in Brooklyn while staging one of his usual "inspections."

By this time Weyman was rather disgusted with military careers and switched to medicine. Soon "Doctor" Weyman was off for a year to Lima, Peru, in the service of a construction company as its medical consultant. He carried off his act there rather well by doing practically nothing medically, assigning all duties to local doctors.

Instead Weyman spent all his time throwing lavish parties in a villa he had rented, sending the bills back to the New York office. Never having had a medical man who was such a spendthrift, the firm decided to check his credentials a bit more thoroughly. Soon, Weyman was returning to the United States, his medical career aborted, at least for a time.

In 1921 Weyman evidently took stock of his career and found it wanting. He was either always in jail or flat broke. He decided to mend his ways. He did so in a not very socially accepted manner.

Princess Fatima of Afghanistan was at the time visiting America, and she was in residence in a suite at the Waldorf Astoria. One morning a Lieutenant Commander Weyman showed up as the U.S.

State Department's head of protocol. The princess was very pleased
since up until then the U.S. government had paid her no mind.
The commander arranged for her to go to Washington to meet
President Harding, and he even posed with Fatima and the president for official White House photographs. He also got $10,000
from the Princess, after explaining to her that it was customary for
guests to this country to distribute gratuities to the junior officials
who handled the details for her visit to the capital. He gladly handled the matter for Fatima and said he would also take care of her
hotel bill.

Exit Lt. Commander Weyman. A New York newspaper photo
editor was to see the pictures of Weyman's White House call.
Throwing the prints in the air, he shouted, "That little S.O.B.'s
done it again!"

The next year, however, Weyman was apprehended while posing as a hospital official who had greeted Dr. Adolf Lorenz, the
world-famed bloodless surgeon from Vienna, before he had even
disembarked from his liner. Weyman came aboard by launch and
in fact acted as Dr. Lorenz's interpreter with the reporters who
interviewed him. Dr. Lorenz found Weyman indispensable—until
it was discovered the latter was extracting fees from patients the
Viennese surgeon was examining as a courtesy. Weyman got a year
for that one, plus two years for the Fatima matter.

In 1926 Weyman was living in obscurity in Brooklyn when
Rudolph Valentino, the Great Lover of the silent movies, died. Actress Pola Negri hurried to New York just to inform the press how
crushed she was, especially since she and Valentino were secretly
engaged. La Negri insisted her own health was endangered by her
grief.

Out of Brooklyn came Dr. Weyman to take care of her. At first
the actress thought the little man was a bit cracked, but when he
agreed that her condition was fragile indeed, she realized he obviously knew his stuff. The knight errant medico issued bulletins to
reporters on Negri's condition. The *Times* also reported to its readers that the doctor was the author of a highly regarded (if non-
existent) volume entitled *Weyman on Medico-Jurisprudence*.

Dr. Weyman accompanied Negri to Campbell's Funeral Home
for a last look at her departed lover. When a woman in the crowd
fainted, Weyman was right there with his smelling salts. It was his
finest hour.

Even his later greeting of Queen Marie of Rumania as an under secretary of state could not match the high drama of the Valentino funeral, but it was still a tour de force. He conned his way

past the queen's secret service guards and, in the course of greeting her, got her to answer all sorts of questions. Actually a roguish newspaper of the day, the *New York Graphic* had hired him to quiz the queen, who had refused the press all interviews. Weyman, the impostor, was becoming a genuine journalist.

But he went back to the wrong during World War II, when he set himself up as a "selective service consultant," giving instruction in draft-dodging to pupils interested in how to simulate deafness or, in the case of the particularly dim-looking candidates, how to fake feeblemindedness.

That one got Weyman seven long years in the slammer. In 1948, fresh out of prison, Weyman turned up at the United Nations at Lake Success, of all places, working for a small news service and radio station. Weyman hobnobbed with the likes of Warren Austin, the chief American delegate, and Andrei Gromyko, his Russian counterpart. The delegation from Thailand was so impressed with Weyman's style that, in 1950, it offered him a job as its press officer with full diplomatic accreditation. Weyman was thrilled at the prospect but first wrote to the State Department inquiring if taking such a post would affect his American citizenship. The State Department had had some experience with Stanley Clifford Weyman, and he was soon back on the street, his chances for a diplomatic career dashed.

Weyman sort of faded away after that, or at least was unheard of again until 1960, when he was working as a night manager in a New York hotel. He was shot to death by a thief he had tried to stop from robbing the hotel safe. Oddly, in his last act in real life, the mad imposter ended up playing the role of hero.

The Cherry Sisters (fl. 1893–1903)

BEST OF THE WORST

For a decade at the turn of the century, the Cherry Sisters became the best known if not the best loved stage performers in America. In 1893 the sisters—Lizzie, Effie, Jessie, and Addie, aged 17 to 22— strutted on to a stage in Cedar Rapids, Michigan, to perform a sketch of their own composition in an amateur program. They didn't win. In fact they were, by popular opinion, absolutely terrible. Only the sisters themselves thought they had merit, and soon they pushed on to the most fantastic career in the history of the American theater—certainly so, considering the talent involved.

They played in vaudeville houses throughout the Midwest, giving performances that were so ludicrously bad that audiences pelted them with garbage and overripe tomatoes. Finally they could only perform with a wire-mesh screen in front of them. We are told, and there is much reason to believe, that the Cherry Sisters did not regard themselves individually as subpar performers. Each was sure she was the best of the bunch, that if there was any bad reaction from the audience it was due to her three sisters.

Inevitably they played to packed houses; this fact might cause a psychiatrist today to deduce that the audiences were letting out their aggressions by going to see, and reacting to, the Cherry Sisters.

Inevitably, Broadway beckoned—in the person of the great impresario Oscar Hammerstein, who had in the years just prior to 1896 staged a number of shows that died. Good talent, Hammerstein decided, was no guarantee to success. Could the worst do better? He gave the Cherry Sisters a contract guaranteeing $1,000 a week.

On November 16, the sisters opened at the Olympia Theater, strangely if stunningly clad in fiery-red dresses, hats, and woolen mittens. Their garb was the high point of their act, which hit rock bottom when they opened their mouths. New York audiences, being a bit more sophisticated than their country cousins, sat in goggle-eyed silence as the sisters launched into their first number, "Cherries Ripe Boom-de-ay!" Jessie slammed away on the bass drum while her three sisters belted out:

> Cherries ripe Boom-de-ay!
> Cherries red Boom-de-ay!
> The Cherry sisters
> Have come to stay!

The rendition was, to put it charitably, grotesque, but the sisters were thrilled. Not a single New Yorker hurled a missile at them, at first. This remarkable development could only be explained by the fact that the audience had come ill-prepared, a situation that would change rapidly thereafter.

The first-night reviews were ghastly. Lizzie, probably to the delight of her sisters, was singled out by one critic who said, "A locksmith with a strong rasping file could earn ready wages taking the kinks out of Lizzie's voice." The *New York World* was more kind, saying, "It was awful," while the *New York Times,* a model of restraint, declared, "It is sincerely hoped that nothing like them will ever be seen again." Thereafter, even New York audiences knew to come armed with vegetables and empty beer bottles, and the trusty screen, by now the sisters' trademark, was called upon once again for duty.

A cynic might say the Cherry Sisters laughed all the way to the bank; when they retired in 1903 to live the farm life with their fortune of $200,000, they truly believed they were among the world's finest actresses, that only jealous professional competitors had ever attacked them. In fact, in later interviews they insisted that they had never been targets of any garbage or slop, that no one had ever thrown a thing at them. How could that have been, they asked, when they always played to full houses? One journalist noted that the Christians and the lions had also packed them in at the Roman circus.

Manville, Tommy (1895–1967)

THE CONSTANT BRIDEGROOM

Heir to the Johns-Manville asbestos fortune, Thomas Franklyn Manville, better known as Tommy Manville, became America's constant bridegroom, as he ran through 11 wives in 13 marriages—he remarried twice. There is no evidence he did anything else of a worthwhile nature during his lifetime.

Truly erratic and proud of his record of collecting blonde wives, Manville was the darling of the Sunday supplements. In 1936, a story under his byline appeared in the *American Weekly* when he was temporarily unattached in which he predicted he'd soon marry another blonde—almost any blonde.

The next year he took full-page advertisements in New York newspapers, publicly seeking a new attorney to represent him in his marital disputes. He later erected a sign at the entrance of his mansion, which read:

"BEWARE. MARRYING MANVILLE LIVES HERE."

Manville was 17 years old in June 1911, when he met a chorus girl named Florence Huber under a Broadway marquee. They were married five days later. Tommy's father, traveling from Europe to the United States, announced he would have the match annulled when he got to New York.

Tommy immediately arranged a second wedding ceremony in New Jersey, tried to have another in Maryland, and said he would, if need be, remarry his bride in as many of the remaining states as need be. When his father cut him off from family funds, Tommy took a $15-a-week job, for the first and last time doing anything productive.

That he was launching on a bridegroom career was not readily apparent, since that first marriage lasted 11 years. In September 1925, Tommy took his father's 22-year-old stenographer, Lois Ar-

Asbestos heir Tommy Manville, here with his 11th and final bride, Christina Erdlin, refuted the theory that blondes have more fun. (Wide World)

line McCoin, as his second wife. The next month his father died
and left him about $10 million of a $50 million estate.

Now Tommy was in business. His second wife charged him with
desertion in 1926 and won a settlement of $19,000 a year. By this
time Manville was describing himself to the press as "a retired businessman." He was not however retired from matrimony.

The rest of his marriage slate went as follows:

#3. Follies girl Avonne Taylor in May 1931. Her third mar-
riage. They separated after 34 days.

#4. Marcelle Edwards, a showgirl, in October 1933. They di-
vorced in 1937, with Marcelle getting a $200,000 settlement.

#5. Twenty-two-year-old showgirl Bonita Edwards in Novem-
ber 1941. They were divorced three months later.

#6. Wilhelmina Connelly (Billy) Boze, a 20-year-old actress in
October 1942. They divorced in February 1943, and, a rarity
among the Manville wives, she refused to take any money in settlement.

#7. Macie Marie (Sunny) Ainsworth in August 1943. She had
been married four times before she was 20. They separated after
eight hours and were divorced in October.

#8. British-born Georgina Campbell in December 1945. She
was 27 and Manville was 50. They were already separated when
Georgina was killed in an automobile collision in 1952.

#9. Anita Frances Roddy-Eden in July 1952. She obtained a
Mexican divorce in August.

#10. Twenty-six-year-old Pat Gaston. They were married in
May 1957 and divorced the following November.

#11. Christina Erdien, who was 20 when they married in 1960.
This marriage finally took, and she was at his bedside when he died
October 8, 1967.

A newspaper reporter once asked Tommy Manville if it was
true that blondes have more fun. "No," Tommy replied. "*I* have
more fun."

All through the years Manville had maintained a bequest of
$50,000 in his will for his first wife. However, not long before he
died, Manville had cancelled it.

Sidis, William James (1898–1944)

THE INFANT PRODIGY

He was recognized as the most accomplished child prodigy of his era; aspiring parents sought to have their own offspring emulate his example. He was also sadly warped by his conditioning. At the age of four in 1902, two years after his father had given him alphabet blocks, William James Sidis was typing in English and French. At five he had worked out a formula by which he could instantly name the day of the week for any date in history. At six his teacher admitted she could not keep up with his mathematical theories. At nine he completed his first year of high school and applied for admission to Harvard. He was rejected, not for lack of scholarship but because it was believed he was too emotionally immature for college life. He was accepted when he was 11.

Probably more than any child ever, Sidis was a creation of his parents. His mother was a Russian-born physician and his father, also Russian-born, was Boris Sidis, a Harvard professor of abnormal psychology. Dr. Sidis' pet theory was that geniuses were not born but made, and he was determined to demonstrate that fact with his son, starting to mold him into a genius while he was still in his cradle. He said that if parents encouraged a babe's intellectual curiosity, he would tend to learn faster than a jack rabbit runs.

By young Sidis' freshman year at Harvard, he certainly seemed to have borne out his father's theory of intellectual force-feeding. As a freshman Sidis proceeded to deliver a lecture on the fourth dimension that even most of his professors probably did not grasp.

Then at the age of 12, he suffered a nervous breakdown. After being treated at his father's sanitorium in New Hampshire, he returned to his studies, and at 16 he graduated cum laude. After that he breezed through law school and taught for a short time at Rice Institute. Then suddenly he quit. Some time before that he had told the press, "I want to live the perfect life. The only way to live the perfect life is to live it in seclusion." What Sidis was saying especially was that he wanted nothing to do with his parents, whom he had grown to despise for the pressure they had put on him.

He took menial jobs and became an ardent Marxist, joining both the Socialist and Communist parties. In 1919 he was convicted in Roxbury, Massachusetts, of shouting during a May Day rally, "To hell with the American flag." He was sentenced to 18 months in prison but he appealed his conviction and eventually the charge was dropped.

Shortly thereafter Sidis moved to New York City, where he worked as an adding machine operator. Physically not attractive and ponderous of movement, he was regarded by co-workers as something of a freak. Office girls wrinkled their noses and opined he could use more frequent baths. Sidis couldn't care less, desiring only to be left alone. When a friend informed him his father had died, Sidis berated him for bothering him with such trivialities.

Sidis put away all his interests in intellectual and scientific pursuits, developing a passion for collecting streetcar transfers. He wrote and published a book on the delights of his hobby, calling it *Notes on the Collection of Transfers*.

In 1937 the *New Yorker* located him working in obscurity in a Boston office and resurrected the story of the man who was an eccentric genius. Sidis took such offense at that description that he filed suit against the publication, charging libel and invasion of privacy. After some court decisions that the public's right to know about the fate of a child prodigy exceeded Sidis' rights to privacy, the case was settled out of court.

In 1944 Sidis died of an inner cranial hemorrhage at the age of 46. It was left to Stanford psychologist Lewis Terman—who conducted a study of 1,400 precocious children in the 1920s and found almost all of them to have achieved success and happiness far above the average—to provide a sort of epitaph. "Sidis' case was a rare exception. I think the boy was largely ruined by his father, giving him so much bad publicity. The Quiz Kids radio program has done a lot to dispel the popular notion that gifted children are queer."

West, James Marion, Jr. (1903–1957)

"SILVER DOLLAR" WEST

Even for a multimillionaire oil-man, James Marion West, Jr., was a mite bizarre. In fact, it may be said that he did more to establish the stereotype of what a Texas oil-man is like than any of his free-spending, wild-living contemporaries. He gained the nickname of "Silver Dollar" West because of his habit of dispensing such coins to kids, pedestrians, waitresses, and whomever else struck his fancy.

The story was told that when he had completed building his River Oak Boulevard mansion in Houston, he inspected his six-car garage and found only five pairs of fins protruding from the stalls. "Buy me another Cadillac immediately to fill that hole," he snapped to his secretary. The story is probably apocryphal. He owned 40 Cadillacs.

While he inherited a great fortune and multiplied it through shrewd investment and enterprise in oil, cattle, and lumber, making money was not a particularly high priority with West. A magazine once ran a story about him entitled "How to Have Fun with 100 Million Dollars." West's true passions in life were (not necessarily in order of preference) butter, silver dollars, Cadillacs, firearms, and crime fighting.

He lived, with his Cadillacs, in a $500,000 castle, and went about Stetson-hatted and cowboy-booted, wearing a diamond-encrusted Texas Ranger badge. One of his main methods of having fun was to scatter rolls of silver dollars in the street and watch people scamper after them. Dining in a restaurant, West brought along a vat of butter churned on his own farm and if the establishment's service pleased him, he tipped the waitress with a stack of 80 silver dollars.

Obsessed with the crime problem, West was a close friend of scores of Texas policemen and law enforcement officers; an insomniac, he rode the streets of Houston with a police officer at his side in one of his radio-equipped Caddies. The Houston police, with a certain reputation of their own for unconventional behavior, furnished him with a uniformed partner, Lieutenant A. C. Martindale. It was never too clear what the lieutenant's exact duties were—to assist West in the administering of his duties or to keep him from going hog wild. In any event, so the story goes, Martindale ended up taking a shot in the foot when West, forever fast on the trigger, cut loose at a fleeing bandit.

West's crime-fighting Caddy could better be described as a fortress on wheels, sporting among other items in its arsenal a 30-30 carbine, a shotgun, a Tommy gun, and a goodly supply of tear gas. Naturally, West did not go about his appointed rounds without at least one .45-caliber pistol strapped to his hip.

West could chortle at making kids scramble in chase of his pieces of silver, but he could not bear up well as the butt of humor. One Halloween night a group of costumed trick-or-treaters surrounded his automotive arsenal and rocked it violently, demanding a tribute in silver dollars. West's answer was to loose a cannister of tear gas in their midst and send them off sobbing. West thought it humorous but the children's parents did not. Some newspapers even raised the suggestion that perhaps the time had come to fence in the self-appointed minion of the law. West was outraged. As he once put it, "The press has always had fun at my expense."

West was hardly socially perceptive enough to understand that the harsh criticism of him represented a city coming culturally of age. Nor was he amused when a journalist stated after an interview with him that he was overwhelmed with a "perfectly preposterous emotion. . . . I was feeling sorry for a hundred million dollars."

When Silver Dollar West cashed in his chips in December 1957, there were those who observed that at last the days of the frontier were over.

Slattery, Jimmy (1904–1960)

"GREATEST LIVER WHO EVER FOUGHT"

The folklore of boxing has many candidates for the wildest man of the ring, the erratic if not punch-drunk fighter, the battler who went from the Garden to the gutter. There is no doubt that boxing's number-one nutball was an idol of the Golden Twenties, a fighting machine named Jimmy Slattery.

There are many who considered him, as did Gene Tunney, to be the greatest natural boxer of modern times. Gentleman Jim Corbett paid Slats the high compliment of never missing a Slattery bout. Sportswriters commented that this was because Corbett saw his own greatness mirrored in the lean Irishman out of Buffalo, New York. But if there were those who called him "the greatest fighter who ever lived," there were even more who regarded him "the greatest liver who ever fought."

Out of 122 fights, he lost only 12 and won the light-heavyweight championship. Everyone agreed he would have reigned longer and lost far fewer fights had he not combined the elbow-bending talents of John L. Sullivan with the delicate accomplishments of Casanova.

In Buffalo he became a local god when he outpointed Young Stribling shortly before he went on to New York and the big time. There he astonished boxing men and sportswriters by toying with tough Jack Delaney. They watched in awe as this handsome Irish kid, with his black hair gleaming under the ring lights like patent leather, danced around Delaney. Delaney never so much as mussed Slats' hair. The fight was limited to six rounds because of 20-year-old Slattery's tender years. At the time Slats was a model boy. He didn't smoke or drink. His mom sewed the first pair of green tights he wore in the ring.

Some said that something about the Big Town got to Slats. Some said it was automobiles. Others liquor. Yet others insisted

Jimmy Slattery (second from left), a formidable presence in the ring, was given to frequent disappearing acts outside the arena. (Wide World)

women were the bottom of Slats' woes. There is much to be said for each school of thought.

Slats certainly took to automobiles. He owned in succession a black Ford, a blue Dort, a blue Hudson, a green Cadillac, a yellow Lincoln, a green Lincoln, three more Lincolns of varying hues, another Ford and a red Cadillac sedan.

Once, wearing a sweatshirt after jogging through Manhattan streets, Slats entered an auto salesroom and asked a snooty salesman the price of a gleaming model. The salesman quoted a price tag of $5,200, then walked off with a disdainful air. Slats immediately peeled $5,200 from a roll he carried and bought the car from another salesman. Reminded by a friend that he had just bought a car, Slats said, "I know, but I didn't like the way the guy acted."

Slats asked only one thing from his cars, that they go fast. His greatest nemeses, in order, were telephone poles and traffic cops. There is no record of him ever hitting the latter, but if a motorcycle cop stopped him for speeding, the ever-mirthful Slats would frequently steal the cop's motorcycle for a fast getaway.

Slats also had a fondness for taxicabs. After one fight at Madison Square Garden he stepped out to the street and hailed a cab for a 300-mile ride to the Adirondacks. Slats was always on the go like that. Once he and manager Red Carr arrived in New York to take in the Sharkey–Maloney bout, and Slats said he was leaving their hotel to buy a straw hat. He returned three days after the fight, by which time the frantic Carr had given the police a missing-persons notice and enlisted the personal assistance of Mayor Jimmy Walker. He strongly suspected his fighter had been kidnapped. Asked where he'd been, Slats said vaguely, "Just around." He didn't even have a straw hat.

On another occasion Slats disappeared five days before an important bout. Then Carr got a wire from the police chief of Elkhart, Indiana. Slats had been arrested as a vagrant after being caught riding the freights with some newfound friends. He also had a case of blood poisoning in his toe. He hadn't the vaguest idea how that had happened.

On a European jaunt Slats turned up missing in Venice. His companions were about to have the canals dragged when he turned up, drifting aimlessly in a stolen gondola. Well, not aimlessly: he had a lady friend along.

There is no doubt that if Slats had trained, he would have been the leading fighter of the twenties and thirties. Once, for a bout with James J. Braddock in 1929, Slats vowed to stay in training and did so for four whole days. On the fifth he was riding down the

Great White Way on top of taxis, drinking champagne. What was amazing is that he still held the tough Braddock dead even for nine rounds until put down by a haymaker.

One thing Slats never wondered about was what that paper stuff was that flew through his fingers. He spent money on cars, on women, on clothes, on tips, for moochers, for a general good time. He earned and hurled away $438,000, dollars of the kind that conservatively are estimated to be worth ten times that amount today. His oft-stated credo was, "What the hell, Jack."

He fought three memorable fights with Slapsie Maxie Rosenbloom, winning two of them, a triumph of Buffalo beer over Brooklyn brew. Rosenbloom of course cultivated his image as a ring eccentric in a later show-business career, but between the two, Slats came out way ahead in the mad-behavior department.

Slats was the scourge of the physicians charged with examining fighters at weigh-ins. Told to cough, Slats had the terrifying habit of clutching suddenly at certain portions of the doctor's anatomy and declaring they would cough in unison or not at all. One physician never examined Slats without first fully protecting himself.

By the time he was 28, Slats was washed up as a fighter. Five years later he was back in Buffalo, working on the WPA. He had lost the home he had built for his mother and was flat broke. By the time he was 33, his father, mother, two brothers, and a sister were dead. People said that was why Slats went roaring through the city every payday. He was trying to forget.

Still, having gone from riches to rags, he hadn't changed. He still loved riding cabs but often had a bit of trouble paying for them. And he still took to disappearing. At work his foreman asked him to buy him some cigars, so Slats roared away in a power truck—and came back the next day.

A lesser personage could be fired for such indiscretions, but not Buffalo's Slattery. Later Slats' health deteriorated, and he moved for a time to the drier climate of Arizona. When his funds ran out, his old friends, and even many of the moochers who had clung to him in his heyday, raised $10,000 to pay his medical expenses.

Slats died in a modest hotel room in Buffalo in 1960. He was 56. To the end he maintained the Slattery philosophy about what might have been. "Suppose I had invested my money?" he told an interviewer. "I'd only have lost it in the crash, wouldn't I? I had a hell of a good time. What the hell, Jack."

Brach, Helen (1911–?)

THE CINDERELLA RECLUSE

Soon after candy company founder Frank Brach met and married hatcheck girl Helen Vorhees in 1952, the millionaire and his wife turned into a reclusive couple, almost never socializing. This was quite a change, at least for the gregarious millionaire. Clearly, it was Helen's decision. Chicago society whispered that Helen, who came from a long line of postal employees, was fearful of rebuffs in social circles.

The Brachs did not even associate with their neighbors in exclusive Glenview, Illinois, where they lived in a stone mansion on seven wooded acres. "She would wave when she went by in one of her [five] pink cars," a neighbor said. "And that was all."

Brach died in 1970 at the age of 80, and nothing much changed for Helen, who inherited $21 million. Her life continued as before, except that she became, if anything, more eccentric. An employee once said she would rather eat carryout chicken than dine in a fancy restaurant. As was the case when Brach was alive, Helen gave no parties. Her main interest was psychic phenomena. She consulted a card-reading fortune-teller by phone almost daily, and she produced a drawerful of psychic writings while in an trancelike state. Suspicious of most people, Helen preferred the companionship of her nine thoroughbred horses and her mongrel dogs—Candy, Luvey, Tinkerbelle, and Beauty—to whom she fed filet mignon. She once chartered a plane from the Bahamas to be at a dying dog's bedside.

Then in 1977 the calls to the fortune-teller stopped. After a visit to Minnesota's Mayo Clinic, she just disappeared. According to her chauffeur, he drove her to Chicago's O'Hare Airport for a vacation in Florida. She never turned up there. Police searched her estates, as well as a farm in Illinois and a summer home in Ohio, all to no avail. There were no clues.

There was just a hole in the life of Helen Brach. So far as anyone knew, she had no close friends, no place to hide. There was no indication that she vanished with any of her funds. The crypt she had designed and built for herself—it looks like a candy box—still lies empty in Unionport, Ohio.

"She had total privacy before," one investigator was quoted as saying. "She has even more now." Hampering the police search for

Helen was the fact that they did not even have any recent photographs of her. Helen refused to pose for many pictures and appeared to have destroyed most of those that were taken.

In 1984 the courts moved to find her legally dead, so that her estate could be distributed. Helen's will called for relatively small sums to go to her chauffeur and a brother, but well over $20 million was left to the Helen Brach Foundation she had organized to help animals.

Meanwhile, Everett Moore, the estate's administrator, has maintained Brach's house, grounds, horses, and financial affairs, as though the heiress were just on vacation. If Helen Brach comes home today, she can sit right down and catch up reading the back issues of *Classic,* her favorite horse magazine.

Wendel Sisters (fl. 1914–1932)

FAMILY OF MISERS

No family held to a life of miserliness with more determination than the Wendels, often described by journalists as New York's oddest millionaires. Individually, the six Wendel sisters may not have been any more odd than the likes of Hetty Green or the two Collyer brothers. But that does not alter the fact that, as a family grouping, they remain the most compleat recluses and misers in American history.

The founder of the family in New York, in the late 18th century, was a shrewd German immigrant, John Gottlieb Matthias Wendel, who married the sister of John Jacob Astor and was Astor's partner in amassing furs and lands. The grandson of the first Wendels, John Gottlieb Wendel, succeeded as head of the family upon the death of his father, John Daniel Wendel, in 1876. He far increased the family's real estate holdings, becoming one of New York's biggest single landlords.

Some have sought to impute eccentricity to this last of the male Wendels; but, without doubt, he was the epitome of the saying "crazy like a fox." To imply that there was anything bizarre in his behavior because of his oft-announced principle of "buy, but never sell New York real estate" flies in the face of one of the most successful business techniques utilized during the past century to accumulate great wealth. When times were good, Wendel bought; when times were bad, Wendel bought. True, Wendel gained a measure of celebrity by his actions. Once he rejected an offer of $6 million from real-estate promoters for the family mansion's courtyard at 442 Fifth Avenue. He pointed out blandly that his sister Ella's white poodle needed the yard for exercise, making the little beast perhaps the most expensively maintained since Roman emperor Caligula's celebrated horse.

Of course the tycoon was merely emphasizing his stand that Wendel land was not for sale under any circumstances. Other such tales abound about Wendel. Typical is the one about the broker who offered him prime real estate at the corner of Broadway and Liberty Street—where the future Westinghouse building would be built—for a mere $750,000. Wendel disappeared and 15 minutes later was back counting out the full purchase price in cash. When the broker protested at the thought of having to carry such a huge amount on his person, Wendel snapped, "Young man, the Wendel terms are cash, nothing but hard cash." The broker swallowed hard and went on with the deal.

No doubt, by conventional standards Wendel was on the odd side. However he was a man of the world, an expert horseman, a hunter, a deep-sea fisherman, and certainly an immensely cultured person, often writing dinner invitations in Latin. He may be said to have aged cantankerously; in later years he carried an umbrella every day, rain or shine. But eccentricity truly ran amok in the Wendel family among John's six sisters, the Misses Wendel, as they were listed in 1897 in the *Elite Directory*, a forerunner of the *Social Register*. They were noted as being domiciled at 442 Fifth Avenue at Thirty-ninth Street. Thereafter there was only silence from the organs of society, despite the fact that the Wendel wealth at the time approached some $75 million.

Papa Wendel had always warned the girls against fortune hunters, and their brother diligently attempted to see that they obeyed their father's edict, so that there would never be any dissipation of the estate via romance or marriage. The relatively worldly younger male Wendel so dominated the sisters that he kept five of them forever unmarried, virtual prisoners in the house for decades.

There was Henrietta Dorothea, the oldest, who was the first to die; Mary Eliza Astor, known as Ella, who lived long but achieved little distinction other than as a proud owner of poodles; Auguste

Antonia, destined to spend many years in a Pennsylvania asylum; and Josephine Jane, poor Josie, the sweetest of the girls, who so wanted children but ended up in a lonely room, with dream children playing around her. Then there were two other sisters, more vital than the others: Rebecca Antoinette Dew—Miss Becky—the best looking of them all, and the one who broke out and married, albeit at the age of 60, to Luther A. Swope, who had tutored the children of the Four Hundred; and finally Georgiana Geisse Reid—Miss Georgie—the most strong willed of the sisters, and the one most likely to stand up to her brother. Unfortunately she had an unsound mind that dominated her actions more and more as time went by.

Much of the public's disaffection for John Gottlieb Wendel stemmed from its belief in Miss Georgie's frequent cries of persecution. Most of her claims, as it turned out, sprang from her own increasingly neurotic hallucinations. Before her death in 1929, it was thought she was living somewhere in the many rooms of the mansion. Actually she had been locked away in a suburban mental institution for almost 20 years.

Was Wendel a monster to his sisters? The fact was that, when he died in California at the age of 79 in 1914, all the titles to the Wendel properties, then valued at $80 million, were solely in his name. But that may well have been because he thought little of the girls' intellects, that he did not wish to allow them any money out of fear of fortune hunters. That he was zany about frugality can hardly be argued. He dictated their wardrobes, which consisted of the round sailor hats popular in the 1860s and 1870s, and decreed they wear old-fashioned, full-skirted black dresses which they made themselves without the aid of such newfangled contraptions as sewing machines.

With Wendel's death, the Misses Wendel could not be said to have broken loose from their yoke of oppression. They remained in their now-seedy mansion, with its tattered window curtains keeping out the stares of the curious. Where once hundreds of gaslights shone on a wealth of treasures, only a few now lighted the scene or showed off the hand-carved grand staircase of natural oak. It has been speculated that the Wendel mansion's forlorn desolation might have provided Charles Addams with the inspiration for his grotesque caricatures. Like the Collyer brothers, the Misses Wendel were besieged by newspaper reporters seeking to crack their determined wall of seclusion. It was not an easy task; reporters found the door bell offered them no entree since, as one journalist stated, it "hadn't been connected since Dewey took Manila."

The newspapers, which had for years labeled the male Wendel a "monster," suddenly discovered virtues in him that did not exist in Miss Becky, who took over the administration of the family estates. It turned out that John Wendel had contributed the free use of a flower garden on a lot at Seventh Avenue and Thirty-eighth Street, and had also walled off a tract of land on West Broadway for a playground for tenement children. Miss Becky canceled out such "foolish generosity" forthwith. There is every indication that she reined in her sisters more harshly than ever before. Family servants who considered granting an interview to lady journalists quickly repented in fear of being fired by Miss Becky.

By this time the Wendel estate was worth about $100 million, but Miss Becky held to the Wendel no-selling policy, especially of the courtyard kept for Miss Ella's pet, Tobey, which by the 1920s was the third poodle of the same name. Enterprising cameramen seeking photos of the Misses Wendel mounted cameras with telescopic lenses in nearby office buildings but were rewarded with little more than Tobey lifting a leg in what was beyond a doubt the most expensive dog run in the world.

The 1920s saw the deaths of all but two of the sisters. When Miss Becky died in 1930 at the age of 87, only Miss Ella was left. She lived alone, save for dutiful servants, in this midtown mausoleum. All the treasures of the mansion remained, although pipes had rusted, marble had cracked, and the upholstery was worn and torn. In the cellar, vintage wines, untouched since the late brother's day, had turned to vinegar. Tobey ate at a special dog table while his mistress ate silently at the long, otherwise empty banquet table. When the pair retired to an upstairs bedroom, Miss Ella slept in one twin bed and Tobey in an adjoining one.

Extravagantly rich and horribly lonely, Miss Ella died in 1932. She departed this world, never having had a telephone, electricity, or an automobile, and the only dress she owned was one that she had made herself—about 25 years earlier.

John G. Wendel had left no will, because he "didn't want any lawyer making money out of the property," and now no less than 2,303 "relatives" and other claimants swooped down to claim part of the Wendel millions. The most outspoken claimant among them was one Thomas Patrick Morris of Scotland, who said he was the illegitimate son of John G.

The long court case concluded with Morris being convicted of false claims and being sentenced to prison. Finally, in 1939, the Wendel millions were ordered disposed of according to Miss Ella's will. As a fitting counter to many decades of Wendel greed, almost all the money was given to charity—churches, missions, hospitals. A sum estimated to be $16 million went to Flower Memorial Hospital, because sometime in the dim past a staffer there had ministered to one of Miss Ella's Tobeys when no veterinarian was available. The sum certainly stands as the largest veterinary payment in history.

Bovar, Oric (1917–1977)

THE CHARISMATIC MASTER BOVAR

As a cult leader and mystic, Oric Bovar attracted some 200 devoted followers in New York and California in the 1970s. An apostle of clean living—with strictures against drinking, smoking, drugs, and extramarital sex—he attracted such show-business celebrities as Bernadette Peters and Carol Burnett.

As one of his longtime adherents put it, "His advice had always been good and he had helped us so much before and we had come to trust him so much we just went along with him."

The degree of control the charismatic Bovar exerted over his followers was striking. When a person came into a room, he might say to a woman follower, "This is your husband: you must marry him." And they usually did. In addition, Bovar maintained a strict prohibition against doctors, and several women had babies without consulting physicians.

Oric Bovar was of course rather mad, a condition that became more evident in the early 1970s, when he suffered a breakdown. By the time he reappeared before his converts, he had changed from a slightly bloated-looking redhead to a skinny, white-haired man.

At about this time he announced he was Jesus Christ; henceforth, Christmas was to be observed on August 29, his own birthday, instead of December 25. This more than anything else drove a number of adherents away, although a large group celebrated Christmas 1976 during the summer, as per his instructions. By this time Peters and Burnett had left him; those who remained devoted to Bovar broke off all friendships with the defectors.

Charismatic cult leader Oric Bovar resurrected neither himself nor his flagging flock.

By autumn, in his increasing madness Bovar had announced that he had godly powers and could resurrect the dead. When New York Bovarite Stephanos Hatzitheodorou died of cancer, his death was not reported to authorities. Bovar and five of his flock—a college criminal justice teacher, a writer, a Wall Street clerk, a railroad employee, and an Evelyn Wood speed-reading instructor—stood vigil over the decomposing body in a New York City apartment for two months, chanting, "Rise, Stephan, rise."

There is no telling how much longer they might have kept at it. In December, police, acting on a tip from a woman who identified herself as Mary Magdalene, raided the place. "I've never seen anything like it in my twenty years on the job," Detective Sergeant Raymond Treubert said, describing the scene in the seventeenth-floor apartment, where the corpse, covered with a shroud, lay on a bed surrounded by six chanting men. It was learned that Bovar had been paying the deceased's rent so that their religious efforts to raise the dead could continue without interference.

Bovar and his followers were charged with failure to report a death and were scheduled to appear in court the following April to answer the charge. On April 14, 1977, Bovar jumped to his death from his tenth-floor apartment window. It is not absolutely certain that it was suicide. Bovar had been reportedly assuring his dwindling flock that he could jump out of a window and come back without dying.

Dym, Rose (1917–   )

BROADWAY ROSE

Just as many a small town has acquiesced in the eccentricities of its village idiot, Manhattan for years put up with Rose Dym, a raucous, bedraggled female who made her rounds wearing a torn calico dress and scuffed red bedroom slippers. She became a world-famous celebrity as Broadway Rose. Tales about her made Broadway columns such as Winchell's with regularity.

Born Anna Dym, Rose was the exceedingly homely daughter of a Brooklyn pushcart peddler. She descended upon Broadway in 1929, when she was 17. She hung around stage doors in quest of autographs, bowling her way through crowds to get to a star. Upset by her bulldozing methods, some celebrities tried to ignore her, a tactic that brought forth screeches and snarls. In time, in fact, she developed a knack for making such a pest of herself that people obliged her at whatever she asked. Soon she graduated from autographs to cash, in time eschewing coin for folding money only.

Restaurant and nightclub doormen quaked at her approach upon their domain. Would she demand entrance? If so, dare they refuse? Eventually, the tack became to ignore her, "just like pimples," one doorman explained, and hope she would go away. If she entered, it was every man for himself. Even ex-boxing champion Jack Dempsey fled in panic from his Broadway restaurant when she marched in to put the touch on customers. At the Stage Door Delicatessen, it could only be hoped a $10 bill from the head waiter would persuade her to go elsewhere. And it was even said that gang leader Lucky Luciano once had a bodyguard cut her off with money when he saw her approaching.

Eventually, it became the fashion for tourists to search for Broadway Rose as one of the shining lights of the Great White Way. Seeing her was one thing, but giving her money was another. She had prospered to such an extent that she could refuse a donation from the unheralded with a sneer. "Go get yourself a reputation, jerk, before I'll take your scratch," she'd say.

Eventually in the post–World War II era, Broadway started losing much of its glitter and glamor, and even Broadway Rose was gone, fading into a much deserved obscurity.

Keys, John R. (?–1943)

THE $1.27-A-WEEK MISER

A lifelong Philadelphian, John R. Keys must stand as one of the greatest, if now unsung, American misers. Through the 1920s, thirties, and early forties, he boasted to friends that he could and did live on $1.27 a week. That was quite an accomplishment even in the Depression years, when butter was only 37 cents a pound, cheese 23 cents a pound, and coffee 18 cents a pound. But Keys did it, working at odd menial jobs always within walking distance from his home, so that he could save on transportation.

In the early 1940s, Keys decided it was time for him to retire to warmer climes, and he moved to Hawaii, working for his passage aboard a freighter. In Honolulu, Keys became a sort of elderly beach bum, surviving on bread, cheese, milk, and an abundant supply of pineapples. The record does not show if he continued to hold to his $1.27-a-week upkeep, but there is no reason to suspect otherwise. Certainly his estate indicated, when he died, that he never spent a penny too much for anything. A search of his quarters by authorities found bank notes, bonds, and other securities worth some $800,000.

Herzog, Helene (?–1945) and Beatrice (?–1934)

REFUGEES FROM CRIME

Crime, or at least the fear of it, experts tell us, is changing the way of urban life in America in the late 20th century. People who previously were night people now stay at home, ceasing to eat out, go to the theater, or even visit friends. Many of us are becoming, it is said, "behavioral recluses."

However, much as we may regard the past as the Good Old Days, things have not really changed; "drop outs" from crime were always with us. Easily two of the most bizarre of these in the 1920s were the sisters Herzog—Beatrice and Helene—who in 1927 ensconced themselves in the Le Marquis, a New York hotel in what was then still the ritzy East Thirties. They had been living at the Park Avenue Hotel with their mother the two years previous to their move, until the old woman died. They then decided to take rooms at the Le Marquis, where they would be within sight of their brownstone home, diagonally opposite, on the next block at 45 East Thirty-first Street.

On registering, the sisters did not say much to the manager, although Helene did point out the brownstone front and say, "That's our family home. Burglars drove us from it."

As he escorted the ladies to their second-floor suite, the manager, making small talk, asked them if they had notified the police that their house had been burglarized. The inquiry was met with icy stares.

If the manager thought the ladies a bit odd, he had to admit they added a touch of old-fashioned elegance to the hotel, with their long skirts, tightly fitted bodices and jackets, and plumed hats. They paid for the first week's rent of $5 a day for a bedroom, living room, and bath with a $50 bill. The manager noted the bill had a musty smell to it. So did the others, as the sisters paid their rent promptly each week.

Within a short time, the sisters telephoned the desk and announced they had decided to say on indefinitely. They rented the next suite as storage for all their trunks. They also wanted their piano, which was still in their home across the street. The manager came to their door with a lease to be signed. Helene Herzog was appalled. She stepped out to the hallway. "No gentleman," she announced rather cuttingly, "ever enters a lady's room."

This was true not only for the manager but for the bell captain, Billy Curley, who brought up the ladies' food from the hotel restaurant, an establishment the Herzogs never entered. He would leave the trays outside the door and come back in an hour to retrieve them, after the sisters had eaten.

News was received often about the Herzog mansion. Police constantly investigated the building, which was robbed regularly until all the furniture had been stolen. Vandals broke every window. Once the police responded to an intruder alarm, and the burglar fled just ahead of them, leaving the floor littered with, of all things, Spanish doubloons. The Herzog sisters could have had the doubloons simply for the claiming, but they never did so. They also never paid any more taxes on the property. Eventually the city took it over and it was torn down.

James Birch, the manager of the Corn Exchange Bank at Fourth Avenue and Twenty-ninth Street, advised the sisters on financial matters. He tried to get them to reclaim their house. They refused, informing him their life-style was their own business. The bank had charge of the sister's affairs, including their inheritance of their father's estate. The father, Philip Herzog, was a pioneer radio and camera inventor, who had retired a millionaire.

The sisters and their mother had lived in the mansion after Herzog died until burglars broke into the house. That frightening event sent the three of them to live in the Park Avenue Hotel and later, the two sisters had fled to the Le Marquis.

Birch knew why the sisters always paid their rent in cash. They had a terrible time writing checks. Once, while the mother was alive, they had written checks and lost quite a bit of money in some kind of transaction. Thereafter they only signed anything under the direst of circumstances.

Over the succeeding years, manager Birch saw the Herzogs only on rare occasions when they wandered out of their hotel refuge, bewigged and out of date, counterparts of Charles Dickens–style recluses. These occasions were only when they needed money and their signatures were required to sign some stocks so they could be sold.

After the market crash of 1929 the sisters went on the same as before. They continued to pay their rent regularly and tipped the bell captain generously for his services. They still appeared to be very rich; certainly no one had reason to doubt that was the case.

Then in 1934 Beatrice died. A coachman from the days when the Herzogs lived in their mansion came for the coffin. No one in the hotel knew where the burial was. Helene never stirred from her room.

Helene lived another 11 years. Often the bell captain heard nothing from her room, and other times he'd hear Helene sitting at the piano, banging out Spanish tunes on her old grand for hours on end. Sometimes the door was open for ventilation purposes and the captain caught a glimpse of Helene in a Spanish lace evening gown, the kind popular a half-century earlier.

In 1945 Helene was found near death. She hadn't picked up her food tray. A carpenter had to take the door off the hinges so hotel employees could enter. Helene lay in bed, in a black lace dress, an artificial red rose in her black wig. She had pneumonia.

At the time of her death Helene was behind in her rent some $1,800. The hotel owners had not had the heart to evict her. They found no will, no written documents, her bank accounts were long closed. All that was left of the Herzog inheritance was Helene's possessions—some moth-eaten furs and gowns dating back 50 years or so, 22 suitcases, 16 trunks, 20 clocks, two pianos, and dozens of lipsticks.

The hotel did not know where to bury her. Management had no idea where Beatrice Herzog had been interred. Helene was saved from a pauper's grave only because the hotel's owner paid for one in Silver Mound Cemetery on Staten Island.

Some half-dozen years after Helene's death, an enterprising reporter discovered her sister Beatrice's burial place. It was in Woodlawn Cemetery in the Herzog family plot. Mr. and Mrs. Herzog were buried there, as was Felix Herzog, their son, and Beatrice. There was yet room for two more interments but Miss Helene had left no record of the family plot. She had cut herself off from the family mansion years before and in death, undoubtedly inadvertently, she had deprived herself of a final resting place with her family. She remained buried alone in an untended grave on Staten Island.

Demara, Ferdinand Waldo, Jr. (1921–1982)

THE GRAND IMPOSTOR

Ferdinand Waldo Demara, Jr., was without doubt the busiest impostor in 20th-century America. He was also surely the most skilled; he carried off hoaxes that fooled so many experts in so many fields that some observers saw in him the Renaissance Man reborn, a man capable of teaching himself advanced concepts so well that he was readily accepted as a brilliant scholar in whatever field he chose.

Demara clearly suffered from a compulsion to impersonate people, but he never picked easy shots for himself, preferring to fool the establishment with sweeping flourishes. When he was a doctor—a lush field for impostors—he did not limit himself to a cautious practice but engaged in surgery, very successful surgery at that.

Demara was in fact a high school dropout. Bored with the idea of a conventional existence, he was a young man in a hurry, and he needed no degree or certificate to master his chosen calling. In his twenties and thirties, despite a youthful crewcut appearance, he was able to palm himself off as, among other things, a doctor of philosophy teaching college psychology courses, a zoologist, a Trappist monk serving in a Kentucky monastery, a biologist involved in cancer research, a law student, a deputy sheriff, a hospital orderly, a guidance counselor in a Texas maximum-security prison, a soldier, and a sailor.

He was most skillful at forging documents of accreditation, giving references with post office box addresses. He then answered the inquiries with glowing tributes to himself on official-looking letterheads. But more importantly, he seemed eminently qualified for the positions he applied for, because of his great acting ability and intensive study of the subject matter involved. Degrees and certifications, Demara proved, were of secondary importance.

Perhaps Demara's crowning impersonation occurred during the Korean War. Masquerading as a lieutenant-surgeon in the Canadian Navy, he performed a number of major operations under severe battle conditions. Faced with the varied problems of pulling teeth, removing tonsils, or amputating limbs aboard ship, Demara simply retreated to his quarters and boned up on the area in question, hurriedly reading the medical texts. His most astonishing operation involved successfully removing a bullet from within a

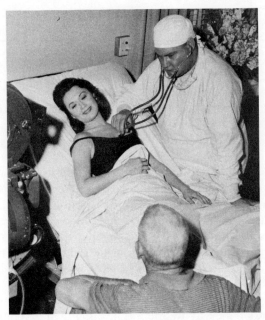

Fred Demara proved so charming an imposter that Hollywood not only filmed his life story, but also cast him in a minor epic called *The Hypnotic Eye*, in which he played the doctor (one of his favorite real-life roles). **(Wide World)**

fraction of an inch of a soldier's heart. Those who assisted or observed the operation gave a cheer when he completed the harrowing operation. Despite being officially unqualified for his position, Demara never lost a patient. Undoubtedly he saved several lives.

Unfortunately for Demara, it was his very success that led to him being unmasked. News stories about his amazing medical exploits were wired back to Canada, where someone started checking on his bogus identity. When it was determined that Demara was an impostor, he was ordered back to Canada, drummed out of the navy, and given all pay due him. The authorities merely assumed he had enlisted under a false name. No one thought he was not a doctor!

Almost invariably, whenever Demara was exposed as a fraud, he was banished with considerable regret by his victims. The Trappist monks hated to see such a dependable individual leave their monastery, and Texas prison officials felt they would never find another expert who would so earn the respect of the convicts.

In 1956 Demara was unmasked posing as an accredited teacher in Maine—the siren call of academia was a particular weakness of his—and he was jailed for a few months for "cheating by false premises." The longest sentence he ever got was a year and a half, and his exploits brought him national fame in the form of a book on his life, or many lives. In the Hollywood film about him, he was portrayed by Tony Curtis. Demara was frequently asked to explain his odd compulsion. His answer: "Rascality, pure rascality."

When Ferdinand Demara died in 1982, he had been unheard from since the 1960s—which meant either he had reformed or had become more adept at his great impersonations.

The Romero Family (fl. 1924 –late 1950s)

THE GUESTS WHO WOULDN'T CHECK OUT

The hotels of New York City hold their share of recluses. They are of a different cloth than house recluses such as the Collyer brothers, who could slip in and out of their mansion under the protective cover of darkness. Not so in a hotel. It is impossible to leave without being seen by elevator operators, doormen, desk clerks, bellhops, and the like.

Yet in another respect the hotel hermit enjoys a more favored sanctuary. If he can afford it, he need never leave his room or suite at all. Deliveries can take care of his needs. Groceries can be delivered, cooked meals requested, newspapers and prescriptions ordered—all by telephone. There is no reason for the hotel hermit to wander beyond the safe confines of his or her residence. The Romero family thusly gained a journalistic reputation as the "Hermits of Dream Street."

The Romeros—Señor José Romero de Cainas, his wife Michaela, and their 18-year-old daughter Acacia—were sugar-plantation-rich Cubans who settled on New York's West Forty-seventh Street in 1924. So secretive were they that their odd existence did not become general knowledge until 1942. That was possible on "Dream Street," the short block between Sixth and Seventh avenues, so nicknamed by O. O. McIntyre because it was, early in the century as it still is today, a favorite haunt of narcotics sellers. In the booming twenties, the bootleg and desperate thirties, and the wartime forties, it was easy to get lost in the melee of that bustling block.

In the twenties, the Romeros ensconced themselves in a hotel called The America, when that establishment was in its better days. By World War II The America had changed considerably, by then housing a number of business women who used the premises for calls with passing clients. Not that the Romeros were particularly aware of the changes. They had, so far as could be determined, never so much as left their suite. The closest they seemed to come to the teeming humanity of Dream Street was when, occasionally, a lace curtain in a window parted slightly and an indistinguishable figure peered out.

There was no need for the Romeros to leave their refuge. They were very rich, and each month money flowed to them from their plantation at Manzanillo. Money was supplied directly to the hotel each month, some to cover the rent and the balance for food, tips, and incidentals.

Then one day in 1930 Señor José developed pneumonia, and he died the following day. The female Romeros were pictures of grief. They knelt beside the dead man in a desperate effort to revive him. They refused to send for an undertaker. Only after the manager insisted he would have to call the police did they relent. Afterwards they closed their door on this intrusion of visitors and remained alone once more with their grief.

Life, such as it was—as far as the outside world was concerned—continued on in the same way. A news dealer on the corner sent up a copy of the Spanish language newspaper, La Prensa. The bell captain carried up an expensive black cigar and three table d'hôte dinners to the suite. When The America closed its dining room as part of its general decline, the bell captain trotted over to the nearby Somerset Hotel to get the meals.

Only occasionally did anyone get to enter the Romero suite. Once a plumber had to come in to repair a leak in the bathroom. The two women—black-clad in mourning—stood facing the wall the entire time he labored.

Then in 1942, The America became the object of police raids; finally a major flush-out of prostitutes cleaned out every room in the place, save for the Romero suite. A representative from the Cuban consulate vouched to the police for the Romero women. They were, however, ordered to move by the Emigrant Savings Bank, the assignees of the raided property. The hotel was to be closed.

Edouard Portales of the Cuban consulate was resummoned to explain to the Romero women through their locked door. Unable to make headway, Portales explained he would have to send for Señor Juarez, their estate manager in Cuba. Together they tried to explain to the women, who insisted they could not leave. Such a move would confuse Señor José, they insisted. Did they really believe their husband and father was still alive, to return to them one day? Or were they using any argument to attempt to ward off the inevitable? The denizens of Dream Street waited impatiently for their departure, to catch a sight of the Romero women the first time they stepped out onto the street in 18 years.

It never happened.

One day the women were gone. They had taken up residence at the Hotel Ashley up the street, but they had never descended *to* the street.

A newspaper reporter tried to find out how they had made the shift. A news dealer explained. "It was Juarez, from the plantation, and Portales from the consulate." The pair had convinced the women to go to the Ashley, and the women agreed only when they were told they could make the move over the roofs of buildings, the path being approved by the police. They occupied a seventh-floor suite in the Ashley, their luggage, two huge trunks, and numerous suitcases being transferred along the street by hand truck.

Life went on for the Romero women as before. There were the same three meals sent up at regular hours, and the inevitable cigar.

As late as the early 1950s the Romeros were still there. Acacia was in her late forties, and the mother in her eighties. At times they admitted an elderly Spanish doctor or Portales from the consulate or their plantation manager. Sometimes the two black-clad women walked the corridors of the seventh floor, turning their faces whenever other hotel guests passed them. Acacia sometimes called down to the bell captain, and he brought up some perfume or a box of chocolates. Sometimes she said a few words to him, explaining she had devoted her entire life to her mother. "She's been such a good mother. I am all she has left."

She spoke of the beautiful home the family maintained in Havana, deserted all these years save for caretakers. "Someday I go back," Acacia said.

Probably she never did. This was the 1950s, and the Castro revolution exploded in Cuba. The story of the Romeros ends here. Today no one on Dream Street knows what became of them. It is the complete hermit tale. They excluded society not only from their lives but from their ultimate fate. All we are left with are the tantalizing facts about their strange existence, and even those facts are unclear.

True, they ordered three meals. Was one of them for the departed Papa José? Or did they simply eat a lot? We do know that neither of them smoked the expensive black cigars. But the word from employees of the Ashley in the fifties was that even the cigar was not for Papa but rather for Mama Michaela's rheumatism. Acacia would soak it in water and poultice her mother's leg with it. Eventually the cure lost its powers, and they stopped ordering the cigar.

Thus a little mystery about the Romeros was answered, but their big secret remains unsolved.

West, Sandra Ilene (1940–1977)

A FERRARI IS FOREVER

During her brief but eventful life, Texas-born millionairess Sandra Ilene West had a love affair with automobiles; it was often said she would buy a flashy car on impulse as quickly as another might buy a box of chocolates. When she died in 1977, at the age of 37, she made it clear in her will she could not bear the thought of being separated from her favorite sportscar, a baby-blue Ferrari. She requested she be buried "next to my husband . . . in my Ferrari, with the seat slanted comfortably."

Not surprisingly, her executors had their doubts about the legality of her request, and West's body was stored in a San Antonio funeral parlor pending a court decision. Happily a California court ruled her request "unusual but not illegal" and released the Ferrari for shipment back to Texas. Mrs. West was duly interred in her car, wearing her favorite lace nightgown. To foil would-be vandals, West and the Ferrari were first placed in a wooden crate and then covered over with two truckloads of cement.

Morris Pop Corn (fl. 1950s–1970s)

POP CORN FOR THE SUCKERS

Within the social circles of New York racetracks, few aficionados do not know Morris Pop Corn. Had he been born only slightly earlier he would no doubt have been immortalized by Damon Runyon. Few if any race-goers know him as anything other than Morris or more commonly Morris Pop Corn, a moniker hung on him some decades ago when a horse named Pop Corn was ridden in a race by that champion of jockeys, Eddie Arcaro.

Jockeys generally become immune to the taunts of horseplayers, but it is doubtful if Arcaro was ever more irritated than by the grating taunts of Morris. Morris' voice had a deep, guttural, East European accent, that summoned up all the agony of downtrodden peoples in a wail of protest, albeit a protest tinged with rebellion. On this particular afternoon at Belmont Race Track Morris became obsessed with the idea of a fixed race. Morris was in fact always obsessed with the idea of fixed races, but it was hardly likely in this race. Arcaro's mount, a rather dependable nag called Pop Corn, was seemingly a "lock," or sure winner. Pop Corn was bet down to one to five, meaning a gambler had to bet $2 to win 40 cents.

Morris had been studying, and at times lecturing, his *Morning Telegraph*, that bible of the betting gentry and predecessor to the *Daily Racing Form*. He crumpled it up and stuffed it into his coat pocket as the horse started the parade to the post.

"*Goniffs!*" he yelled. "*Goniffs, goniffs, goniffs!*" *Goniff* is the Yiddish word for crook or cheat. As Arcaro rode by Morris yelled, "Arcaro, you *goniff*, you are cheating the people! Pop Corn for the suckers." Then he turned to address the crowd at track level. "Do not bet on this cripple," he screamed. "This is a race to rob the public!"

The race went off and, true to Morris' words (at least to the extent that Pop Corn did not win), the heavy favorite ran out of the money. The crowd typically booed Arcaro on his return to the paddock. First and foremost of course was Morris, still screaming "Pop Corn for the suckers." Then he turned and looked up high in the stands to where the stewards were located, waved a fist, and screamed again, "*Goniffs!*"

It was then that the Pinkerton security guards came along and ushered Morris out of the track. He was warned not to return until he could behave with the decorum befitting a horseplayer.

Morris came back, to be thrown out time and again. He would pore over his *Telegraph*, mumbling to himself about the rank dishonesty all about him. Seldom did he appear to bet. Undoubtedly his disinclination was based on the horseplayer's timeworn belief that a bettor could not beat the races but he could beat a race. Morris clearly was a spot bettor. It is between Morris and the IRS if he ever came out ahead, but Morris Pop Corn was famed for being able to pick losers, usually favorites who did not win. He would rave about their presence in the race and insist it was part of a gigantic hoax on the part of the tracks to separate a horseplayer from his money.

Tales are legion about other bettors trying to edge near Morris Pop Corn to hear his personal handicapping. Morris Pop Corn mumbled as he read his racing sheet, running through the potential of each horse, often casting aspersions on the creature's ancestors. Sometimes a bettor asked him outright about a nag's chances, but Morris continued his mumbling. When Morris Pop Corn handicapped he was oblivious to the human race.

One day a bookmaker arrived at the old Jamaica Race Track with $10,000 to "lay off" on a certain race. He had too much action on one horse and planned to bet it through the window to cut his potential losses if it won (and at the same time drive down the price he would have to pay out on the balance of the bets he had accepted). A crony informed him Morris Pop Corn was screaming the horse couldn't win. Now bookmakers generally are not betting men; rather they are bookkeepers who bring their action in line so that, no matter what the result is in any race, they end up making a bit more money than they lose. In this case however our bookie decided to tempt the fates. It was worth it since he had Morris Pop Corn on his side.

It was a wise decision. The nag ran out of the money, allowing the bookie to pocket the $10,000. And Morris Pop Corn raced about denouncing the *goniffs*.

Eventually poor Morris Pop Corn was dealt the cruelest of fates. The Pinks took his picture and conducted him off the premises. He was warned that he was banned from the racetrack for life. It was a sad spectacle to see Morris thereafter trying to enter the racetrack, sometimes with a hat pulled down over his eyes. Always he was denied entrance.

For the true horseplayer, this was purgatory. Morris Pop Corn was seen from time to time marching along Broadway or Seventh Avenue in the New York garment district, forever studying his racing sheet. Did he bet with a bookie and later, when it became legal, with Off Track Betting? But Morris Pop Corn had always eschewed such action. "You must be at the track to see the horses to know how to bet," he once explained. "I must see if the horses are sweating or taking a crap on the track. If a horse takes a crap on the track he is either nervous or the *goniffs* have put him off his feed to throw him off his running rhythm."

In the end Morris Pop Corn was forced to lower himself to attending the night trotting tracks. It was a blow to him. "If God wanted horses to race with wheels," he once propounded, "He would have made them with wheels instead of legs." Morris Pop Corn hated the trotters. Were they more dishonest? "More dishonest," he sneered. "These *goniffs* are so dishonest and money hungry they even let me in!"

Eventually justice prevailed for Morris Pop Corn. He discovered that Garden State Racetrack in New Jersey would admit him. It was, as he put it, a bit of a *"schlep,"* but joy, if not decorum, returned to Morris. And then came the crueliest blow of all . . . Garden State burned to the ground and closed.

Morris Pop Corn was seen at the trotters after that, but he hardly muttered an insult. To the few persons he talked to from time to time, he allowed that it was time for him to retire, perhaps to California. "They have year-round racing there," he observed.

Someone noted he never worked by day and he never worked by night. "So how can you retire?" he was asked.

Morris Pop Corn was enraged. "How do you know what kind of money I have? Do *you* know how to pick winners? Do you know how to pick *losers?*"

In the past few years Morris Pop Corn has disappeared from New York. Those who know him hope he has not crossed that great finish line that even horseplayers cannot avoid, and that he has indeed ventured out to California—where the *goniffs* are.

INDEX